SF

4

WITHDRAWN

THE
LANGUAGE OF EMOTION

PERSONALITY AND PSYCHOPATHOLOGY:

A Series of Monographs, Texts, and Treatises

1. The Anatomy of Achievement Motivation, *Heinz Heckhausen.* 1966
2. Cues, Decisions, and Diagnoses: A Systems-Analytic Approach to the Diagnosis of Psychopathology, *Peter E. Nathan.* 1967
3. Human Adaptation and Its Failures, *Leslie Phillips.* 1968
4. Schizophrenia: Research and Theory, *William E. Broen, Jr.* 1968
5. Fears and Phobias, *I. M. Marks.* 1969
6. Language of Emotion, *Joel R. Davitz.* 1969

THE

LANGUAGE OF EMOTION

JOEL R. DAVITZ

Department of Psychology
Teachers College
Columbia University
New York, New York

ACADEMIC PRESS   New York and London   1969

ACADEMIC PRESS, INC.
111 Fifth Avenue, New York, New York 1000

United Kingdom Edition published by
ACADEMIC PRESS, INC. (LONDON) LTD.
Berkeley Square House, London W.1

LIBRARY OF CONGRESS CATALOG CARD NUMBER: 77-84236

PRINTED IN THE UNITED STATES OF AMERICA

PREFACE

The aim of this volume is to introduce a line of inquiry concerned with the language of emotion. Beginning with a series of intensive interviews and written reports about a variety of emotional experiences, investigation was focused on a systematic description of the language used to describe emotional states. The results of this work are summarized in a dictionary of emotional meaning reflecting the consensus of verbal reports about experiences associated with words commonly used to label emotional states. On the basis of these definitions, an underlying structure of emotional meaning was identified, and this structure is considered in relation to a number of theoretical interpretations of emotional phenomena. Following this basic descriptive material, the final section of this volume deals with an extension of this research into several interrelated lines of psychological inquiry.

The basic problems of this research are neither new nor limited to the interests of psychologists. Philosophers, psychiatrists, social workers, and educators have long been concerned with questions about emotional phenomena, and indeed there is an extraordinarily extensive theoretical and research literature dealing with these questions from numerous points of view. But many of the fundamental questions in this field remain unanswered, and undoubtedly other important questions about emotion have not yet been formulated systemically. It would seem as if the difficulties encountered in any field of psychological investigation are somehow multiplied in the area of emotion.

There are, of course, intrinsic difficulties involved in the study of any phenomenon as varied and complex as emotion, but notwithstanding these intrinsic difficulties, it seems likely that investigators have added some problems of their own making. These have derived largely from assumed commandments about what "Thou shalt" and what "Thou shalt not" study, sometimes leading investigators in this field into uncomfortable, if not impossible, *cul de sacs.*

v

Recent emphasis of the cognitive aspects of emotion promises a way out of some of these *cul de sacs,* and with further developments along this line, the next few years of work in this area might well result in significant gains in knowledge. The research reported in this volume, however, begins with a point of view somewhat different from that of most other psychologists currently working on problems of emotion—particularly American psychologists working in the mainstream of behaviorism.

Essentially, I began with the naive assumption that emotions are phenomena experienced by people, and that careful, systematic observation of how people describe their emotional states is one of the essential first steps in developing a meaningful approach to investigation in this area. This led to a focus on language, the design of methods that would serve as a basis for obtaining quantifiable observations, and the development of a point of view which might be characterized as a "social phenomenology."

The main part of this volume is descriptive, and the research was conducted with minimal theoretical superstructure—although certain assumptions are implicit in the ways in which the work was pursued. The descriptive results, however, suggest a resolution of some of the differences among various theories of emotion, and this resolution is discussed in relation to a proposed structure of emotional meaning. Thus, the empirically oriented, descriptive approach characteristic of most of this work eventually led to a consideration of theoretical issues.

As in any work that is carried on over a period of years, it would be impossible for me to acknowledge individually all of those who contributed in one way or another to this research. However, I should like to express my appreciation to the hundreds of people who have cooperated in various parts of the investigation, many of whom contributed many hours of intensive, hard work to the tasks involved in the research. I should like to thank Professor E. Belvin Williams, Mrs. Beatrice Mittelman, and, in particular Mr. Victor Diamond of the Teachers College Computer Center for their patience, industry, and ingenuity in dealing with my inordinate requests, and I am also most appreciative of Professor Rosedith Sitgreaves' consultation on statistical problems encountered during the course of this work.

A number of people have made helpful comments about various parts of the manuscript, but I should like to express my special appreciation to Professor Auke Tellegen for his careful critical review of an earlier draft of this report and the suggestions be made that led to major revisions and clarifications in the final draft of the manuscript.

I am also deeply indebted to Mrs. Norma Chenkin for her invaluable help at every stage of this research, from collecting and analyzing data to preparing the many drafts of this report. And finally, to my wife, Lois, for her encouragement and support and the countless hours we have shared working and discussing every phase of this research, I extend my deepest love and appreciation.

JOEL R. DAVITZ

May, 1969

CONTENTS

PREFACE   v

1.   The Problem and the Method of Investigation

First Steps in the Investigation ·   5

Procedure   7
    Subjects   8
    The Terms   10
    Data Collection   11
    Analysis of Results   12
    Presentation of Results   13

2.   A Dictionary of Emotional Meaning ·   32

3.   Comments on the Dictionary, The Model, and the Method

Overlap and Specificity of Definitions ·   87

The Model and the Method ·   88
    The Model   88
    The Method   89
    A Revised Check List   92
    Other Methods   93

4.   The Structure of Emotional Meaning

Cluster Analysis of Items   106
    The Clusters   108
    Summary of Cluster Analysis   114

Interrelationships among Clusters ·   114
    Patterning of Clusters in Emotional States   122

ix

5.   Comments on the Structure of Emotional Meaning

Dimensions of Emotion 128
    Activation   128
    Relatedness   129
    Hedonic   Tone   132
    Competence   133
    Summary   135

Notes toward a Theory of Emotion 136
    Propositions   136
    A Final Comment 149

6.   Studies of the Language of Emotion

Development of the Language of Emotion 156
    Results   157

Individual Differences in Reported Emotional Experiences
and Perceptual–Cognitive Style · 164
    Method   166
    Results   167
    Discussion   168

Similarity of Reported Emotional Experiences and
Genetic Background 170
    Method   171
    Results   172
    Discussion   172

A Comparison of Emotional Experiences Reported by
Adolescents in Uganda and the United States 172

Method and Procedures · 173
    Results   178
    Discussion   183

Questions for Further Investigation 190

Bibliography. 193

AUTHOR INDEX 195

SUBJECT INDEX 196

CHAPTER 1

The Problem and the Method
of Investigation

This research began with a problem encountered in writing the final chapter of *The Communication of Emotional Meaning* (Davitz, 1964), which dealt with nonverbal aspects of emotional communication. In this earlier work, subjects were presented with various stimuli and asked to identify the meaning of each stimulus in terms of emotional labels such as Happy, Angry, or Sad. For example, we frequently used recordings of speakers saying the same sentence repeatedly, each time trying to express a different emotional meaning, and we asked listeners to identify these vocal expressions by assigning a given set of emotional labels.

Although our research procedures obviously differed from communication in everyday interaction, the general paradigm from which our research derived was a conversation in which one person determines that another person is happy or sad, angry or loving, or is expressing any of a variety of emotional states. Therefore, in preparing the final summary of our empirical work and trying to set the findings within a conceptual framework relevant to the general paradigm of conversation, a central question became apparent: *What does a person mean when he says someone is happy or angry or sad?*

For purposes of this earlier work, our concern was limited to the labeling process itself, and to a certain extent this limitation was useful. At least it permitted our research to get on without falling into philosophical pitfalls of theoretical interpretation. But within the broader context of interpreting our findings in terms of everyday communication, this was not a very satisfactory solution for it stopped inquiry at the level of labeling without considering the meaning of the labels. As a matter of fact, the title of this earlier work might better have focused on the communication of emotional *labels* rather than on emotional meaning.

A review of psychological literature dealing with emotion provides little help in understanding what people mean when they say someone is happy

1

or sad. This is not due to the inadequacies of previous work, but it reflects the fact that psychological work in this area has by and large dealt with aspects of emotion quite different from the question raised by our research. For the most part, investigations have been concerned with predicting and controlling various emotional phenomena or with identifying antecedents, correlates, and consequences of emotional reactions. Our question, however, requires a descriptive or definitional answer about how people use language in referring to emotional states.

As a first naive step in this line of inquiry, I began by asking people what they meant when they said someone was happy or sad or angry. Among my colleagues the answers reflected their particular professional biases—some emphasized physiological responses, others focused on situational factors, and of course most of them mentioned various kinds of behavior. But among nonpsychologists, it became evident that when people say someone is happy or sad they are usually referring to the *experience* of an emotional state. Without the psychologist's sophisticated awareness of the difficulties involved in knowing anything about experience, apparently most people casually assume experiential referents of the emotional labels they use. Thus, if we are to understand what people mean when they use emotional labels, we must obtain descriptive definitions of these labels as people use them—and to a large extent these definitions refer to experience.

At this point in the history of psychology it hardly seems necessary to belabor the obvious fact that the experience of another person cannot be observed directly. Experience *must* be studied as it is reported through some language system. This implies that one appropriate focus of psychological research is the language that deals ostensibly with experiential referents of emotional labels, recognizing that the primary data are linguistic symbols that probably reflect, to a certain extent, experiential events but cannot be assumed to be direct, unequivocal representations of these events. In a sense, these linguistic events are as "close" as one can come to studying emotional experience.

Although some writers have recognized the language used to describe experience as a legitimate area of inquiry, for one reason or another most psychological investigators have focused their attention on other aspects of emotional phenomena, leaving the language of emotion to poetry, drama, and clinical reports. Knowledge in this area has thus depended upon occasional, brilliant insights and dramatic portrayals of emotional experiences, rather than on systematic and cumulative inquiry.

Perhaps this is because of the connotative taint of problems concerned with experience, a taint deriving from the *cul de sac* of theoretical arguments characterizing the early history of psychology. Having been shocked once by the impossibility of establishing "the basic elements of real experience," most research psychologists seem to have acquired an avoidance reaction that has generalized to any related area of investigation. So the obvious proposition that one can only study the language of reported experience seems to have effectively short-circuited any efforts to study that language.

Nevertheless, psychologists in their professional communications continue to use words like anger, fear, and anxiety—and occasionally even love and happiness. These words, of course, are borrowed from the nontechnical language of everyday conversation. Perhaps because psychologists use these words in their nonprofessional interactions without encountering obvious difficulties, they rarely bother to define these terms as carefully as they might when using such obviously technical phrases as *schedules of reinforcement* or *stimulus generalization*. But if the principal referents of emotional labels as used in everyday conversation are experiential events—and thus by definition are private and subjective— it would seem likely that precisely these kinds of words involve individual differences in meaning that might interfere with accurate communication. When a psychologist uses words like anger, fear, and love in his professional communications, he is likely to bring with him the implicit meanings of these words as used in everyday conversations. This adds a certain human richness to his technical vocabulary, but it also adds a considerable potential for confusion in a field that hardly needs additional sources of noise in the channels of professional communication.

With these considerations in mind, I set out to compile a dictionary of common emotional terms that might be of some use in clarifying communication about emotional phenomena, not by legislating definitions but by describing the commonalities of meaning shared by members of a given language community. In a sense, by identifying areas of intersubjective agreement in the language of experience associated with a given emotional label, one can begin to establish objectively the definition of words used to label emotional states. The general strategy of this research, therefore, was to ask people to describe verbally their experiences of a number of emotional states, and for each state—designated by a particular label such as Anger, Love, Sadness—to identify those aspects of reported experiences agreed upon by a specified portion of the sample.

The limitations of this strategy are obvious. Individual subjects can report only those aspects of an emotional experience for which they have language available. The verbal report of any experience is necessarily filtered through the language of report and is undoubtedly structured and limited by that language. In addition, reports of previous emotional experiences depend upon recall, so one would expect the reports to be influenced by the processes of leveling, sharpening, and forgetting characteristic of any recalled report. Moreover, in dealing with emotional phenomena it is reasonable to expect a certain amount of suppression, repression, and distortion in reports obtained, though using group data might compensate somewhat for these sources of error. The data are also influenced by individual differences in labeling, so that one person's *sadness* might be another person's *depression*—and even within a single individual, the sadness experienced at one time is unlikely to be exactly the same as an experience labeled sadness at another time. Thus, in identifying commonalities of reported experiences, one must necessarily deal with emotional terms at a somewhat abstract level. The agreed upon aspects of the definition of Fear, for example, are unlikely to describe completely any single instance of fear, but rather reflect commonalities abstracted from a number of concrete and somewhat different instances of fear.

Notwithstanding these clear-cut limitations, the development of an empirical basis for defining common emotional labels would seem to be of some value. The primary emphasis in this work, at least in its initial stages, has been on the descriptive aspects of the research task, but the data obtained can be treated from a variety of theoretical viewpoints. For example, one can restrict the interpretation of these data to questions of primarily linguistic concern. As such, the dictionary of emotional meaning developed in this work might serve as a general guide to clarify linguistic behaviors relevant to communication about emotional phenomena. From another point of view one might interpret the data in terms of experiential events to which the words presumably refer, recognizing of course that these are, and can only be, more or less useful inferences from the observed data. Thus, the data might be interpreted theoretically from points of view ranging from behaviorism to phenomenology.

At the present time, one's choice of theoretical stance in psychology is largely a matter of personal taste. Despite the seeming confidence with which some phenomenologists and some behaviorists present points of view that superficially, at least, appear to be mutually exclusive, neither style of theory can reasonably be said to have swept the field on the basis of hard data and consistently meaningful results. From time to time phenomenologically oriented writers announce and applaud the death of behaviorism, and then of neobehaviorism; however, the current research literature suggests that the corpse is remarkably productive. While there does seem to be a certain amount of dissatisfaction with the current style of behaviorism in psychological theory, the methodological muddles into which phenomenology seems regularly to fall cannot be viewed as encouraging. At the present time, therefore, probably the most charitable, and perhaps the most useful, view of theory in psychology is one that permits a variety of perspectives, leaving the researcher free to pose what seem to be potentially significant questions, recognizing that the immediate problem of evaluating significance in many instances is currently a matter of fashion, taste, and chance. In any research, then, the major emphasis that can be shared among psychologists of various theoretical persuasions is a focus on the data, on the observations that in fact concretely define the research.

Specifically, in regards to the present research, this position suggests that major emphasis be placed on the descriptive task of defining the ways in which people use language to describe a variety of emotional experiences. Regardless of whether one prefers behavioristic or experiential constructs in discussing these data, the central research problem is a descriptive one, and the primary criterion for initially evaluating the model underlying the research is the degree to which apparent demands of the phenomena investigated are satisfied by the descriptive techniques.

My own point of view, which undoubtedly influenced the way in which the general problem was attacked, might be characterized as a naive and skeptical phenomenology. It is naive in that I believe the words a subject uses in describing an emotional experience do indeed reflect or refer to some aspect of that experience. When he says, "I feel my heart pounding," I believe these words do reflect the experience of his heart pounding—and I can imaginatively "understand" his words in terms of my own experiences. But I am also skeptical enough to believe that these words reflect only part of the experience, that they are almost always gross and abstract reflections, and that we shall never be able to obtain a full and completely valid description of any experience. Moreover, it would be unreasonable to assume that verbal reports are determined only by the referential experience—other determinants, such as linguistic habits, verbal ability, and response sets unquestionably influence the results obtained. Some of these limitations and distortions can be reduced or minimized, but there are always likely to be rather severe limits to the knowledge we can gain about experiential events. Perhaps the best we can do is try to reduce the magnitude of our ignorance, and certainly our current ignorance allows plenty of room in which to work.

First Steps in the Investigation

Having defined the problem in terms of developing a dictionary of emotional meanings dealing with reported experiences, the first step involved a series of intensive interviews designed to elicit as full a description of emotional experiences as I could obtain. Using a short list of emotional labels based on the tests of sensitivity we had developed in earlier research (Affection, Anger, Anxiety, Boredom, Cheerfulness, Confidence, Impatience, Sadness, and Satisfaction), I asked each of 30 people to think of a time in which he experienced a given emotion and to describe that experience. In some instances, we covered the entire list in an hour; in other instances, we could discuss only a few experiences in the hour or two a person was willing to devote to the interview. The results, of course, were hardly worth a detailed analysis because of the relatively unsystematic way in which the information was collected. The interviews themselves, nevertheless, were most significant, for it was obvious that the interviewees were talking about material that had direct and immediate psychological significance for them. Of course, they had varying degrees of difficulty describing their experiences, but the task was clearly a realistic and meaningful one for them. I was thus strongly reinforced to continue this line of investigation, modifying somewhat the fairly unstructured means of gathering observations.

As I began planning the next steps to be taken in preparing the dictionary, a suggestion made by O. H. Mowrer in a conversation we had had many years ago occurred to me. We had been discussing the difficulties of systematically describing experience, and in the course of the discussion, Professor Mowrer suggested that, rather than follow the model of poetry which might use a grand metaphor to capture the essence of a particular experience, we might work more effectively using an atomistic model of modern electronics, borrowing the general idea underlying, for example, the visual presentation of a radar scope or a television screen. These instruments are capable of presenting very complex pictures; but no matter how complex the picture, the visual presentation is comprised of a pattern of many small dots, each of which is either present or absent in a given picture. Drawing the parallel for the purpose of describing emotional experiences, it seemed that a potentially useful method might be based on a similar atomistic approach in which a person would simply be required to make a judgment of "present" or "absent" about a large number of bits of information relevant to emotional phenomena. Each bit might refer to a very small part of the total pattern, but the bits of information taken together might present a useful approximation of the overall experience.

This suggested the development of an extensive check list of statements that could be used to describe an emotional experience. One source of such statements was the series of interviews in which people described their experiences in various emotional states. To supplement this pool 1200 subjects were asked to think of a concrete instance in which they had experienced one of a wide variety of emotional states and to write a description of this experience with as much detail as possible.

From the material contained in the interviews and the writtten reports, thousands of brief statements were obtained, each statement descriptive of some aspect of an emotional experience. The aim of this step was to develop a large and extensive pool of items. Then, these thousands of items were reviewed; synonymous items were eliminated, keeping the statement that occurred most often; highly similar items were rewritten as one statement; and statements that occurred only once in the entire sample were dropped. This filtering and elimination of items certainly was susceptible to my own biases, for it is not likely that others would always have made exactly the same judgments about synonymous or similar items. But throughout the procedure, I tried to favor the error of overinclusion rather than overexclusion, so that the final check list was probably longer than it actually need have been, because it included a number of quite similar statements treated as separate items. The goal, however, was to develop a list of descriptive statements that covered as wide a range of phenomena as I could obtain and a final instrument which provided a basis for making discriminations which seemed reasonable on the basis of the interviews and written descriptions obtained. Therefore, length of the check list was not a major concern in its construction, though I did want an instrument that could be used by a subject to describe a single experience at one sitting without undue fatigue.

The final list is comprised of 556 statements. By far the largest number of items refer to physical sensations, and most of these occur in the first part of the check list. These are followed by statements describing one's perception of and relation to the external situation or the world in general. Next are a number of items describing various cognitive events, followed by statements concerning one's relation to others, and a group of items generally referring to one's self, though not in terms of a specific physical sensation. These are followed by items describing impulses to behave or control behavior, including expressive behaviors, and finally, there are a number of items describing the formal aspects of the experience, such as how long it lasts and the course it takes over time. The final check list as used in collecting data for the dictionary is presented at the end of this chapter.

Procedure

The data upon which the dictionary is based were obtained from 50 subjects, each of whom used the check list to describe 50 different emotional experiences identified by the terms included in the dictionary. Thus, the definition of a term such as Affection depends upon the reports of

50 people who have described their experiences of an emotional state they have labeled "Affection." The dictionary therefore represents a tabulation of the common descriptive statements the subjects used for each emotional term.

SUBJECTS

The sample was comprised of 25 men and 25 women, all volunteers, ranging in age from 20 to 50, and including both white and Negro subjects. Because of the demanding and time-consuming nature of the task, it was necessary to use subjects who could be counted on for cooperation far beyond that required in most psychological researches. It should be noted that of those who initially volunteered, only two failed to complete the task and had to be replaced. In addition to high motivation and capacity to persist at a high level of performance throughout the long and psychologically strenuous data collection, the fairly complex verbal demands of the task required subjects of relatively high verbal ability. All the subjects, therefore, were college graduates; a majority were currently either full- or part-time graduate students, though none of them were students in psychology, and others were members of the secretarial and administrative staff at Columbia University. A few were obtained from outside the university through friends and associates, but once again, none of these had any special training or professional interest in psychology. Although almost all parts of the country were represented, a large majority of subjects were from the Northeast, and of course all of them were native speakers of English. Table 1-1 presents the relevant descriptive data for each of the subjects in the final sample.

Obviously the sample upon which the dictionary is based is not representative of the population of the United States. In particular, this is a well-educated, verbally intelligent group, and thus the results presented in the dictionary are distinctly limited in the degree to which they can be generalized to the national population. Nevertheless, for what it is worth, an informal observation made during the interviews should be shared. The 30 people who participated in these interviews ranged in educational level from high school graduates to those with advanced graduate degrees in a variety of fields. In this small sample, it was clear that educational level had nothing at all to do with one's ability to describe emotional experiences or with the nature of the descriptions. This mitigates, somewhat, the limits of generalization implied by the educational level of the final sample, though this does not at all discount the necessity of exploring this problem in more detail in future research. Suffice to say that the dictionary reports here is only a first step in this general direction of

TABLE 1-1
Description of Sample

Subject	Sex	Age	Geographical Background[a]
1	Male	20–30	New York
2	Male	20–30	New Jersey
3	Male	40–50	New York City
4	Male	20–30	New York City and Vermont
5	Male	20–30	New Jersey
6	Male	40–50	New York City
7	Male	20–30	New York
8	Male	20–30	New Jersey
9	Male	20–30	Pennsylvania
10	Male	30–40	Texas
11	Male	20–30	Pennsylvania
12	Male	20–30	Pennsylvania
13	Male	30–40	Ohio
14	Male	20–30	New York City
15	Male	40–50	Missouri
16	Male	20–30	New York City
17	Male	30–40	Virginia
18	Male	20–30	Wisconsin
19	Male	40–50	New York City
20	Male	20–30	Indiana
21	Male	40–50	New York
22	Male	20–30	Michigan
23	Male	20–30	New York City
24	Male	20–30	New York
25	Male	20–30	Pennsylvania
26	Female	20–30	Connecticut
27	Female	20–30	New York
28	Female	20–30	Oklahoma
29	Female	20–30	New Jersey
30	Female	20–30	Massachusetts and New York
31	Female	40–50	Missouri
32	Female	40–50	Middle Atlantic States
33	Female	20–30	New York
34	Female	20–30	Canada
35	Female	40–50	New York City
36	Female	40–50	New York
37	Female	20–30	Pennsylvania
38	Female	20–30	Washington, D.C.
39	Female	30–40	New Hampshire
40	Female	20–30	New Jersey
41	Female	30–40	New York
42	Female	20–30	New York
43	Female	20–30	North Dakota
44	Female	30–40	West Virginia

TABLE 1-1 *(continued)*

Subject	Sex	Age	Geographical Background[a]
45	Female	20–30	Virginia
46	Female	20–30	Virginia
47	Female	30–40	New York
48	Female	50–60	New York
49	Female	20–30	New York City
50	Female	20–30	Massachusetts

[a] Geographical background indicated by state except for those Ss who are from New York City.

investigation, and one would hope that further work will correct the defects and remedy the deficiencies of this initial effort. At this early stage in this area of investigation, with all the clumsiness of a newly developed instrument and the severe demands required of the subjects, it seemed wisest to sacrifice representativeness of the sample in favor of high motivation and ability required by the task.

THE TERMS

To obtain terms people used to label emotions, all of the entries in a *Roget's Thesaurus* were scanned, and every word that seemed at all likely to be used as the label of an emotional state was noted. Over 400 words were thus obtained, and these were then read to 40 subjects selected from the same general population as the final sample whose reported experiences formed the basis of the dictionary. These 40 subjects were asked to indicate each of the words they would use to label an emotion. Of the total list presented to this group, 137 were agreed upon as emotional labels by over half the subjects, and from these 137 terms, 50 were chosen on an intuitive basis to represent as wide and varied a range as possible of emotional states. These are the terms included in the dictionary and are listed in Table 1-2.

For the most part, the terms are obviously common and familiar labels of emotions, some of which, such as Anxiety and Anger, have been the focus of a good deal of psychological research. Many of the words, however, refer to emotional states that are commonly recognized, but have received little formal attention in previous investigations. Such words, for example, are Awe, Delight, Disgust, and Remorse. A few of the terms, such as Admiration and Solemnity, though apparently used by nonpsychologists to label emotional states, may be somewhat questionable to some psychologists as appropriate terms for a list of emotions. The aim of the dictionary, however, was to describe the language as it is commonly

TABLE 1-2

Terms Included in the Dictonary of Emotional Meaning

Term	Lorge-Thorndike frequency[a]	Term	Lorge-Thorndike frequency[a]
Admiration	29	Gratitude	22
Affection	3	Grief	45
Amusement	22	Guilt	14
Anger	A	Happiness	A
Anxiety	22	Hate	A
Apathy	3	Hope	AA
Awe	17	Impatience	9
Boredom	1	Inspiration	18
Cheerfulness	5	Irritation	5
Confidence	A	Jealousy	17
Contempt	18	Love	AA
Contentment	8	Nervousness	3
Delight	A	Panic	19
Depression	25	Passion	A
Determination	19	Pity	A
Disgust	21	Pride	A
Dislike	23	Relief	A
Elation	2	Remorse	7
Embarrassment	9	Resentment	12
Enjoyment	13	Reverence	14
Excitement	43	Sadness	11
Fear	AA	Serenity	2
Friendliness	6	Shame	A
Frustration	1	Solemnity	5
Gaiety	5	Suprise	AA

[a] Frequencies reported were obtained from *The Teacher's Word Book of 30,000 Words* by Edward L. Thorndike and Irving Lorge, 1944. Frequencies are reported on the basis of the number of times a given word occurred in each 1,000,000 words counted. A designation of *A* indicates the frequency is greater than 50 per 1,000,000 words, and *AA* indicates the frequency is greater than 100 per 1,000,000 words.

and nontechnically used, and therefore such words were included in the final list used in constructing the dictionary.

DATA COLLECTION

Before the actual data collection, subjects were informed of the general purpose of the research, and the overall procedure was explained with emphasis on the aim of obtaining each person's own description of his emotional experiences. A critical incident technique was used; for each emotion, a subject was asked to think of a specific instance in which he had experienced that emotional state. He was asked to describe the situation briefly and then to read through the check list carefully, checking each statement that described his experience.

A subject received a separate booklet with instructions and check list for each emotion, and each subject described the 50 emotional experiences in a different random order. The booklets were filled out at the subject's own convenience and at his own pace. The time required to describe each experience varied from subject to subject and emotion to emotion, sometimes requiring over an hour to think of and describe a single experience, but generally averaging about 30 min. for each emotion. Since subjects worked on the project at their convenience and at times when they felt able to recall and describe given emotional experiences, the overall time required to complete the entire procedure for the 50 emotions varied considerably, ranging from ten days to eight weeks.

ANALYSIS OF RESULTS

The basic data for the dictionary of emotional meaning consist of the number of times each of the 556 items was checked by the 50 subjects in describing each of their 50 emotional experiences. The definition of each term is based on the items most frequently checked by the subjects in their descriptions of experiences they chose as representative of that term. Obviously individual differences in descriptions were expected and obtained; the major aim of the research, however, was to identify the commonalities among descriptions of experiences reported under the same emotional label. Thus, it was necessary to establish a specific frequency with which an item was checked as a cutoff point for determining whether or not that item should be included in the definition of a given term. There was no previous work to serve as a guide in this respect; entries in other dictionaries usually represent the author's opinion of the "correct" definition of a word or his opinion about the meaning conventionally associated with the common usage of a term. In this study, there was at least an empirical basis for estimating the relative frequency of statements used to describe (and thus define) each term, but the decision establishing the frequency which operationally defined a particular statement as part of the definition of an emotional state was necessarily arbitrary. Recognizing both the arbitrariness of the decision, as well as the fact that the final product is to some extent influenced by this decision, one can only proceed on the basis of what seems reasonable at this stage of research, and then make the decision explicit and consistent. Therefore, on the basis of an inspection of the final tabulations, I decided to include in the definition of a term every statement that was checked by over one-third of the subjects in their descriptions of the emotional experiences labeled

by that term. Intuitively, this seems to represent a fairly low level of
agreement for a definition of "commonality," but this might be compen-
sated for by including in each definition the percentage of subjects who
checked each item in the definition so that a reader who might choose
a higher level of agreement can make the appropriate omissions.

In addition, as a check on the adequacy of the results obtained, the
definitions included in the dictionary were submitted to a sample of 20
independent judges selected from the same general population as the sample of 50 subjects whose responses served as the basic data. These judges
were asked to rate the adequacy of each definition on the basis of their
own emotional experiences, considering the definition of an emotional
state both in terms of how fully it describes their experiences as well
as how much is included that is inconsistent with their own experiences.
These judges were given the following instructions:

> This booklet contains definitions of the fifty words used to label emotional states.
> The definitions consist of descriptions of the experience of these emotions, and
> your task is to rate the adequacy of these definitions. Read through the definition
> of each term carefully, and then rate its adequacy on the basis of: (1) how
> fully or comprehensively it describes the experience of the emotion; and (2) the
> accuracy or validity of the statements in terms of how consistent they are with
> your own experience of the emotion.

Ratings for each definition were obtained using the following scale:

1. *Adequate:* presents a comprehensive and accurate description of the
emotional experience.

2. *Fairly Adequate:* presents a fairly comprehensive and fairly accurate
description but either does not contain a significant aspect of the experience or presents some aspect inaccurately.

3. *Fairly Inadequate:* either omits more than one significant aspect
of the experience and/or presents more than one aspect inaccurately.

4. *Inadequate:* does not describe the experience accurately and/or omits
a good deal of the experience.

PRESENTATION OF RESULTS

The dictionary of emotional meaning presented in Chapter 2 contains
50 terms used to label emotional states. For each term, there is a brief
statement of its etymology presented merely for possible interest in relating
a term's etymology to its current usage. Then, agreement among subjects
in describing the experiences under a given term is indicated in several
ways: (*a*) the number of items checked by at least one-third of the subjects; (*b*) the range in percentage of agreement of items contained in

the definition; and (c) the number of items checked by at least 50% of the subjects for that term.

For each term, the median adequacy rating is presented, followed by the definition of the term listing the items checked by over one-third of the sample. After each statement, in brackets, is the percentage of the total sample that checked the item in describing their experiences under the particular emotional term. In almost all instances, the statements are presented as they occur in the check list, but occasionally, to eliminate repetition of the same introductory phrase for successive items in a definition, these noncritical phrases have been omitted.

The various statements presented in each definition are grouped in terms of clusters identified in an analysis of the items. These clusters are discussed in Chapter 4. Essentially, this provides a framework for grouping similar items within a definition. The clusters are presented in order, from the cluster containing the most statements in the definition of a given term to the cluster containing the fewest statements. This is followed by a miscellaneous group of statements that do not fit into any cluster, with a final grouping of those statements which refer to the formal aspects of the experience. Within each cluster in the definition, the statements are ordered on the basis of percentage of subjects who checked each item. The end of each item as it occurs in the check list may be identified by the brackets containing the appropriate percentage of subjects for that item. To facilitate reading the definitions, successive items which are highly similar are separated by commas, while relatively less similar items are separated by semicolons.

Check List of Descriptive Statements Used in Obtaining Definitions of Emotional Terms

_____ 1. weakness across my chest

_____ 2. seem to be immediately in touch and appreciative of immediate physical sensations

_____ 3. I feel soft and firm

_____ 4. as if I'm suffocating or smothering

_____ 5. there is a heavy feeling in my stomach

_____ 6. I'm not aware of what's going on inside

_____ 7. I'm easily irritated, ready to snap

_____ 8. there is a clutching, sinking feeling in the middle of my chest

_____ 9. my senses are perfectly focused

_____ 10. a gnawing feeling in the pit of my stomach

_____ 11. I'm excited in a calm way

_____ 12. my blood pressure goes up; blood seems to rush through my body

_____ 13. I'm more aware of what's going on inside of me

_____ 14. I feel taller, stronger, bigger

_____ 15. there's a lump in my throat

_____ 16. my head spins

_____ 17. there's a combination of pain and pleasure

_____ 18. there is no sensation; I'm numb, desensitized

_____ 19. as if I'm out of touch, seeing things from far away

_____ 20. my hands are shaky

_____ 21. I'm cold, yet perspiration pours out of me

_____ 22. there is an inner warm glow, a radiant sensation

_____ 23. I sweat

_____ 24. muscular rigidity

_____ 25. I feel empty, drained, hollow

_____ 26. my body seems to soften

_____ 27. a sense of being dried up

_____ 28. breathing becomes shallower

_____ 29. I feel like fainting

_____ 30. slightly headachy, as if my brain were tired

_____ 31. my head shakes and shivers

_____ 32. I can't hear as well as I normally do

_____ 33. clammy hands

_____ 34. I'm shivery

_____ 35. I'm really functioning as a unit

_____ 36. my feelings seem dulled

_____ 37. as if everything inside, my stomach, my throat, my head is expanding to the utmost, almost bursting

Check List (*continued*)

_____ 38. my nose runs

_____ 39. my head seems ready to explode

_____ 40. blood rushes to my head as if I'm intoxicated

_____ 41. there's an itchiness

_____ 42. there is a general release, a lessening of tension

_____ 43. my body seems to speed up

_____ 44. muscle tone is suddenly enhanced

_____ 45. I feel sexually excited

_____ 46. I feel nauseated, sick to my stomach

_____ 47. a narrowing of my senses, my attention becomes riveted on one thing

_____ 48. I breathe more deeply

_____ 49. I feel strong inside

_____ 50. a sense that somehow I can't experience things wholly, as if there is a lid or some sort of clamp which keeps me from perceiving

_____ 51. there are moments of tremendous strength

_____ 52. an inner ache you can't locate

_____ 53. things seem to waver, as if I'm looking at them through water; everything seems to be covered by a sheet of glass.

_____ 54. I feel heavy, logy, sluggish

_____ 55. I'm jumpy, jittery

_____ 56. an intensified focus to my sensations

_____ 57. my arms and legs feel heavy, leaden

_____ 58. I'm loose, relaxed

_____ 59. there's absolute physical turmoil

_____ 60. I'm breathless

_____ 61. warmth in the pit of my stomach

_____ 62. hot and cold flashes

_____ 63. my hands and legs are cold

_____ 64. a feeling of warmth all over

_____ 65. a tight knotted feeling in my stomach

_____ 66. as if I'm all loose inside

_____ 67. there's an excitement, a sense of being keyed up, overstimulated, supercharged

_____ 68. there's an intense awareness of everything; I seem to experience things with greater clarity; colors seem brighter, sounds clearer, movements more vivid

_____ 69. there's a quickening of heartbeat

_____ 70. I stop breathing for a moment

_____ 71. there's a throbbing in my throat

_____ 72. there is a sharp pain where my heart is

_____ 73. there is a dull sensation of pain in my chest

Check List (*continued*)

_____ 74. everything seems out of proportion

_____ 75. my hands go limp

_____ 76. warm, yet simultaneously cold

_____ 77. I feel my mouth drooping

_____ 78. my heart seems to shiver

_____ 79. I'm unfocused and I can't focus

_____ 80. there's an increased awareness of essential things like hot and cold, texture and smell

_____ 81. there's tension across my back, my neck, and shoulders

_____ 82. sense of vitality, aliveness, vibrancy, an extra spurt of energy or drive

_____ 83. my teeth grind against each other

_____ 84. weakness in my back or neck

_____ 85. feeling of suspension in my stomach

_____ 86. like I'm a mass of jelly inside

_____ 87. there is a pushing pressure behind my eyes

_____ 88. my eyes twitch

_____ 89. a creeping sensation all over my body, my flesh seems to crawl

_____ 90. a special lift in everything I do and say; I feel bouncy, springy

_____ 91. there is a burning in my chest

_____ 92. there is a tightness, a constriction across my chest

_____ 93. I feel effervescent, bubbly

_____ 94. I'm jumpy inside as if my viscera are trembling, shivering

_____ 95. my head aches, throbs

_____ 96. my sensations are blurred

_____ 97. fists are clenched

_____ 98. my heartbeat slows down

_____ 99. I have no appetite; I can't eat

_____ 100. I feel bloated

_____ 101. I'm full, yet simultaneously empty

_____ 102. a floating, soaring sensation

_____ 103. like having a warm lump inside your chest

_____ 104. there's an icy burning inside

_____ 105. like a gnawing inside without pangs

_____ 106. there is an inner buoyancy

_____ 107. I feel dizzy

_____ 108. I'm thirsty

_____ 109. my face and mouth are tight, tense, hard

_____ 110. my whole body is tense

_____ 111. I feel understimulated, undercharged

_____ 112. my body seems to get smaller

_____ 113. there's a deep, intense pain

Check List (*continued*)

_____ 114. I seem more alert	_____ 136. my knees and legs tremble
_____ 115. I feel choked up	_____ 137. there is a hollow pang in my stomach
_____ 116. warm excitement	
_____ 117. I'm physically less responsive	_____ 138. my senses aren't working quite right
_____ 118. there is a churning inside	_____ 139. I become conscious of my breathing
_____ 119. my heart pounds	
_____ 120. I seem to sense everything and experience everything immediately	_____ 140. there is a cold wave down my back
	_____ 141. my vision is slightly out of whack
_____ 121. my mouth gets dry	_____ 142. weakness in my legs or arms
_____ 122. I begin to gag, feel I will vomit	_____ 143. there is a hot red flame inside of me
_____ 123. I feel tired, sleepy	
_____ 124. something inside seems to go, seems cut loose	_____ 144. hands are moist
	_____ 145. my body tingles
_____ 125. there's a sharp, acute pain	_____ 146. a sense of lightness, buoyancy and upsurge of the body
_____ 126. my heart seems to ache	
_____ 127. my teeth are clenched	_____ 147. my hair stands on end
_____ 128. my throat is tight, constricted	_____ 148. there is a queasy feeling in my stomach
_____ 129. tension in my arms and legs	
_____ 130 a shiver goes up my spine	_____ 149. I need to take a deep breath
_____ 131. there is a ringing or twisting feeling in my chest	_____ 150. as if everything inside has stopped
	_____ 151. as if there were a tight, cold fist inside
_____ 132. there's an inner imbalance	
_____ 133. I have to urinate	_____ 152. my body seems to slow down
_____ 134. I'm wound up inside	_____ 153. my body wants to contract, draw closer to myself
_____ 135. a sense of harmony and peace within	
	_____ 154. every pain is magnified

Check List (*continued*)

_____ 155. my reactions seem to be exaggerated

_____ 156. my temples throb

_____ 157. I'm hypersensitive

_____ 158. there's a sagging of muscles

_____ 159. a sense of well being

_____ 160. I feel that I'll burst or explode, as if there is too much inside to be held in

_____ 161. I get diarrhea

_____ 162. there's a sense of weakness

_____ 163. all my senses seem to be completely open

_____ 164. I feel off balance

_____ 165. my breathing slows down

_____ 166. there is an odd taste in my mouth

_____ 167. I'm chilled, cold all over

_____ 168. I feel hot and flushed

_____ 169. my body movements are awkward and clumsy

_____ 170. a sense that I'm experiencing everything fully, completely, thoroughly; that I'm feeling all the way

_____ 171. I feel wide awake

_____ 172. I ache all over

_____ 173. a tugging sensation inside

_____ 174. a sense of fullness

_____ 175. there seems to be a lack of feeling inside

_____ 176. red heat in my eyes

_____ 177. a sense of being exceptionally strong or energetic

_____ 178. my ears feel blocked

_____ 179. there's some difficulty in breathing; I can't take a full breath

_____ 180. my stomach shivers and trembles; there's a tremor in my stomach

_____ 181. all excitement, vitality is gone

_____ 182. as if I'm breaking apart inside, with pieces flying off in all directions

_____ 183. I can hear my heart beat

_____ 184. I'm especially sensitive to everything around me

_____ 185. there's no thinking, just feeling

_____ 186. my diaphragm feels constricted

_____ 187. as if there's a lump in my stomach

_____ 188. I get hungry

_____ 189. there's a sensation of my heart sinking

_____ 190. a tingling movement inside

_____ 191. my breathing becomes faster

Check List (*continued*)

_____ 192. my movements are graceful and easy, I feel especially well coordinated

_____ 193. numbness alternates with pain

_____ 194. my senses are sharp but can't be focused on anything for any length of time; as though I'm flitting from thing to thing

_____ 195. my pulse quickens

_____ 196. my chest feels like it will burst

_____ 197. there's a heaviness in my chest

_____ 198. my throat aches

_____ 199. my head seems too large

_____ 200. there's a mellow comfort

_____ 201. I can't sleep

_____ 202. everything—breathing, moving, thinking—seems easier

_____ 203. I have to swallow frequently

_____ 204. a sense of being dead inside

_____ 205. everything seemed artificial

_____ 206. a sense of wandering, lost in space with nothing solid to grab onto

_____ 207. everything is going right for me

_____ 208. a sense of being totally unable to cope with the situation

_____ 209. the world seems a vast panorama I'm viewing from outside

_____ 210. I'm alternately detached and then keenly aware of my surroundings

_____ 211. everything seems unimportant and trivial

_____ 212. a strong sense of interest and involvement in things around me

_____ 213. sense of "rightness" with oneself and the world; nothing can go wrong

_____ 214. it seems as if the world is going to end

_____ 215. there seems to be religious overtones

_____ 216. a sense of being removed from daily chores

_____ 217. I'm just carried along by what is happening—adrift without an anchor

_____ 218. there's a renewed appreciation of life

_____ 219. there's a sense of tenuousness or disintegration of the world

_____ 220. things seem to be out of time, out of space, eternal, just there

_____ 221. I'm optimistic and cheerful; the world seems basically good and beautiful; men are essentially kind; life is worth living

_____ 222. the world seems no good, hostile, unfair

_____ 223. everything seems chaotic

_____ 224. I'm in tune with the world

Check List (*continued*)

_____ 225. I'm very aware of my surroundings

_____ 226. the air seems heavy

_____ 227. sense of being gripped by the
situation

_____ 228. a sense of being close to something unknown

_____ 229. there's a sense of the unknown

_____ 230. I'm at peace with the world

_____ 231. sounds and sights seemed muted
and dulled; the world outside of
me is a shadow, as if there were
a veil over me, over everything

_____ 232. I want to give thanks to God

_____ 233. a sense that another dimension
has been added and everything
has a greater intensity

_____ 234. I want to look away but somehow I'm fascinated

_____ 235. I feel a need to pray

_____ 236. as if God is in his heaven and all
is right with the world

_____ 237. everything seems useless, absurd,
meaningless

_____ 238. everything seems quiet

_____ 239. I have a sense of running endlessly, not knowing where to turn
next, getting nowhere

_____ 240. particularly acute awareness of
pleasurable things, their sounds,
their colors, and textures—
everything seems more beautiful,
natural, and desirable

_____ 241. I have a sense of strangeness,
unreality, as if I'm temporarily
in another world

_____ 242. I feel as if I am in a vacuum

_____ 243. nothing is a burden; problems
fade away and I'm free from
worry

_____ 244. I have a sense that there is
simply no place to go, no way of
ever getting out

_____ 245. I feel close to God

_____ 246. everything looks rotten, dirty,
black

_____ 247. the world seems to be characterized by an ebbing and flowing
fullness

_____ 248. as if I am in a dream and nothing
is real

_____ 249. I become aware of the vastness
and spaciousness of the world
around me

_____ 250. I seem to be immediately in
touch with the world; a sense of
being very open, receptive, with
no separation between me and
the world

_____ 251. there's a lack of involvement and
not caring about anything that
goes on around me

_____ 252. I seem to be caught up and overwhelmed by the feeling

_____ 253. everything seems in place,
ordered, organized

_____ 254. a sense of anticipation, waiting
for something to happen

Check List (*continued*)

_____ 255. there is a sense of regret	_____ 272. I seem to be functioning intellectually at a higher level
_____ 256. there is a sense of longing	
_____ 257. there is a sense of loss, of deprivation	_____ 273. I try to stop thinking of the situation and try to think of other things
_____ 258. I can only think of what caused the feeling	_____ 274. I want to understand but I can't
_____ 259. I keep wondering if I'm doing the right thing	_____ 275. I seem to be going around in a daze
_____ 260. I'm stunned	_____ 276. I have many different thoughts going through my head
_____ 261. I think of death	
_____ 262. I feel disoriented	_____ 277. I can't control my thinking rationally
_____ 263. thoughts just race through my head without control	_____ 278. all sensations, sounds, images, ideas crowd together, overlap
_____ 264. my thoughts just keep going around and around in a vicious circle never getting anywhere, thinking the same thing over and over again	_____ 279. I become forgetful
	_____ 280. I keep searching for an explanation, for some understanding; I keep thinking, "why?"
_____ 265. a sense that I'm losing my understanding of things around me	_____ 281. I am unable to think or reason correctly
_____ 266. I can't form thoughts	_____ 282. there is a sense of nostalgia as old memories crop up and I think of the past
_____ 267. I try to escape into dreams and fantasies	
	_____ 283. I think of suicide
_____ 268. I am able to think clearly, understand everything	_____ 284. all judgment, reason is suspended
_____ 269. I feel my brain is just a jungle of junk	_____ 285. I keep blaming myself for the situation
_____ 270. I keep thinking about what happened over and over again	_____ 286. I begin to think about what I can do to change the situation
	_____ 287. I'm extremely distractable, unable to concentrate
_____ 271. there's a sense of disbelief	

Check List (continued)

_____ 288. I'm completely free from worry

_____ 289. my mind goes blank and I can't think

_____ 290. I wish I could go back in time

_____ 291. I become introspective, turn inwards

_____ 292. my thinking is rapid

_____ 293. I think about beautiful things

_____ 294. I'm completely uncertain of everything

_____ 295. I'm haunted by terrible thoughts that I can't stop

_____ 296. I keep thinking of past successes

_____ 297. my mind wanders

_____ 298. I'm not too alert

_____ 299. there's a sense of increased clarity and understanding of the world

_____ 300. I keep asking myself a thousand questions

_____ 301. I feel mentally dull

_____ 302. I can't believe what's happening is true

_____ 303. I keep thinking of getting even, of revenge

_____ 304. there's a sense of not knowing where to go, what to do

_____ 305. as if everything has stopped, is standing still

_____ 306. somehow my sense of time is disturbed, disrupted

_____ 307. a state of timelessness

_____ 308. I'm optimistic about the future; the future seems bright

_____ 309. a sense that this is the end; there is no future in sight

_____ 310. as if there is a great dividing line between the time before and what's happened now

_____ 311. there's an intense concern for what will happen next

_____ 312. a feeling that time has passed and its too late

_____ 313. there is a very strong sense that time seems to slow down, to drag

_____ 314. I'm less aware of time

_____ 315. I become very concerned with the past

_____ 316. a sense of eternity or permanency

_____ 317. time seems to stand still

_____ 318. things are slowing down or stopping

_____ 319. I'm completely wrapped up in the moment, the present, the here and now, with no thought of past or future

_____ 320. time seems to speed up, to rush by

_____ 321. a sense of uncertainty about the future

Check List (*continued*)

_____ 322. there is no sense of the past, no present, no future; I'm suspended in time

_____ 323. as if I'm living from moment to moment

_____ 324. I want to hold back time, capture the moment

_____ 325. there's a desire to give of myself to another person

_____ 326. a sense that people don't like me

_____ 327. a sense of trust and appreciation of another person

_____ 328. sense of confidence in being with another person

_____ 329. I want to be noticed, have others pay attention to me

_____ 330. a sense of being deserted, betrayed and the world indifferent to me

_____ 331. a sense of being a stranger in the world

_____ 332. there's a sense of complete understanding of the other person

_____ 333. I want to talk to someone

_____ 334. a sense of empathic harmony with another person; in tune, sharing and experiencing the same feelings and thoughts

_____ 335. I want others (or the other person) to feel the same as I do

_____ 336. I want to touch, hold, be close physically to the other person

_____ 337. I want to talk to someone about my feelings

_____ 338. a sense of being wanted, needed

_____ 339. I want to be with friends

_____ 340. a sense of loving everyone, everything

_____ 341. I feel no respect for others around me

_____ 342. I want to reach out to everyone I meet

_____ 343. I keep thinking of what the other person has, how successful or how lucky he is

_____ 344. there is an intense positive relationship with another person or with other people; a communion, a unity, a closeness, friendliness and freedom, mutual respect and interdependence

_____ 345. a sense of unrelatedness to others; everyone seems far away; I am out of contact, can't reach others

_____ 346. realization that someone else is more important to me than I am to myself

_____ 347. I don't want to communicate with anyone

_____ 348. I want to help, protect, please another person

_____ 349. I want to feel with the other person, experience with the other person with every sense; to be psychologically in touch with another person

Check List (continued)

_____ 350. I want to be comforted, helped by someone

_____ 351. there is a total concentration on another person, an intense awareness of the other person

_____ 352. I feel outgoing

_____ 353. I want to avoid all stimulation

_____ 354. there is an impulse to hurt, to hit or to kick someone else

_____ 355. a sense of belonging with another person, a belonging from which other people are excluded

_____ 356. I don't want to talk to anyone about how I am feeling

_____ 357. I am very aware of myself in relation to others

_____ 358. I feel more understanding of others

_____ 359. I want to make others happy

_____ 360. a feeling of a certain distance from others; everyone seems far away

_____ 361. I'm just out of contact with the other person, I can't reach him

_____ 362. a sense of belonging with others

_____ 363. a sense of tolerance and acceptance of others

_____ 364. I want to communicate freely, share my thoughts and feelings with everyone around

_____ 365. a sense of giving, doing something for another person

_____ 366. I keep thinking about how bad it is for the other person

_____ 367. I want to withdraw, disappear, draw back, be alone, away from others, crawl into myself

_____ 368. I seem to be unable to communicate, unable to make another person understand

_____ 369. I want to be tender and gentle with another person

_____ 370. there is a sense of aloneness, being cut off, completely by myself

_____ 371. I don't care what anyone else thinks

_____ 372. a sense of being very integrated and at ease with myself, in harmony with myself

_____ 373. there is a heightened selfawareness

_____ 374. a sense of selflessness or surrender of myself; absolutely no self consciousness, I completely lose myself

_____ 375. a sense of not feeling or being me, of being unreal

_____ 376. I feel invulnerable

_____ 377. I feel insignificant

_____ 378. a sense of being important and worthwhile

_____ 379. I have a sense of innocence

_____ 380. seems that nothing I do is right

Check List (*continued*)

_____ 381. I feel vulnerable and totally helpless

_____ 382. I feel safe and secure

_____ 383. my mind and body seem totally unified

_____ 384. a sense of being more alive

_____ 385. a sense of being a bit ajar within myself

_____ 386. I forget my physical self; I don't care how I look

_____ 387. I have a tremendous sense of being in a hurry, in a rush

_____ 388. a sense of smiling at myself

_____ 389. I feel dirty and ugly

_____ 390. I don't care what happens to me

_____ 391. I feel aimless

_____ 392. I feel I can't go on

_____ 393. I'm intensely here and now

_____ 394. as if I'm standing outside of myself as an observer

_____ 395. a sense of being incomplete; as if part of me is missing

_____ 396. there is something complete within me

_____ 397. it hurts to be alive

_____ 398. I feel lost

_____ 399. a sense of being wild and reckless

_____ 400. I feel as if I'm under a heavy burden

_____ 401. my whole existence seems to be changed

_____ 402. I have a sense of sureness

_____ 403. a sense of being superior

_____ 404. I lose all confidence in myself and doubt myself

_____ 405. a sense that I am about to break down completely

_____ 406. there is a sense of detachment from myself, that I'm not my whole self anymore

_____ 407. I feel mechanical, like a robot, an automaton

_____ 408. sense of being split, disintegrated, fragmented

_____ 409. I am free of conflict

_____ 410. my attention is completely focused on myself, I'm preoccupied with myself

_____ 411. a tremendous self-consciousness, a sense that I can't get myself off my back, that I'm very aware of myself

_____ 412. I feel clean

_____ 413. I feel as if I look especially good

_____ 414. there is a sense of accomplishment, fulfillment

Check List (*continued*)

_____ 415. I get mad at myself for my feelings or thoughts or for what I've done

_____ 416. I have a sense of being no good, worthless

_____ 417. I feel let down

_____ 418. I have a sense of power

_____ 419. I have a feeling of being here, but not here

_____ 420. there's a feeling that no obstacle is too great for me

_____ 421. sense of being low, close to the ground

_____ 422. I feel expansive

_____ 423. I feel I can really be myself

_____ 424. there's a sense of being more substantial, of existing, of being real

_____ 425. there's a sense of dissociation of mind and body

_____ 426. as if part of me is watching the other part of me, half uncontrollable, and the other half watching and condemning

_____ 427. I keep thinking how lucky I am

_____ 428. I feel sorry for myself

_____ 429. I am peaceful, tranquil, quiet

_____ 430. a sense of being carefree but within balance

_____ 431. I seem to be acting without effort or compulsion, just going along with things as they come, in no hurry

_____ 432. I seem to be fighting myself

_____ 433. a sense of more confidence in myself; a feeling that I can do anything

_____ 434. I can't smile or laugh

_____ 435. I'm concerned that my speech won't come out right

_____ 436. I have trouble talking; my voice gets more or less unsteady; I stutter, stammer, hesitate

_____ 437. tears come to my eyes, the sort of tears not just from my eyes, but my whole self is crying

_____ 438. I'm torn between acting and not acting

_____ 439. it's a state of release

_____ 440. there is a lot of aimless physical activity, lots of insignificant, unnecessary little things

_____ 441. there is a yearning, a desire for change; I want things to hurry up and begin to change

_____ 442. a sense that I have no control over the situation

_____ 443. I seem to act on reflex, without thinking

_____ 444. I can't control my body motion

_____ 445. I want to cry, but I can't

Check List (*continued*)

_____ 446. I am afraid of expressing or releasing the feeling

_____ 447. I want to hide my feeling

_____ 448. I seem to lose all will power

_____ 449. I want to act, but I can't

_____ 450. there is an impulse to hide, to escape, to run, to get away

_____ 451. there's no desire to live; I don't want to go on

_____ 452. I'm on the verge of laughing and crying

_____ 453. a general apathy, "I don't care" attitude, as if my will to do anything were lost

_____ 454. I feel like laughing

_____ 455. I have a sense of being trapped, closed up, boxed, fenced in, tied down, inhibited

_____ 456. I don't want to move; I just want to stay motionless, immobile

_____ 457. it's an effort to do anything

_____ 458. the pitch of my voice goes up

_____ 459. I wish I could care, but I can't

_____ 460. I can't complete anything I start doing

_____ 461. I get giggly

_____ 462. I want to put things in order

_____ 463. my speech gets softer

_____ 464. I can't express my feelings

_____ 465. I feel like singing

_____ 466. my speech becomes very rapid

_____ 467. there is a great desire to let myself go completely

_____ 468. I want to express my feelings but somehow I can't

_____ 469. I am greatly concerned about doing the wrong thing

_____ 470. a longing to have things the same as before

_____ 471. I feel driven to move, be active, do something, anything, dance, jump, run, move—anything but sitting or standing still

_____ 472. I don't want anything changed

_____ 473. tears well up

_____ 474. I have no control of myself; I lose my sense of self-control

_____ 475. I'm momentarily immobilized; paralyzed; unable to act or move

_____ 476. I want to run

_____ 477. my speech slows down

_____ 478. I talk as if I'm hoarse; my voice sounds strange, different to me

_____ 479. I can't talk

_____ 480. I have an impulse to chatter and talk a lot; I keep talking and talking almost incoherently

Check List (continued)

_____ 481. I have a sense of being free, uninhibited, open, no longer blocked. I feel uninhibited and spontaneous—anything goes

_____ 482. there is nothing spontaneous, only deliberately, carefully controlled action

_____ 483. I want to do something, anything, to change the situation and relieve the tension

_____ 484. I want to try new things

_____ 485. I cry

_____ 486. I want something but I don't know what

_____ 487. I've got to do something with my hands

_____ 488. there is an impulse to strike out, to pound, or smash, or kick, or bite; to do something that will hurt

_____ 489. the feeling seizes me and takes over. I feel totally incapable of controlling, handling or stopping it

_____ 490. I want to clap my hands

_____ 491. my movements are sharper and quicker

_____ 492. I feel like smiling

_____ 493. a sense of being passive together with a desire to be active

_____ 494. I want to scream and yell

_____ 495. I feel like slouching, just being limp, completely relaxed

_____ 496. I become concerned and worried that I won't be able to control myself

_____ 497. I want to lie down somewhere and die

_____ 498. my voice gets much louder

_____ 499. I am completely silent as if I'm mute.

_____ 500. I want to strike out, explode, but I hold back, control myself

_____ 501. I have no desire, no motivation, no interest; wants, needs, drives are gone

_____ 502. I'm afraid that others will know how I feel

_____ 503. I want to say something nasty, something that will hurt someone

_____ 504. there is an irregular, undirected, disorganized rhythm to the feeling

_____ 505. it's an almost intangible sort of feeling

_____ 506. there doesn't seem to be much change in the intensity of the feeling; it pretty much stays at one level

_____ 507. it's a confused, mixed-up feeling, involved with other feelings

_____ 508. it's primarily a visceral feeling

_____ 509. the feeling seems to linger; to last a long time, with no immediate release

Check List (*continued*)

_____ 510. it seems to be a clearly formed tangible sort of feeling

_____ 511. the feeling is all involuntary, there is no anticipation on my part, it all just comes

_____ 512. the feeling seems to be all over, nowhere special, just not localized

_____ 513. a sense that the feeling will never end

_____ 514. it's a feeling that comes without warning

_____ 515. it just seems to peter out, to ebb away gradually

_____ 516. there is a steady, organized, regular, rhythm to the feeling

_____ 517. the feeling is on the surface

_____ 518. a sense that I'll never get over the feeling

_____ 519. a sense that I can't overcome the feeling

_____ 520. it's more an "inner" than an "outer" feeling

_____ 521. the feeling seems to go on and on, boundless, endless, limitless

_____ 522. the feeling is only brief in time; it's over quickly

_____ 523. the feeling goes slowly

_____ 524. it's an erratic, changing feeling

_____ 525. the feeling flows from the inside outwards

_____ 526. it's a very personal feeling

_____ 527. the feeling is very deep inside; I seem to feel it at the pit of my being

_____ 528. there is a slow rhythm to the feeling

_____ 529. the feeling begins with a sharp sudden onset

_____ 530. it's a very bland sort of feeling

_____ 531. the feeling starts somewhere in middle and then fills my whole body

_____ 532. it's a bottomless feeling

_____ 533. there is a slow gradual swelling intensity of feeling, until a peak is reached

_____ 534. I seem to nurture the feeling within myself; I want the feeling to continue, to keep going

_____ 535. I'm afraid and concerned that the feeling will end

_____ 536. I experience it, but the feeling doesn't really seem to touch me very much

_____ 537. I'm completely focused on the feeling; nothing intrudes; all other feelings cut out; it fills my whole being, spreading over everyone and everything. I lose myself completely in the feeling and experience

_____ 538. the feeling seems to be mostly in my muscles

_____ 539. I'm afraid of the feeling

Check List (continued)

_____ 540. it's as if I were in quicksand: the harder I struggle to get out of the feeling, the deeper I'm drawn in; I can't and don't know how to get rid of or pull out of the feeling

_____ 541. the feeling seems to come over me gradually, without my being aware of when it starts

_____ 542. it's a steady, ongoing feeling

_____ 543. there is this throbbing swell of intensity of feeling

_____ 544. it's involved with other feelings

_____ 545. the feeling suddenly stops and then starts again and suddenly stops again

_____ 546. it's a very complex sort of feeling

_____ 547. want to fight against it, not let the feeling overcome me

_____ 548. the feeling recurs again and again, in cycles

_____ 549. it all seems bottled up inside of me

_____ 550. the feeling fills me completely

_____ 551. there is a sharp, sudden end to the feeling

_____ 552. the feeling seems to be localized primarily in my head

_____ 553. it's a simple, pure feeling

_____ 554. there is a fast, rapid rhythm to the feeling

_____ 555. it seems to build up more and more

_____ 556. the feeling seizes me, takes over, I don't know how to stop the feeling

CHAPTER 2

A Dictionary of Emotional Meaning

ADMIRATION (from the Latin *admīrārī*, meaning "wonder at")
Number of items: 28
Range of agreement: 34–66%
Number of items at least 50% agreement: 2
Adequacy rating: 2.0

DEFINITION

there's a renewed appreciation of life (48), I'm optimistic and cheerful; the world seems basically good and beautiful; men are essentially kind; life is worth living (46); I feel like smiling (44), there is an inner warm glow, a radiant sensation (42); the future seems bright (38); there is a feeling of warmth all over (36), a sense of well-being (34); I think about beautiful things (34)

I'm excited in a calm way (52), I feel wide awake (46), my sense are perfectly focused (44); there is a strong sense of interest and involvement in things around me (42), a sense of vitality, aliveness, vibrancy, an extra spurt of energy or drive (36), a warm excitement (36), an inner buoyancy (36), a sense of being more alive (34)

there's a sense of trust and appreciation of another person (66), a total concentration on another person, an intense awareness of the other person (42), an intense positive relationship with another person or with other people; a communion, a unity, a closeness, friendliness and freedom, mutual respect and interdependence (40), a sense of confidence in being with another person (36), a sense of empathic harmony with another person; in tune, sharing and experiencing the same feelings and thoughts (34)

I feel strong inside (40); I seem to be functioning intellectually at a higher level (34)

I keep thinking of what the other person has, how successful or how lucky he is (48) it's involved with other feelings (42); it's more an "inner" than an "outer" feeling (40); it's a steady, ongoing feeling (36); it's a very personal feeling (34)

AFFECTION (from the Latin *affectio,* meaning "influence," "state of mind," or "favorable disposition")
Number of items: 45
Range of agreement: 34–72%
Number of items at least 50% agreement: 14
Adequacy rating: 1.5

DEFINITION

a sense of trust and appreciation of another person (62), an intense positive relationship with another person or with other people; a communion, a unity, a closeness, friendliness and freedom, mutual respect and interdependence (56); a sense of giving, doing something for another person (56), I want to be tender and gentle with another person (56); a sense of empathic harmony with another person; in tune, sharing and experiencing the same feelings and thoughts (52), a sense of complete understanding of the other person (52); I want to help, protect, please another person (48); there is a sense of confidence in being with another person (44); I want to touch, hold, be close physically to the other person (44); a sense of being wanted, needed (42); I feel soft and firm (40); there is a desire to give of myself to another person (40), a realization that someone else is more important to me than I am to myself (38); I want to make others happy (38); I feel outgoing (36); I want to feel with the other person, experience with the other person with every sense; to be psychologically in touch with another person (34)

I feel like smiling (72), there is an inner warm glow, a radiant sensation (68), a feeling of warmth all over (62), a sense of well being (54), I'm loose, relaxed (52), there is a sense of harmony and peace within (48); I'm optimistic and cheerful; the world seems basically good and beautiful; men are essentially kind; life is worth living (46); there is a mellow comfort (42); there is a renewed appreciation of life (42); my body seems to soften (38), I feel safe and secure (36), I think about beautiful things (36), I'm optimistic about the future; the future seems bright (34), I'm in tune with the world (34), my mind and body seem totally unified (34)

I'm excited in a calm way (52); there is an inner buoyancy (50), a warm excitement (48), a sense of being more alive (38), a sense of lightness, an upsurge of the body (34), I feel wide awake (34)

there is a sense of being important and worthwhile (44)

it's a very personal feeling (64), it's more an "inner" than an "outer" feeling (46); it's a simple, pure feeling (44), a steady, on-going feeling (42); the feeling seems to be all over, nowhere special, just not localized (38); the feeling flows from the inside outwards (36); it's involved with other feelings (36)

AMUSEMENT (taken from the French *amuser,* meaning "divert" or "occupy with trifles")
Number of items: 32
Range of agreement: 34–82%
Number of items at least 50% agreement: 6
Adequacy rating: 2.0

DEFINITION

I feel like smiling (82), I'm loose, relaxed (64); there is a sense of well-being (58), a sense of smiling at myself (48); there is an inner warm glow, a radiant sensation (46), a general release, a lessening of tension (44); I'm optimistic and cheerful; the world seems basically good and beautiful; men are essentially kind; life is worth living (38); there is a feeling of warmth all over (36), a mellow comfort (36), a sense of being carefree but within balance (34); I am free of conflict (34); there is a renewed appreciation of life (34); I'm in tune with the world (34)

I feel effervescent, bubbly (56), wide awake (48); there is an inner buoyancy (46), a warm excitement (44), a sense of lightness, an upsurge of the body (42), a sense of vitality, aliveness, vibrancy, an extra spurt of energy or drive (42), a sense of being more alive (42), a special lift in everything I do and say; I feel bouncy, springy, (40), more alert (38); my senses are perfectly focused (36), I'm excited in a calm way (34)

I feel like laughing (76); I feel outgoing (48); I get giggly (42); I'm completely wrapped up in the moment, the present, the here and now, with no thought of past or future (42); I seem to nurture the feeling within myself; I want the feeling to continue, to keep going (40); I'm less aware of time (34) it's a simple, pure feeling (54); the feeling is all involuntary, there is no anticipation on my part, it all just comes (36)

ANGER (from the Scandinavian; a comparable word in Icelandic is *angr,* meaning "grief" or "sorrow")
   Number of items: 34
   Range of agreement: 34–72%
   Number of items at least 50% agreement: 15
   Adequacy rating: 1.0

DEFINITION

my blood pressure goes up; blood seems to rush through my body (72), there is an excitement, a sense of being keyed up, overstimulated, supercharged (58); my pulse quickens (56), my body seems to speed up (54), there is a quickening of heartbeat (52); I feel that I'll burst or explode; as if there is too much inside to be held in (48); there is a churning inside (40), my heart pounds (40), its as if everything inside, my stomach, my throat, my head is expanding to the utmost, almost bursting (34)

my fists are clenched (52); there is a narrowing of my senses, my attention becomes riveted on one thing (52); there is an impulse to hurt, to hit, or to kick someone else (50), an impulse to strike out, to pound, or smash, or kick, or bite; to do something that will hurt (50); I want to strike out, explode, but I hold back, control myself (46); I want to say something nasty, something that will hurt someone (42); I keep thinking of getting even, of revenge (40)

I'm easily irritated, ready to snap (64); my face and mouth are tight, tense, hard (60), my whole body is tense (60), my teeth are clenched (52), there is a muscular rigidity (40), a tight knotted feeling in my stomach (38)

I seem to be caught up and overwhelmed by the feeling (64); there is a sense of being gripped by the situation (54)

there is an intensified focus to my sensations (34), my senses are perfectly focused (34)

I keep thinking about what happened over and over again (44), I can only think of what caused the feeling (38); my reactions seem to be exaggerated (38); I'm completely wrapped up in the moment, the present, the here and now, with no thought of past or future (36); I keep searching for an explanation, for some understanding; I keep thinking, "why?" (34)

the feeling begins with a sharp, sudden onset (42); it's involved with other feelings (40), a confused, mixed-up feeling (38)

ANXIETY (from the Latin *anxietas,* meaning essentially the same as anxiety in English)
Number of items: 23
Range of agreement: 34–60%
Number of items at least 50% agreement: 3
Adequacy rating: 1.0

DEFINITION

I'm wound up inside (60), my whole body is tense (48), I'm jumpy, jittery (48); I want to do something, anything, to change the situation and relieve the tension (44); there is a tight knotted feeling in my stomach (40), a tension across my back, my neck, and shoulders (38)

there is a sense that I have no control over the situation (54), a sense of being gripped by the situation (48); there's a sense of uncertainty about the future (46); I seem to be caught up and overwhelmed by the feeling (40); everything seems out of proportion (34)

I have no appetite; I can't eat (42), there is a queasy feeling in my stomach (38), a clutching, sinking feeling in the middle of my chest (38), a gnawing feeling in the pit of my stomach (36)

there is a yearning a desire for change; I want things to hurry up and begin to change (36); I try to stop thinking of the situation and try to think of other things (34)

there is an intense concern for what will happen next (56), a sense of anticipation, waiting for something to happen (50); there is a sense of aloneness, being cut off, completely by myself (40); there is a narrowing of my senses, my attention becomes riveted on one thing (36); I want to fight against it, not let the feeling overcome me (34)

it's involved with other feelings (38)

APATHY (from the Latin *apáthīa;* originally from the Greek *apatheia,* meaning "insensibility")
Number of items: 37
Range of agreement: 34–72%
Number of items at least 50% agreement: 10
Adequacy rating: 1.0

DEFINITION

> a general "I don't care attitude," as if my will to do anything were lost (72); I have no desire, no motivation, no interest; wants, needs, drives are gone (58); I feel understimulated, undercharged (56); there seems to be a lack of feeling inside (56); I'm physically less responsive (54); I feel mentally dull (54), my feelings seem dulled (54); all excitement, vitality is gone (50), there is no sensation; I'm numb, desensitized (48); I'm not too alert (48); it's an effort to do anything (46); I feel empty, drained, hollow (44), heavy, logy, sluggish (42), my body seems to slow down (40), I feel tired, sleepy (40); there's a sense of being dead inside (38)

> there's a lack of involvement and not caring about anything that goes on around me (66); everything seems unimportant and trivial (52); I feel aimless (46); it's as if I'm out of touch, seeing things from far away (42); everything seems useless, absurd, meaningless (42); there's a feeling of a certain distance from others; everyone seems far away (40); there is a sense of being incomplete; as if part of me is missing (38); I want to withdraw, and disappear, draw back, be alone, away from others, crawl into myself (38); there is a sense of unrelatedness to others; everyone seems far away; I am out of contact, can't reach others (38), a sense of aloneness, being cut off, completely by myself (36); there is a sense of wandering, lost in space with nothing solid to grab onto (36)

> my mind wanders (42), I'm just carried along by what is happening—adrift without an anchor (38), I'm unfocused and I can't focus (38); I feel mechanical, like a robot, an automation (38); I wish I could care, but I can't (36), I seem to be acting without effort or compulsion, just going along with things as they come, in no hurry (34); my sensations are blurred (34)

> the feeling seems to be all over, nowhere special, just not localized (40); it's a very bland sort of feeling (40), there doesn't seem to be much change in the intensity of the feeling; it pretty much stays at one level (34)

AWE (from the Scandinavian; a comparable word in Icelandic is *agi,* meaning "fear")

> Number of items: 25
> Range of agreement: 34–66%
> Number of items at least 50% agreement: 3
> Adequacy rating: 2.0

I'm excited in a calm way (66), I feel wide awake (50), there's a warm excitement (46); my senses are perfectly focused (44), I'm very aware of my surroundings (40); there is an intensified focus to my sensations (40), all my senses seem to be completely open (38); there is a strong sense of interest and involvement in things around me (36), a sense that I'm experiencing everything fully, completely, thoroughly; that I'm feeling all the way (36), that I seem to sense everything and experience everything immediately (34)

I seem to be caught up and overwhelmed by the feeling (40); there is a sense of being gripped by the situation (38); I feel insignificant (38)

there is a renewed appreciation of life (50), an inner warm glow, a radiant sensation (38)

there is a quickening of heartbeat (44), an excitement, a sense of being keyed up, overstimulated, supercharged (44)

I become aware of the vastness and spaciousness of the world around me (42); there is a narrowing of my senses, my attention becomes riveted on one thing (40); I'm less aware of time (36); there seems to be religious overtones (34); there is a sense that another dimension has been added and everything has a greater intensity (34)

it's more an "inner" than an "outer" feeling (42), a very personal feeling (40); the feeling fills me completely (34)

BOREDOM (origin unknown)

Number of times: 32
Range of agreement: 34–60%
Number of items at least 50% agreement: 11
Adequacy rating: 1.5

I feel tired, sleepy (60), I'm physically less responsive (58); I feel heavy, logy, sluggish (58), understimulated, undercharged (58), mentally dull (56); all excitement, vitality is gone (52); my feelings seem dulled (50), I'm not too alert (44), there seems to be a lack of feeling inside (40); my body seems to slow down (40), I feel let down (38)

there's a lack of involvement and not caring about anything that goes on around me (54); I feel aimless (46), everything seems unimportant and trivial (44); there is a sense of aloneness, being cut off, completely by myself (42); I try to escape into dreams and fantasies (40); I feel as if I'm in a vacuum (40); as if I'm out of touch, seeing things from far away (38), a feeling of a certain distance from others; everyone seems far away (36); a sense of unrelatedness to others; everyone seems far away; I'm out of contact, can't reach others (36)

there is a yearning, a desire for change; I want things to hurry up and begin to change (52), I begin to think about what I can do to change the situation (44)

my mind wanders (56); there is a very strong sense that time seems to slow down, to drag (56); I have a sense of being trapped, closed up, boxed, fenced in, tied down, inhibited (40); time seems to stand still (36); it's as if I'm suffocating or smothering (36); I feel driven to move, be active, do something, anything, dance, jump, run, move—anything but sitting or standing still (34); I'm easily irritated, ready to snap (34) the feeling seems to be all over, nowhere special, just not localized (38); it seems to come over me gradually, without my being aware of when it starts (36); it's a very bland sort of feeling (34)

CHEERFULNESS (from the Old French [before 1400] *chere;* going back to the Latin *cara,* meaning "face")

Number of items: 69
Range of agreement: 34–76%
Number of items at least 50% agreement: 26
Adequacy rating: 1.0

DEFINITION

I feel like smiling (76); I'm loose, relaxed (74); there is a renewed appreciation of life (68), I'm optimistic and cheerful; the world seems basically good and beautiful; men are essentially kind; life is worth living (66); there is a sense of well-being (66), an inner warm glow, a radiant sensation (64); everything is going right for me (58); a sense of being very integrated and at ease with myself, in harmony with myself (54); I'm optimistic about the future; the future seems bright (50); I'm in tune with the world (50), there is a sense of being carefree but within balance (48), I'm completely free from worry (48); there is a sense of harmony and peace within (48), a feeling of warmth all over (46), a sense of "rightness" with onself and the world; nothing can go wrong (46); I am free of conflict (44), I'm really functioning as a unit

(44), I'm at peace with the world (44), I feel safe and secure (44), I feel I can really be myself (42); I think about beautiful things (42); everything—breathing, moving, thinking—seems easier (40), my movements are graceful and easy, I feel especially well coordinated (40); there is a sense of smiling at myself (40), a general release, a lessening of tension (40), a sense of fullness (34); nothing is a burden; problems fade away and I'm free from worry (34)

there is a special lift in everything I do and say; I feel bouncy, springy (74), a sense of vitality, aliveness, vibrancy, an extra spurt of energy or drive (66), a lightness, buoyancy and upsurge of the body (64); I feel wide awake (60), more alive (58), excited in a calm way (56), more alert (54); there is a particularly acute awareness of pleasurable things, their sounds, their colors, and textures—everything seems more beautiful, natural, and desirable (54); there is a strong sense of interest and involvement in things around (52); there is an inner buoyancy (50), a warm excitement (48); I feel effervescent, bubbly (46); my senses are perfectly focused (44), there is an intense awareness of everything; I seem to experience things with greater clarity; colors seem brighter, sounds clearer, movements more vivid (40); I seem to be immediately in touch with the world; a sense of being very open, receptive, with no separation between me and the world (38); I seem to be immediately in touch and appreciative of immediate physical sensations (36); I'm very aware of my surroundings (34), there is a sense that I'm experiencing everything fully, completely, thoroughly; that I'm feeling all the way (34)

I have a sense of sureness (58); I feel strong inside (54); I feel taller, stronger, bigger (46); I feel as if I look especially good (42); I feel clean (40), expansive (40); I keep thinking how lucky I am (40); there is a sense of being more substantial, of existing, of being real (36); a sense of being exceptionally strong or energetic (36), of being important and worthwhile (36); a sense of more confidence in myself; a feeling that I can do anything (34)

I feel outgoing (60), I want others or the other person to feel the same as I do (52); there is a sense of loving everyone, everything (42), I want to make others happy (40); there is an intense positive relationship with another person or with other people; a communion, a unity, a closeness, friendliness and freedom, mutual respect and interdependence (40); I feel more understanding of others (40), there is a sense of tolerance and acceptance of others (38); I want to be with friends (36); there is a sense of trust and appreciation of another person (34)

I feel like singing (50); I seem to nurture the feeling within myself; I want the feeling to continue, to keep going (48)

the feeling seems to be all over, nowhere special, just not localized (52); it's a simple, pure feeling (44)

CONFIDENCE (from the Latin *confidentia,* meaning "reliant" or "firmly trusting")

Number of items: 58
Range of agreement: 34–68%
Number of items at least 50% agreement: 19
Adequacy rating: 1.5

DEFINITION

I feel safe and secure (62); I'm really functioning as a unit (56); there's a sense of well-being (52), a sense of "rightness" with oneself and the world; nothing can go wrong (52); there is a sense of accomplishment, fulfillment (52); I'm optimistic about the future; the future seems bright (50), everything is going right for me (50), I'm optimistic and cheerful; the world seems basically good and beautiful; men are essentially kind; life is worth living (46); I feel like smiling (46), I'm in tune with the world (44); there is a sense of harmony and peace within (44), a sense of being very integrated and at ease with myself, in harmony with myself (42), everything seems in place, ordered, organized (42); there is an inner warm glow, a radiant sensation (42); I feel I can really be myself (40), I am free of conflict (38), my mind and body seem totally unified (38); there is a renewed appreciation of life (38); nothing is a burden; problems fade away and I'm free from worry (38); there is something complete within me (36); there is a mellow comfort (36), I'm at peace with the world (36); everything—breathing, moving, thinking—seems easier (34)

I have a sense of sureness (68), I feel strong inside (60); I seem to be functioning intellectually at a higher level (52), I am able to think clearly, understand everything (50); I feel taller, stronger, bigger (50), there are moments of tremendous strength (48); there is a sense of more confidence in myself; a feeling that I can do anything (48); a sense of being important and worthwhile (46); my movements are graceful and easy, I feel especially well coordinated (44); I feel as if I look especially good (36); there is a feeling that no obstacle is too great for me (36), a sense of being exceptionally strong or energetic (36), my muscle tone is suddenly enhanced (34); my thinking is rapid (34), there is a sense of increased clarity and understanding of the world (34); I keep thinking how lucky I am (34)

I feel wide awake (58), more alert (58), excited in a calm way (58); my senses are perfectly focused (54); there is an inner buoyancy (52), a sense of vitality, aliveness, vibrancy, an extra spurt of energy or drive (50), a sense of being more alive (48); there is a strong sense of interest and involvement in things around me (42); I seem to be immediately in touch with the world; a sense of being very open, receptive, with no separation between me and the world (42); there is a special lift in everything I do and say; I feel bouncy, springy (36)

I feel outgoing (52); there is an intense positive relationship with another person or with other people; a communion, a unity, a closeness, friendliness and freedom, mutual respect and interdependence (38); there is a sense of confidence in being with another person (34), a sense of trust and appreciation of another person (34)

I seem to nurture the feeling within myself; I want the feeling to continue, to keep going (40); I am very aware of myself in relation to others (36)

it's a very personal feeling (40); it seems to be a clearly formed tangible sort of feeling (38); it's more an "inner" than an "outer" feeling (36)

CONTEMPT (from the Latin *contemptus,* meaning "scorn")
Number of items: 14
Ranger of agreement: 34–58%
Number of items at least 50% agreement: 2
Adequacy rating: 2.0

DEFINITION
my face and mouth are tight, tense, hard (58), my whole body is tense (50); I'm easily irritated, ready to snap (48), I'm wound up inside (46)

I want to say something nasty, something that will hurt someone (46); I want to strike out, explode, but I hold back, control myself

(44); there is an impulse to strike out, to pound, or smash, or kick, or bite; to do something that will hurt (42)

my blood pressure goes up; blood seems to rush through my body (40), there is a quickening of heartbeat (34)

there is a sense of disbelief (38); I keep searching for an explanation, for some understanding; I keep thinking, "why?" (36); I seem to be caught up and overwhelmed by the feeling (34)

it's a confused, mixed-up feeling, involved with other feelings (40), it's involved with other feelings (36)

CONTENTMENT (from the Latin *contentus,* meaning "satisfied")
  Number of items: 49
  Range of agreement: 34–84%
  Number of items at least 50% agreement: 22
  Adequacy rating: 1.0

DEFINITION

I'm loose, relaxed (84), there is a sense of well-being (78), harmony and peace within (76), I am peaceful, tranquil, quiet (74); there is a general release, a lessening of tension (72); there is an inner warm glow, a radiant sensation (68); I'm optimistic and cheerful; the world seems basically good and beautiful; men are essentially kind; life is worth living (66); I am free of conflict (66), safe and secure (64); there is a renewed appreciation of life (62); I'm at peace with the world (62), there is a mellow comfort (60); I feel like smiling (60), everything is going right for me (58); I'm completely free from worry (58); there is a sense of fullness (52); nothing is a burden; problems fade away and I'm free from worry (52), I'm in tune with the world (50), there is a sense of "rightness" with oneself and the world; nothing can go wrong (50); there is a sense of being very integrated and at ease with myself, in harmony with myself (50); there is a feeling of warmth all over (50); I'm optimistic about the future; the future seems bright (48); I think about beautiful things (44); everything seems quiet (42); my mind and body seem totally unified (42), everything—breathing, moving, thinking—seems easier (40); there is a sense of being carefree but within balance (38); my body seems to soften (38); it's a state of release (36); I feel I can really be myself (36)

there is an inner buoyancy (44); a particularly acute awareness of pleasurable things, their sounds, their colors, and textures—

everything seems more beautiful, natural, and desirable (44); I seem to be immediately in touch and appreciative of immediate physical sensations (40); there is a sense of being more alive (40)

I feel strong inside (38); I have a sense of sureness (38), a sense of more confidence in myself; a feeling that I can do anything (36); I keep thinking how lucky I am (36)

there is a sense of loving everyone, everything (36); a sense of confidence in being with another person (36); I feel soft and firm (34)

I seem to nurture the feeling within myself; I want the feeling to continue, to keep going (46); I'm less aware of time (44); there is a sense of being removed from daily chores (42); I want to hold back time, capture the moment (40); there is a sense of accomplishment, fulfillment (38)

the feeling seems to be all over, nowhere special, just not localized (50); it's a simple, pure feeling (38); a steady, ongoing feeling (36); it's more of an "inner" than an "outer" feeling (34)

DELIGHT (from the Old French *delitier;* going back to the Latin *dēlectāre,* a verb form of *dēlicere,* meaning "allure")
Number of items: 53
Range of agreement: 34–74%
Number of items at least 50% agreement: 16
Adequacy rating: 1.0

DEFINITION

I feel like smiling (74); there is an inner warm glow, a radiant sensation (68), a sense of well-being (66), a renewed appreciation of life (60); I'm optimistic and cheerful; the world seems basically good and beautiful; men are essentially kind; life is worth living (60); everything is going right for me (52); there is a feeling of warmth all over (48); I'm in tune with the world (46), I'm loose, relaxed (42), optimistic about the future; the future seems bright (42); there is a sense of "rightness" with oneself and the world; nothing can go wrong (40); there is a mellow comfort (40); I think about beautiful things (40); I have a sense of being very integrated and at ease with myself, in harmony with myself (38), I am free of conflict (38); there is a general release, a lessening of tension (38), a sense of harmony and peace within

(36), I feel safe and secure (36); there is a sense of being carefree but within balance (34); a sense of smiling at myself (34)

there is a warm excitement (70); I feel effervescent, bubbly (70), excited in a calm way (64); there is an inner buoyancy (62), a special lift in everything I do and say; I feel bouncy, springy (58), a sense of vitality, aliveness, vibrancy, an extra spurt of energy or drive (56), a sense of lightness, buoyancy and upsurge of the body (52), a sense of being more alive (46); there is an intense awareness of everything; I seem to experience things with greater clarity; colors seem brighter, sounds clearer, movements more vivid (46); I seem more alert (44); there is a particularly acute awareness of pleasurable things, their sounds, their colors, and textures—everything seems more beautiful, natural, and desirable (40); I feel wide awake (38); I seem to sense everything and experience everything immediately (36); a sense that I am experiencing everything fully, completely, thoroughly; that I'm feeling all the way (36); there is a sense of interest and involvement in things around me (34)

I feel outgoing (48), a sense of loving everyone, everything (44); there is an intense positive relationship with another person or with other people; a communion, a unity, a closeness, friendliness and freedom, mutual respect and interdependence (40); there's a sense of trust and appreciation of another person (40); I want to make others happy (34)

I keep thinking how lucky I am (46); I feel expansive (36), strong inside (34); my movements are graceful and easy, I feel especially well coordinated (34)

there is an excitement, a sense of being keyed up, overstimulated, supercharged (50); there is quickening of heartbeat (40)

I seem to nurture the feeling within myself; I want the feeling to continue, to keep going (54); I feel like singing (52), like laughing (44); I want to hold back time, capture the moment (34)

it's a simple, pure feeling (44); it's a very personal feeling (40); the feeling seems to be all over, nowhere special, just not localized (34)

DEPRESSION (from the Latin *deprimere,* meaning "to press down")
    Number of items: 83
    Range of agreement: 34–60%

Number of items at least 50% agreement: 16
Adequacy rating: 1.0

DEFINITION

I feel empty, drained, hollow (60), understimulated, undercharged (52), heavy, logy, sluggish (52); my feelings seem dulled (52), I am physically less responsive (50), all excitement, vitality is gone (50); there is a sense of being dead inside (50); I feel let down (46), tired, sleepy (44); it's an effort to do anything (42), I have no desire, no motivation, no interest; wants, needs, drives are gone (42); it's as if everything inside has stopped (40); I feel mentally dull (40); my body seems to slow down (40); there is a sense that somehow I can't experience things wholly, as if there is a lid or some sort of clamp which keeps me from perceiving (36)

there is a sense of uncertainty about the future (52); I feel sorry for myself (50); a sense of being gripped by the situation (50); everything seems out of proportion (48); a sense of being totally unable to cope with the situation (44), there is simply no place to go, no way of ever getting out (44), a sense of not knowing where to go, what to do (42); I lose all confidence in myself and doubt myself (42); I feel lost (40); I seem to be caught up and overwhelmed by the feeling (38); I feel vulnerable and totally helpless (36), off balance (36), as if I were in quicksand; the harder I struggle to get out of the feeling, the deeper I'm drawn in; I can't and don't know how to get rid of or pull out of the feeling (34); I'm completely uncertain of everything (34); I feel insignificant (34)

there is a sense of aloneness, being cut off, completely by myself (56); I want to withdraw, disappear, draw back, be alone, away from others, crawl into myself (52); I feel aimless (46), wandering, lost in space with nothing solid to grab on to (42); I become introspective, turn inwards (42); everything seems useless, absurd, meaningless (42); there is a lack of involvement and not caring about anything that goes on around me (42); there is a sense of being incomplete; as if part of me is missing (40); a feeling of a certain distance from others; everyone seems far away (38), as if I'm out of touch, seeing things from far away (36); there is a sense of unrelatedness to others; everyone seems far away; I am out of contact, can't reach others (36); I feel as if I am in a vacuum (36); I don't want to communicate with anyone

(36); there is a sense of being deserted, betrayed and the world indifferent to me (34); my body wants to contract, draw closer to myself (34)

there is a heavy feeling in my stomach (58); a sense of loss, of deprivation (52); there is an inner ache you can't locate (52); I have no appetite; I can't eat (48); there is a clutching, sinking feeling in the middle of my chest (46), there is a heaviness in my chest (44), I feel as if I'm under a heavy burden (44); there is a lump in my throat (42); I'm slightly headachy, as if my brain were tired (42); I can't smile or laugh (38); there is a gnawing feeling in the pit of my stomach (36); a sensation of my heart sinking (34); it's as if I'm suffocating or smothering (34); it hurts to be alive (34)

there is a sense of longing (46), a yearning, a desire for change; I want things to hurry up and begin to change (42); there is a sense of weakness (40); it seems that nothing I do is right (36); I begin to think about what I can do to change the situation (34)

I'm easily irritated, ready to snap (44); I feel choked up (36), wound up inside (34)

I keep searching for an explanation, for some understanding; I keep thinking, "why?" (38); I want to be comforted, helped by someone (36); I can only think of what caused the feeling (34); I have a sense of being trapped, closed up, boxed, fenced in, tied down, inhibited (34); my attention is completely focused on my myself, I'm preoccupied with myself (34)

the feeling is very deep inside; I seem to feel it at the pit of my being (52), it's more an "inner" than an "outer" feeling (46); it's a confused, mixed up feeling, involved with other feelings (44); the feeling seems to linger; to last a long time, with no immediate release (44); it's a very personal feeling (42); it's involved with other feelings (42); the feeling goes slowly (36), it's a bottomless feeling (36), there is a sense that the feeling will never end (36); it all seems bottled up inside of me (34); it fills me completely (34)

DETERMINATION (from the Latin dētermināre, meaning "to bound," "to limit," or "to fix")
Number of items: 36
Range of agreement: 34–52%

Number of items at least 50% agreement: 6
Adequacy rating: 1.5

DEFINITION

I have a sense of sureness (52); I seem to be functioning intellectually at a higher level (50); there is a feeling that no obstacle is too great for me (46); I feel taller, stronger, bigger (40); I have a sense of more confidence in myself; a feeling that I can do anything (38), a sense of being important and worthwhile (38); there are moments of tremendous strength (38), a sense of being exceptionally strong or energetic (36), I feel strong inside (36), my muscle tone is suddenly enhanced (34)

my senses are perfectly focused (52); I am excited in a calm way (50), more alert (48), wide awake (48), with a sense of vitality, aliveness, vibrancy, an extra spurt of energy or drive (42); there is an intensified focus to my sensations (42)

my body seems to speed up (44), there is an excitement, a sense of being keyed up, overstimulated, supercharged (40); my blood pressure goes up; blood seems to rush through my body (34)

my whole body is tense (44), I'm wound up inside (38), there is a muscular rigidity (34)

there is a sense of being gripped by the situation (52); I'm really functioning as a unit (50); there is a narrowing of my senses, my attention becomes riveted on one thing (48); there is a heightened self-awareness (46); there is an intense concern for what will happen next (44), a sense of anticipation, waiting for something to happen (40); there is nothing spontaneous, only deliberately, carefully controlled action (38); I'm intensely here and now (38); there is a sense of accomplishment, fulfillment (36)

it seems to be a clearly formed tangible sort of feeling (46); it's more an "inner" than an "outer" feeling (40); the feeling is very deep inside; I seem to feel it at the pit of my being (40); it's a steady, ongoing feeling (38); it's involved with other feelings (34)

DISGUST (from the Old French *desgoust* and from the Italian *dis,* implying negation, plus *gusto,* meaning "taste")

Number of items: 14
Range of agreement: 34–50%
Number of items at least 50% agreement: 1
Adequacy rating: 1.5

I'm easily irritated, ready to snap (44); my face and mouth are tight, tense, hard (42); there is a tight knotted feeling in my stomach (40); my teeth are clenched (34), my whole body is tense (34)

I feel nauseated, sick to my stomach (50), there is a queasy feeling in my stomach (40)

there is a sense that I have no control over the situation (38); there is a sense of disbelief (38); I feel let down (34)

it's involved with other feelings (40); the feeling begins with a sharp sudden onset (38), it comes without warning (34); the feeling is all involuntary, there is no anticipation on my part, it all just comes (34)

DISLIKE (from *dis,* implying negation, and *like,* in Old English, *lician;* probably going back to original Teutonic *līko,* meaning "body")
Number of items: 10
Range of agreement: 34–48%
Number of items at least 50% agreement: 0
Adequacy rating: 2.5

I'm easily irritated, ready to snap (48); my face and mouth are tight, tense, hard (36); I'm wound up inside (36), there is a muscular rigidity (34)

there is a narrowing of my senses, my attention becomes riveted on one thing (46); I want to say something nasty, something that will hurt someone (38); I want to strike out, explode, but I hold back, control myself (36)

I begin to think about what I can do to change the situation (40); I try to stop thinking of the situation and try to think of other things (4)

the feeling is only brief in time; it's over quickly (34)

ELATION (from the Latin *ēlātus,* meaning "brought out," "raised," or "exhalted")
Number of items: 63
Range of agreement: 34–78%
Number of items at least 50% agreement: 22
Adequacy rating: 1.0

DEFINITION

I feel effervescent, bubbly (74); there is an inner buoyancy (72), a sense of lightness, buoyancy and upsurge of the body (68), a special lift in everything I do and say; I feel bouncy, springy (68); there is a warm excitement (68), a sense of being more alive (66), wide awake (64), a sense of vitality, aliveness, vibrancy, an extra spurt of energy or drive (62); there is a floating, soaring sensation (52); I seem more alert (48); there is particularly acute awareness of pleasurable things, their sounds, their colors, and textures—everything seems more beautiful, natural, and desirable (44); there is an intense awareness of everything; I seem to experience with greater clarity; colors seem brighter, sounds clearer, movements more vivid (40); all my senses seem to be completely open (36), I'm experiencing everything fully, completely, thoroughly; I'm feeling all the way (36); I'm excited in a calm way (36)

I'm optimistic and cheerful; the world seems basically good and beautiful; men are essentially kind; life is worth living (74); there is a renewed appreciation of life (70); I feel like smiling (70); there is an inner warm glow, a radiant sensation (70); everything is going right for me (62), there is a sense of well-being (60), a sense of "rightness" with oneself and the world; nothing can go wrong (52); I'm optimistic about the future; the future seems bright (48); it's a state of release (46); I'm in tune with the world (44); there is a general release, a lessening of tension (42); there is a feeling of warmth all over (42); I feel safe and secure (40), I'm completely free from worry (38); I think about beautiful things (38); there is a sense of fullness (36), a sense of smiling at myself (36)

I keep thinking how lucky I am (62); there is a sense of being important and worthwhile (54); I feel taller, stronger, bigger (46); I have a sense of sureness (44); I feel strong inside (44), expansive (42); there is a sense of being exceptionally strong or energetic (42), a sense of power (38); a sense of more confidence in myself; a feeling that I can do anything (36)

there is an excitement, a sense of being keyed up, overstimulated, supercharged (78); there is a quickening of heartbeat (50), my body seems to speed up (42), my blood pressure goes up; blood seems to rush through my body (36); I feel driven to move, be active, do something, anything, dance, jump, run, move—anything but sitting or standing still (36); I feel that I'll burst or explode, as if there is too much inside to be held in (36)

I feel outgoing (68), I want to reach out to everyone I meet (40), I want others (or the other person) to feel the same as I do (40); there is a sense of loving everyone, everything (36); I want to talk to someone about my feelings (34), I want to communicate freely, share my thoughts and feelings with everyone around (34)

there is a sense of accomplishment, fulfillment (50); I feel like laughing (48), like singing (46); I seem to nurture the feeling within myself; I want the feeling to continue, to keep going (44); I can't believe what's happening is true (38); I seem to be caught up and overwhelmed by the feeling (38); my whole existence seems to be changed (34)

the feeling seems to be all over, nowhere special, just not localized (48); it fills me completely (46); it's involved with other feelings (38)

EMBARRASSMENT (from the French *embarrasser*, meaning "block" or "obstruct"; derived from *embarras*, meaning "obstacle")
   Number of items: 30
   Range of agreement: 34–58%
   Number of items at least 50% agreement: 4
   Adequacy rating: 1.0

DEFINITION

there is a sense of regret (54); I begin to think about what I can do to change the situation (52); there is a yearning, a desire for change; I want things to hurry up and begin to change (48); I want to hide my feeling (48); I keep blaming myself for the situation (42), I get mad at myself for my feelings or thoughts or for what I've done (38); I try to stop thinking of the situation and try to think of other things (36)

I want to withdraw, disappear, draw back, be alone, away from others, crawl into myself (58); there is an impulse to hide, to escape, to run, to get away (46); my body wants to contract, draw closer to myself (44); there is a sense of aloneness, being cut off, completely by myself (34)

I feel vulnerable and totally helpless (46); there is a sense that I have no control over the situation (40), a sense of being gripped by the situation (40)

my blood pressure goes up; blood seems to rush through my body
(44), my pulse quickens (34), there is a quickening of heartbeat
(34)

I want to do something, anything, to change the situation and
relieve the tension (52), my whole body is tense (40)

there is a clutching, a sinking feeling in the middle of my chest
(38); there is a queasy feeling in my stomach (34)

I keep thinking about what happened over and over again (46);
I'm hypersensitive (44); I can only think of what caused the
feeling (42); I am very aware of myself in relation to others (38);
I'm chilled, cold all over (38); I'm especially sensitive to everything around me (34)

the feeling is all involuntary, there is no anticipation on my part,
it all just comes (40); the feeling begins with a sharp sudden
onset (36); it's a very personal feeling (36)

ENJOYMENT (from the Old French *enjoir,* from *en,* meaning "in," plus
joir, meaning "joy")
> Number of items: 65
> Range of agreement: 34–72%
> Number of items at least 50% agreement: 23
> Adequacy rating: 1.0

DEFINITION

I feel like smiling (72); I'm loose, relaxed (68), there's sense
of well-being (60); I'm completely free from worry (58), I'm
in tune with the world (56); I'm optimistic and cheerful; the world
seems basically good and beautiful; men are essentially kind; life
is worth living (56); there is an inner warm glow, a radiant sensation (56), a renewed appreciation of life (56); there is a sense
of harmony and peace within (56), a sense of being very integrated
and at ease with myself, in harmony with myself (50); everything
is going right for me (48); there is a sense of being carefree
but within balance (48); there is a general release, a lessening
of tension (48); nothing is a burden; problems fade away and
I'm free from worry (46), I'm at peace with the world (46),
I feel safe and secure (46); there is a mellow comfort (44), a
feeling of warmth all over (44); there is a sense of fullness (42);
I feel I can really by myself (42), I am free of conflict (40),
a sense of "rightness" with oneself and the world; nothing can

go wrong (38), I'm really functioning as a unit (36); I think about beautiful things (36); I am peaceful, tranquil, quiet (34); everything—breathing, moving, thinking—seems easier (34); there is a sense of smiling at myself (34)

I'm excited in a calm way (66); I feel wide awake (66), more alive (60); there is a warm excitement (58), an inner buoyancy (56); I feel effervescent, bubbly (54), more alert (52); there's a particularly acute awareness of pleasurable things, their sounds, their colors, and textures—everything seems more beautiful, natural, and desirable (52); my senses are perfectly focused (50); there is an intense awareness of everything; I seem to experience things with greater clarity; colors seem brighter, sounds clearer, movements more vivid (50); there is a special lift in everything I do and say; I feel bouncy, springy (50), with a sense of vitality, aliveness, vibrancy, an extra spurt of energy or drive (48); there is strong sense of interest and involvement in things around me (46); I seem to be immediately in touch and appreciative of immediate physical sensations (40); there is a sense of lightness, buoyancy and upsurge of the body (40); I'm experiencing everything fully, completely, thoroughly; I'm feeling all the way (38); all my senses seem to be completely open (36), I seem to be immediately in touch with the world; a sense of being very open, receptive, with no separation between me and the world (34), I seem to sense everything and experience everything immediately (34)

I feel outgoing (56); I want others (or the other person) to feel the same as I do (38), I want to make others happy (38); there's a sense of belonging with others (38), I want to communicate freely, share my thoughts and feelings with everyone around (38); I want to be with friends (36); there is an intense positive relationship with another person or with other people; a communion, a unity, a closeness, friendliness and freedom, mutual respect and interdependence

my movements are graceful and easy, I feel especially well coordinated (38); I feel strong inside (34); I have a sense of sureness (34)

I'm less aware of time (52); I seem to nurture the feeling within myself; I want the feeling to continue, to keep going (44); I feel like singing (42); I want to hold back time, capture the moment (34) it's a simple, pure feeling (48); the feeling seems to be all over, nowhere special, just not localized (42); it's a very personal feeling (38); it's a steady, ongoing feeling (34); the feeling fills me completely (34)

EXCITEMENT (from the Latin *excitāre,* a verb form of *exciere,* meaning "call forth" or "rouse")
    Number of items: 28
    Range of agreement: 36–76%
    Number of items at least 50% agreement: 7
    Adequacy rating: 1.0

DEFINITION

there is a sense of vitality, aliveness, vibrancy, an extra spurt of energy or drive (66), a sense of being more alive (58), more alert (56), a warm excitement (54), a special lift in everything I do and say; I feel bouncy, spring (50), there is an inner buoyancy (48); there is a strong sense of interest and involvement in things around me (48); I feel effervescent, bubbly (44), wide awake (44); there is a sense of lightness, buoyancy and upsurge of the body (40); I'm excited in a calm way (36)

there is an excitement, a sense of being keyed up, overstimulated, supercharged (76); there is a quickening of heartbeat (56), my pulse quickens (46), my body seems to speed up (46), my blood pressure goes up; blood seems to rush through my body (42)

there is an inner warm glow, a radiant sensation (48); I feel like smiling (42); I'm optimistic and cheerful; the world seems basically good and beautiful; men are essentially kind; life is worth living (38), I'm optimistic about the future; the future seems bright (36)

I feel thinking how lucky I am (44); I feel expansive (36); my movements are sharper and quicker (36)

there is a sense of being gripped by the situation (46), I seem to be caught up and overwhelmed by the feeling (36)

there is a sense of anticipation, waiting for something to happen (44); I feel outgoing (44); I'm wound up inside (40)

FEAR (in Old English before 1100, *fær,* meaning "sudden attack" or "sudden danger")
    Number of items: 50
    Range of agreement: 34–80%

Number of items at least 50% agreement: 10
Adequacy rating: 1.0

DEFINITION

my whole body is tense (80); there is a tight knotted feeling
in my stomach (50), a muscular rigidity (46); I want to do something, anything, to change the situation and relieve the tension
(46); my face and mouth are tight, tense, hard (44); I'm cold,
yet perspiration pours out of me (44); I'm jumpy, jittery (42);
my hands are moist (40); I'm wound up inside (34)

there's a quickening of heartbeat (68), my pulse quickens (60),
my heart pounds (54), my blood pressure goes up; blood seems
to rush through my body (44); there's absolute physical turmoil
(42), an excitement, a sense of being keyed up, overstimulated,
supercharged (40); there is a churning inside (38); I'm stunned
(36); my body seems to speed up (34)

there is a sense of being gripped by the situation (64), I feel
vulnerable and totally helpless (54); I seem to be caught up and
overwhelmed by the feeling (48), there is a sense that I have
no control over the situation (42), being totally unable to cope
with the situation (40); thoughts just race through my head without control (34); there is a sense of not knowing where to go,
what to do (34); I'm momentarily immobilized; paralyzed; unable
to act or move (34)

there is a clutching, sinking feeling in the middle of my chest
(68), a heavy feeling in my stomach (36), a queasy feeling in my
stomach (36), my stomach shivers and trembles; there is a tremor
in my stomach (34); I can't smile or laugh (34) there is an
intense concern for what will happen next (58); I sweat (48);
there is a sense of aloneness, being cut off, completely by myself
(48); there's a narrowing of my senses, my attention becomes
riveted on one thing (46); there is a sense of anticipation, waiting
for something to happen (44); I can't believe what's happening
is true (42); I have clammy hands (42); there is a yearning,
a desire for change; I want things to hurry up and begin to change
(38); I want to be comforted, helped by someone (36); I want
to fight against it, not let the feeling overcome me (36), I'm afraid
of the feeling (36); I'm intensely here and now (36); my reactions
seem to be exaggerated (34)

the feeling fills me completely (50); the feeling is all involuntary,
there is no anticipation on my part, it all just comes (48); the

feeling begins with a sharp sudden onset (46); the feeling seems to be all over, nowhere special, just not localized (38); the feeling is very deep inside; I seem to feel it at the pit of my being (38); it's a feeling that comes without warning (36)

FRIENDLINESS (in Old English, *frēond,* meaning "love")
Number of items: 46
Range of agreement: 34–68%
Number of items at least 50% agreement: 14
Adequacy rating: 1.0

DEFINITION

I'm optimistic and cheerful; the world seems basically good and beautiful; men are essentially kind; life is worth living (68); there is a renewed appreciation of life (66); I feel like smiling (62); there is a sense of well-being (60), an inner warm glow, a radiant sensation (54), I'm loose, relaxed (52), with a feeling of warmth all over (48); there is a sense of harmony and peace within (46), I'm in tune with the world (44), with a sense of being very integrated and at ease with myself, in harmony with myself (42); I feel I can really be myself (42); I feel safe and secure (42); there is a mellow comfort (40), a general release, a lessening of tension (38); everything is going right for me (38); I'm optimistic about the future; the future seems bright (36)

there is a sense of confidence in being with another person (68), a sense of trust and appreciation of another person (64); there is an intense positive relationship with another person or with other people; a communion, a unity, a closeness, friendliness and freedom, mutual respect and interdependence (64); I feel outgoing (56); there is a sense of empathic harmony with another person; in tune, sharing and experiencing the same feelings and thoughts (52); there is a sense of belonging with others (50); a sense of tolerance and acceptance of others (50); there is a sense of complete understanding of the other person (40); a sense of giving, doing something, for another person (40); I feel more understanding of others (36); I want to be with friends (36); there is a sense of being wanted, needed (34)

there is an inner buoyancy (58), a sense of being more alive (48), wide awake (48), a special lift in everything I do and say; I feel bouncy, springy (48); there is a strong sense of interest and involvement in things around me (44); my senses are perfectly focused (42); there is a sense of vitality, aliveness, vibrancy, an extra spurt of energy or drive (40), a sense of lightness, buoyancy and upsurge of the body (40); I seem more alert (38), I feel effervescent, bubbly (38), excited in a calm way (36)

I have a sense of sureness (42); I feel strong inside (40); I have a sense of being important and worthwhile (36); I keep thinking how lucky I am (34)

I seem to nurture the feeling within myself; I want the feeling to continue, to keep going (34)

it's a very personal feeling (46); it's a simple, pure feeling (44)

FRUSTRATION (from the Latin *frustrātus,* meaning "having disappointed" or "having deceived")
> Number of items: 31
> Range of agreement: 34–82%
> Number of items at least 50% agreement: 5
> Adequacy rating: 1.0

DEFINITION

I'm easily irritated, ready to snap (82); my whole body is tense (54), I'm wound up inside (52), with a tight, knotted feeling in my stomach (50); I'm jumpy, jittery (48), my face and mouth are tight, tense, hard (44), there is a tension across my back, my neck, and shoulders (42); I want to do something, anything, to change the situation and relieve the tension (42); I'm hypersensitive (40)

there is a sense of being totally unable to cope with the situation (40), I seem to be caught up and overwhelmed by the feeling (40); I feel sorry for myself (40); there is a sense of being gripped by the situation (36)

I feel as if I'm under a heavy burden (42); I am slightly headachy, as if my brain were tired (36); it's as if I'm suffocating or smothering (36)

I feel that I'll burst or explode, as if there is too much to be held in (42); there is a churning inside (34); my blood pressure goes up; blood seems to rush through my body (34)

I begin to think what I can do to change the situation (54), there is a yearning, a desire for change; I want things to hurry up and begin to change (48)

I want to strike out, explode, but I hold back, control myself (36); there is a narrowing of my senses, my attention becomes riveted on one thing (34)

I feel let down (46); there is a sense of aloneness, being cut off, completely by myself (44); I have a sense of being trapped, closed up, boxed, fenced in, tied down, inhibited (42); there is an intense concern for what will happen (38); I seem to be fighting myself (34)

it's involved with other feelings (44), a confused, mixed-up feeling (36); the feeling goes slowly (34)

GAIETY (from the French *gaieté, gaité,* derived from *gai,* meaning "gay")

Number of items: 71
Range of agreement: 34–74%
Number of items at least 50% agreement: 25
Adequacy rating: 1.0

DEFINITION

I feel like smiling (70); there is an inner warm glow, a radiant sensation (68), a sense of well-being (68); I'm optimistic and cheerful; the world seems basically good and beautiful; men are essentially kind; life is worth living (64); I have a sense of being free, uninhibited, open, no longer blocked; I feel uninhibited and spontaneous—anything goes (54); there is a sense of being care-free but within balance (50); there is a general release, a lessening of tension (50), I'm loose, relaxed (50); there is a renewed appreciation of life (48); everything is going right for me (46), I'm completely free from worry (44); there is a sense of smiling at myself (44); I feel like I can really be myself (44); nothing is a burden; problems fade away and I'm free from worry (42), I'm in tune with the world (42); I'm really functioning as a unit (40), I am free of conflict (40), there is a feeling of warmth all over (40); there is a sense of "rightness" with oneself and the world; nothing can go wrong (38); I feel safe and secure (38), with a sense of harmony and peace within (36) I'm optimistic about the future; the future seems bright (36); I think about beautiful things (34); it's a state of release (34), everything—breathing, moving, thinking—seems easier (34)

I feel effervescent, bubbly (74), there is a warm excitement (72), a sense of vitality, aliveness, vibrancy, an extra spurt of energy or drive (70), an inner buoyancy (70), a special lift in everything I do and say; I feel bouncy, springy (64), a sense of lightness, buoyancy and upsurge of the body (60), a sense of being more alive (60), wide awake (56), excited in a calm way (52); there is a strong sense of interest and involvement in things around me (50); I seem more alert (44); there is a particularly acute awareness of pleasurable things, their sounds, their colors, and textures—everything seems more beautiful, natural, and desirable (44); there is an intense awareness of everything; I seem to experience things with greater clarity; colors seem brighter, sounds clearer, movements more vivid (42); there is a floating, soaring sensation (40); I seem to be immediately in touch with the world; a sense of being very open, receptive, with no separation between me and the world (34); all my senses seem to be completely open (36), I seem to sense everything and experience everything immediately (36)

I feel outgoing (70), loving everyone, everything (52); there is a sense of belonging with others (44); I want to communicate freely, share my thoughts and feelings with everyone around (38); there is a sense of confidence in being with another person (38); I want to make others happy (38), I want to be with friends (36); there is an intense positive relationship with another person or with other people; a communion, a unity, a closeness, friendliness and freedom, mutual respect and interdependence (36); there is a sense of empathic harmony with another person; I'm in tune, sharing and experiencing the same feelings and thoughts (34); there is a sense of trust and appreciation of another person (34)

my movements are graceful and easy, I feel especially well coordinated (52); I feel as if I look especially good (52); I have a sense of sureness (42), a sense of being exceptionally strong or energetic (42); I feel expansive (40); there is a sense of more confidence in myself; a feeling that I can do anything (34), I feel strong inside (34)

there is an excitement, a sense of being keyed up, overstimulated, supercharged (62); my body seems to speed up (40); I feel driven to move, be active, do something, anything, dance, jump, run, move—anything but sitting or standing still (40)

I feel like laughing (56); I'm less aware of time (50); I feel like singing (48); I seem to nurture the feeling within myself; I want the feeling to continue, to keep going (46); I'm completely wrapped up in the moment, the present, the here and now, with no thought of past or future (36); I'm intensely here and now (34); I want to try new things (34)

the feeling seems to be all over, nowhere special, just not localized (40); it's a steady, ongoing feeling (34)

GRATITUDE (from the Latin *grātitūdo,* derived from *grātus,* meaning "pleasing" or "thankful")
>Number of items: 30
>Range of agreement: 34–62%
>Number of items at least 50% agreement: 7
>Adequacy rating: 2.0

DEFINITION

>there is an inner warm glow, a radiant sensation (58), a sense of well-being (54); there is a renewed appreciation of life (52); I'm optimistic about the future; the future seems bright (50); the world seems basically good and beautiful; men are essentially kind; life is worth living (46); I feel like smiling (44); I feel safe and secure (42), nothing is a burden; problems fade away and I'm free from worry (42); there is a feeling of warmth all over (40); there is a general release, a lessening of tension (40); everything is going right for me (40), there is a sense of harmony and peace within (38), a sense of "rightness" with oneself and the world; nothing can go wrong (34); there is a mellow comfort (34)

>there is a sense of trust and appreciation of another person (60); I feel outgoing (40); there is an intense positive relationship with another person or with other people; a communion, a unity, a closeness, friendliness and freedom, mutual respect and interdependence (40); there is a sense of confidence in being with another person (36); there is a sense of giving, doing something for another person (34)

>there is a sense of being more alive (38), a warm excitement (36), an inner buoyancy (34)

>I keep thinking how lucky I am (62); I have a sense of sureness (38)

>I want to give thanks to God (38); I feel choked up (36)

>it's a very personal feeling (50); it's a simple, pure feeling (44); it's more an "inner" than an "outer" feeling (38); it's involved with other feelings (36)

GRIEF (from the Old French *grever,* which goes back to the Latin *gravāre,* meaning "way down")
>Number of items: 53
>Range of agreement: 34–84%

Number of items at least 50% agreement: 18
Adequacy rating: 1.0

DEFINITION

I can't smile or laugh (56); there is a lump in my throat (54); there is an inner ache you can't locate (48); there is a heaviness in my chest (46), my heart seems to ache (46); there is a heavy feeling in my stomach (40), a clutching, sinking feeling in the middle of my chest (40); I have no appetite; I can't eat (36); I feel as if I'm under a heavy burden (34); there is a deep, intense pain (34), it hurts to be alive (34)

there is a sense of regret (54), a sense of longing (46), a longing to have things the same as before (40), a feeling that time has passed and it's too late (34)

there is a sense of being incomplete; as if part of me is missing (40); I don't want to talk to anyone about how I am feeling (36); there is a sense of aloneness, being cut off, completely by myself (34), a sense of wandering, lost in space with nothing solid to grab onto (34)

I feel empty, drained, hollow (64), dead inside (40), all excitement, vitality is gone (38)

I seem to be caught up and overwhelmed by the feeling (54); there is a sense of being gripped by the situation (52), a sense of not knowing where to go, what to do (34)

I feel choked up (50); there is a tight knotted feeling in my stomach (34)

there is a sense of loss, of deprivation (84); there is a sense of disbelief (68); I keep thinking about what happened over and over again (60); tears come to my eyes, the sort of tears not just from my eyes, but my whole self is crying (60); I'm stunned (56); tears well up (54); I keep searching for an explanation, for some understanding; I keep thinking, "why?" (52); I can't believe what's happening is true (50); I think of death (46); I cry (46); there is a sense of nostalgia as old memories crop up and I think of the past (44); my whole existence seems to be changed (42); I can only think of what caused the feeling (38); I forget my physical self; I don't care how I look (34); it's as if there is a great dividing line between the time before and what's happening now (34); there is a narrowing of my senses, my attention becomes riveted on one thing (34) the feeling is very deep inside; I seem to feel it at the pit of my being (62); it's a very personal feeling (62); it fills me completely (54); it's more an "inner" than an "outer" feeling (48); it seems to be all over, nowhere special, just not localized (44); it all seems bottled up inside of me (44); there is a sense that I'll never get over the feeling (42); it's a bottomless feeling (42); a confused, mixed-up feeling involved with other feelings (38); there is a sense that the feeling will never end (36)

GUILT (in Old English, *gylt,* meaning "offense")
    Number of items: 32
    Range of agreement: 34–84%
    Number of items at least 50% agreement: 4
    Adequacy rating: 1.0

DEFINITION

there is a sense of regret (84); I get mad at myself for my feelings or thoughts or for what I've done (58), I keep blaming myself for the situation (52); I begin to think of what I can do to change the situation (52); I try to stop thinking of the situation and try to think of other things (42); I wish I could go back in time (42); I have a sense of being no good, worthless (42); there is a sense of weakness (36); I want to hide my feeling (34)

I feel as if I'm under a heavy burden (48); there is a heavy feeling in my stomach (42), a heaviness in my chest (34), a clutching, sinking feeling in the middle of my chest (34), a tugging sensation inside (34)

I'm hypersensitive (42), wound up inside (38), my whole body is tense (38); I want to do something, anything, to change the situation and relieve the tension (38)

there is a sense of aloneness, being cut off, completely by myself (44); I don't want to talk to anyone about how I am feeling (34)

there is an intense concern for what will happen next (38); there is a sense of being a bit ajar within myself (34); I keep thinking about what happened over and over again (34); I can only think of what caused the feeling (34); there is a sense of being gripped by the situation (34); all excitement, vitality is gone (34)

it's a very personal feeling (46); it's involved with other feelings (46), a confused, mixed-up feeling (42); the feeling is very deep inside; I seem to feel it at the pit of my being (42); it's more an "inner" than an "outer" feeling (40); the feeling seems to linger; to last a long time, with no immediate release (34)

HAPPINESS (taken from the Scandinavian; a comparable world in Icelandic is *happ,* meaning "chance" or "good luck")

Number of items: 66

Range of agreement: 34–82%

Number of items at least 50% agreement: 26

Adequacy rating: 1.0

DEFINITION

there is an inner warm glow, a radiant sensation (82); I feel like smiling (72); there is a sense of well-being (66), a sense of harmony and peace within (66), everything is going right for me (66); I'm optimistic and cheerful; the world seems basically good and beautiful; men are essentially kind; life is worth living (66); there is a renewed appreciation of life (66); I'm optimistic about the future; the future seems bright (58); I'm loose, relaxed (56), in tune with the world (54); there's a feeling of warmth all over (52); I think about beautiful things (46); I feel safe and secure (46), I'm at peace with the world (46); there is a mellow comfort (46), a sense of being very integrated and at ease with myself, in harmony with myself (44); there is a sense of fullness (42), a sense of smiling at myself (40); I am free of conflict (40); there is a sense of "rightness" with oneself and the world; nothing can go wrong (38); my movements are graceful and easy, I feel especially well coordinated (38); there is a general release, a lessening of tension (38), I am peaceful, tranquil, quiet (36), completely free from worry (36); I am really functioning as a unit (34)

there is a sense of being more alive (72), I am excited in a calm way (70); there is an inner buoyancy (64), a warm excitement (64), a sense of vitality, aliveness, vibrancy, an extra spurt of energy or drive (60), a special lift in everything I do and say; I feel bouncy, springy (54), effervescent, bubbly (54), wide awake (48), with a sense of lightness, buoyancy and upsurge of the body (48), more alert (46); there is a particularly acute awareness of pleasurable things, their sounds, their colors, and textures— everything seems more beautiful, natural, and desirable (44); there is an intense awareness of everything; I seem to experience things with greater clarity; colors seem brighter, sounds clearer, movements more vivid (40); I seem to be immediately in touch with the world; a sense of being very open, receptive, with no separation between me and the world (38); a sense that I'm experiencing everything fully, completely, thoroughly; that I'm feeling all the way (38), all my senses seem to be completely open (36); there is a strong sense of interest and involvement in things around me (36)

I keep thinking how lucky I am (56); I have a sense of sureness (52), I feel strong inside (46), taller, stronger, bigger (42); there is a sense of being important and worthwhile (42), a sense of more confidence in myself; a feeling that I can do anything (40); I feel clean (38), as if I look especially good (36); there is a sense of being more substantial, of existing, of being real (36)

I feel outgoing (56), I want to make others happy (50); there is an intense, positive relationship with another person or with other people; a communion, a unity, a closeness, friendliness and freedom, mutual respect and interdependence (50); I want others (or the other person) to feel the same as I do (48); there is a sense of trust and appreciation of another person (42); a sense of loving everyone, everything (38)

I seem to nurture the feeling within myself; I want the feeling to continue, to keep going (54); I feel like singing (50), like laughing (42); there is a sense of accomplishment, fulfillment (40); there is an excitement, a sense of being keyed up, overstimulated, supercharged (40)

it's a very personal feeling (52); a simple, pure feeling (46); it's more an "inner" than an "outer" feeling (42); the feeling flows from the inside outwards (38); the feeling seems to be all over, nowhere special, just not localized (34)

HATE (in Old English, *hatian,* which has essentially the same meaning as *hate* in current English)
>   Number of items: 35
>   Range of agreement: 34–68%
>   Number of items at least 50% agreement: 10
>   Adequacy rating: 2.0

DEFINITION

my whole body is tense (68); I'm easily irritated, ready to snap (58); my face and mouth are tight, tense, hard (48), there is a tight knotted feeling in my stomach (46), I'm wound up inside

(44), there is a muscular rigidity (42); my teeth are clenched (38), my teeth grind against each other (36); there is a tension across my back, my neck, and shoulders (34); I want to do something, anything, to change the situation and relieve the tension (34)

I want to say something nasty, something that will hurt someone (62); there is an impulse to hurt, to hit or to kick someone else (58), an impulse to strike out, to pound, or smash, or kick, or bite; to do something that will hurt (58); I keep thinking of getting even, of revenge (54); I want to strike out, explode, but I hold back, control myself (50); my fists are clenched (46); there is a narrowing of my senses, my attention becomes riveted on one thing (40)

my blood pressure goes up; blood seems to rush through my body (46), I feel that I'll burst or explode, as if there is too much inside to be held in (46); my pulse thickens (40), there is a quickening of heartbeat (38); there is an excitement, a sense of being keyed up, overstimulated, supercharged (34)

there is a sense of being gripped by the situation (52); I seem to be caught up and overwhelmed by the feeling (50)

I can't smile or laugh (42); I feel as if I'm under a heavy burden (34)

I have a sense of being trapped, closed up, boxed, fenced in, tied down, inhibited (40); the world seems no good, hostile, unfair (38); there is a yearning, a desire for change; I want things to hurry up and begin to change (36)

it's involved with other feelings (50), it's a confused, mixed-up feeling (46); it's a very personal feeling (44); it all seems bottled up inside of me (42); the feeling fills me completely (36); it's more an "inner" than an "outer" feeling (36)

HOPE (in Old English, *hopa,* which has essentially the same meaning as *hope* in current English)
    Number of items: 12
    Range of agreement: 34–54%
    Number of items at least 50% agreement: 5
    Adequacy rating: 2.0

DEFINITION
    I'm excited in a calm way (52); there is a warm excitement (38)

I'm optimistic about the future; the future seems bright (44), the world seems basically good and beautiful; men are essentially kind; life is worth living (38)

there is a sense of anticipation, waiting for something to happen (54), an intense concern for what will happen next (54); there is a sense of longing (40); there is a narrowing of my senses, my attention becomes riveted on one thing (38); there is a renewed appreciation of life (34)

it's involved with other feelings (52); it's more an "inner" than an "outer" feeling (50); it's a very personal feeling (40)

IMPATIENCE (from the Latin *impatiens,* meaning "not bearing" or "not enduring")

Number of items: 2;
Range of agreement: 34–80%
Number of items at least 50% agreement: 5
Adequacy rating: 1.0

DEFINITION

I'm easily irritated, ready to snap (8); I'm jumpy, jittery (62), wound up inside (56); my whole body is tense (54); I want to do something, anything, to change the situation and relieve the tension (48); there is tension across my back, my neck, and shoulders (36); my teeth grind against each other (34); I'm hypersensitive (34)

there is a yearning, a desire for change; I want things to hurry up and begin to change (56), I begin to think about what I can do to change the situation (40); I try to stop thinking of the situation and try to think of other things (38)

I seem to be caught up and overwhelmed by the feeling (44); there is a sense that I have no control over the situation (42)

there is a narrowing of my senses, my attention becomes riveted on one thing (46); I feel driven to move, be active, do something, anything, dance, jump, run, move—anything but sitting or standing still (42); I have a tremendous sense of being in a hurry, in a rush (42); there is a very strong sense that time seems to slow down, to drag (40); I have a sense of being trapped, closed up, boxed, fenced in, tied down, inhibited (38); there is a lot of aimless physical activity, lots of insignificant, unnecessary little things (38); my reactions seem to be exaggerated (34)

INSPIRATION (from the Latin *inspīrāre,* meaning "breathe into")
Number of items: 41
Range of agreement: 34–66%
Number of items at least 50% agreement: 11
Adequacy rating: 1.5

DEFINITION

I'm excited in a calm way (66); there is an inner buoyancy (58); I seem more alert (56), more alive (56), with a sense of vitality, aliveness, vibrancy, an extra spurt of energy or drive (56); I feel wide awake (50); my senses are perfectly focused (44); there is a sense that another dimension has been added and everything has a greater intensity (40); there is a warm excitement (40), a sense of lightness, buoyancy and upsurge of the body (38); I seem to sense everything and experience everything immediately (38); there is an intense awareness of everything; I seem to experience things with greater clarity; colors seem brighter, sounds clearer, movements more vivid (36)

I feel strong inside (62); I seem to be functioning intellectually at a higher level (54); there is a sense of more confidence in myself; a feeling that I can do anything (52); I have a sense of sureness (50); I feel taller, stronger, bigger (48); there is a sense of being important and worthwhile (42); there are moments of tremendous strength (40); a sense of increased clarity and understanding of the world (36); my thinking is rapid (34); there is a sense of being exceptionally strong or energetic (34); a sense of being more substantial, of existing, of being real (34)

there is an inner warm glow, a radiant sensation (50); there is a renewed appreciation of life (48); I'm optimistic about the future; the future seems bright (46), the world seems basically good and beautiful; men are essentially kind; life is worth living (42); there is a sense of well-being (42); I feel like smiling (40); I'm really functioning as a unit (36), my mind and body seem totally unified (34); there is a sense of "rightness" with oneself and the world; nothing can go wrong (34)

there is an excitement, a sense of being keyed up, overstimulated, supercharged (46); my body seems to speed up (34)

I seem to be caught up and overwhelmed by the feeling (38); there is a sense of being gripped by the situation (34) there is a sense of accomplishment, fulfillment (40); I seem to nurture the feeling within myself; I want the feeling to continue, to keep going (38)

it's a very personal feeling (46); it's more an "inner" than an "outer" feeling (46); the feeling fills me completely (34)

IRRITATION (from the Latin *irrītātus,* which has essentially the same meaning as *irritate* in English)
    Number of items: 18
    Range of agreement: 34–66%
    Number of items at least 50% agreement: 3
    Adequacy rating: 2.0

DEFINITION

I'm easily irritated, ready to snap (66), my face and mouth are tight, tense, hard (50), I'm wound up inside (48), my whole body is tense (48); my teeth are clenched (42); I'm hypersensitive (38)

I want to strike out, explode, but I hold back, control myself (44); there is a narrowing of my senses, my attention becomes riveted on one thing (38); my fists are clenched (34); I want to say something nasty, something that will hurt someone (34)

I begin to think about what I can do to change the situation (52), there is a yearning, a desire for change; I want things to hurry up and begin to change (38)

my blood pressure goes up; my blood seems to rush through my body (38), my pulse quickens (34)

I have a sense of being trapped, closed up, boxed, fenced in, tied down, inhibited (44), a sense of being gripped by the situation (42)

it seems to be a clearly formed tangible sort of feeling (36); the feeling is only brief in time; it's over quickly (34)

JEALOUSY (from the Latin *zēlōsus,* which was taken from the Greek *zêlos,* meaning "zeal")
    Number of items: 49
    Range of agreement: 34–70%
    Number of items at least 50% agreement: 12
    Adequacy rating: 1.0

I'm easily irritated, ready to snap (64); my face and mouth are tight, tense, hard (50), I'm wound up inside (50), my whole body is tense (50); I'm hypersensitive (44); there is a tight knotted feeling in my stomach (42); I'm jumpy, jittery (40); I feel choked up (36)

I feel sorry for myself (58); I feel insignificant (50); there is a sense of being gripped by the situation (50); I seem to be caught up and overwhelmed by the feeling (42); I want to understand, but I can't (36); there is a sense that I have no control over the situation (34); I lose all confidence in myself and doubt myself (34)

there is a sense of longing (48); I begin to think about what I can do to change the situation (48); I want to hide my feeling (46), I'm afraid that others will know how I feel (38); I try to stop thinking of the situation and try to think of other things (36)

there is a heavy feeling, in my stomach (70); a sense of loss, of deprivation (54); there is an inner ache you can't locate (50), a sensation of my heart sinking (36)

there is a narrowing of my senses, my attention becomes riveted on one thing (42); I want to say something nasty, something that will hurt someone (42); I keep thinking of getting even, of revenge (40); I want to strike out, explode, but I hold back, control myself (38)

there is a sense of aloneness, being cut off, completely by myself (48); there is a sense of being deserted, betrayed and the world indifferent to me (48); I become introspective, turn inwards (36)

I feel let down (70); I keep searching for an explanation, for some understanding; I keep thinking, "why?" (48); I keep thinking about what happened over and over again (44); I'm torn between acting and not acting (42); my reactions seem to be exaggerated (42); I'm afraid of expressing or releasing the feeling (40); I want to fight against it, not let the feeling overcome me (38); there is an intense concern for what will happen next (38); I keep thinking of what the other person has, how successful or how lucky he is (38); everything seems out of proportion (38); there is a churning inside (36); I have many different thoughts going through my head (36); I can only think of what caused the feeling (36); there is a sense of disbelief (34) it's involved with other feelings (52), it's a confused, mixed-up feeling (44); it's a very personal feeling (42), more of an "inner" than an "outer" feeling (38)

LOVE (in Old English *lufu* and *lufian,* which has essentially the same meaning as *love* in current English)
Number of items: 78
Range of agreement: 34–80%
Number of items at least 50% agreement: 38
Adequacy rating: 1.0

DEFINITION
there is an inner warm glow, a radiant sensation (76); I'm optimistic and cheerful; the world seems basically good and beautiful; men are essentially kind; life is worth living (72); there is a feeling of warmth all over (70); I feel like smiling (66), there is a renewed appreciation of life (56); there is a sense of well-being (54), I feel safe and secure (54), I'm optimistic about the future; the future seems bright (52); I think about beautiful things (50); there is a sense of harmony and peace within (46), a sense of "rightness" with oneself and the world; nothing can go wrong (46), I'm at peace with the world (42); I feel I can really be myself (42); there is a sense of fullness (40); everything is going right for me (40), I'm in tune with the world (38); there is a mellow comfort (36), something is complete within me (36); I'm peaceful, tranquil, quiet (36), loose, relaxed (34); there is a sense of being carefree, but within balance (34)

I want to be tender and gentle with another person (80); there is a desire to give of myself to another person (80); I want to touch, hold, be close physically to the other person (76); there is a sense of empathic harmony with another person; in tune, sharing and experiencing the same feelings and thoughts (74); there is a total concentration on another person, an intense awareness of the other person (74); there is an intense positive relationship with another person or with other people; a communion, a unity, a closeness, friendliness and freedom, mutual respect and interdependence (72); there is a sense of trust and appreciation of another person (72), a sense of belonging with another person, a belonging from which other people are excluded (70); there is a sense of confidence in being with another person (68); I want to feel with the other person, experience with the other person with every sense; to be psychologically in touch with another person (62); I want to help, to protect, please another person (62), there is a sense of giving, doing something for another person (60); there's a sense of complete understanding of the other person (60); a realization that someone else is more important to me than I am to myself (58); there is a sense of being wanted, needed (56); I want others (or the other person) to feel the same as I do (52); I feel soft and firm (44); there is a sense of loving everyone, everything (40); I want to make others happy (36)

there is a warm excitement (68), an inner buoyancy (50), a special lift in everything I do and say; I feel bouncy, springy (50), more alive (50); there's a particularly acute awareness of pleasurable things, their sounds, their colors, and textures—everything seems more beautiful, natural, and desirable (50); I'm excited in a calm way (48), with a sense of vitality, aliveness, vibrancy, an extra spurt of energy or drive (46); I seem to be immediately in touch and appreciative of immediate physical sensations (46); there is a sense that I'm experiencing everything fully, completely, thoroughly; that I'm feeling all the way (46); there is a floating, soaring sensation (42); there is an intense awareness of everything; I seem to experience things with greater clarity; colors seem brighter, sounds clearer, movements more vivid (40); I feel effervescent, bubbly (40), with a sense of lightness, buoyancy and upsurge of the body (40)

I keep thinking how lucky I am (60); I have a sense of being important and worthwhile (52), a sense of sureness (48); I feel strong inside (48), taller, stronger, bigger (46); there is a sense of being more substantial, of existing, of being real (36)

there is an excitement, a sense of being keyed up, overstimulated, supercharged (44); there is a quickening of heartbeat (40)

I seem to nurture the feeling within myself; I want the feeling to continue, to keep going (60); I seem to be caught up and overwhelmed by the feeling (46); I feel like singing (42); I want to hold back time, capture the moment (36); I feel sexually excited (36); my speech gets softer (34)

it's a very personal feeling (72), more of an "inner" than an "outer" feeling (58); the feeling seems to be all over, nowhere special, just not localized (54); it fills me completely (52); the feeling is very deep inside; I seem to feel it at the pit of my being (52); the feeling seems to linger; to last a long time, with no immediate release (42); it's a steady, ongoing feeling (42);

it's involved with other feelings (40); the feeling seems to go on and on, boundless, endless, limitless (40), there's a sense that the feeling will never end (38); the feeling flows from the inside outwards (36)

NERVOUSNESS (from the Latin *nervōsus,* meaning "sinewy"; the addition of the suffix, *ness,* denotes a quality or state)
Number of items: 37
Range of agreement: 34–66%
Number of items at least 50% agreement: 12
Adequacy rating: 1.0

DEFINITION

I'm jumpy, jittery (66); there is a tight knotted feeling in my stomach (66); my whole body is tense (62), I'm wound up inside (58); my hands are moist (54); my hands are shaky (48); there is a tension across my back, my neck, and shoulders (42); I want to do something, anything, to change the situation and relieve the tension (42); my face and mouth are tight, tense, hard (36)

there is a quickening of heartbeat (56), my pulse quickens (52), there is a churning inside (44); there is an excitement, a sense of being keyed up, overstimulated, supercharged (44); I've got to do something with my hands (40)

there is a gnawing feeling in the pit of my stomach (52), a queasy feeling in my stomach (46); I feel as if I'm under a heavy burden (44); I have no appetite; I can't eat (42); there is a heavy feeling in my stomach (38)

there is a sense of being gripped by the situation (56), I seem to be caught up and overwhelmed by the feeling (52); I'm extremely distractable, unable to concentrate (36)

I'm greatly concerned about doing the wrong thing (44); there is a yearning, a desire for change; I want things to hurry up and begin to change (42)

there is a sense of anticipation, waiting for something to happen (52); I have clammy hands (50); I sweat (46); I have to urinate (42); there is an intense concern for what will happen next (40); I need to take a deep breath (40); there is a lot of aimless physical activity, lots of insignificant, unnecessary little things (38); there is a sense of being a bit ajar within myself (34); there is a heightened self-awareness (34); I have many different thoughts going through my head (34); I want to fight against it, not let the feeling overcome me (34); there's a narrowing of my senses, my attention becomes riveted on one thing (34)

it's a confused, mixed up feeling, involved with other feelings (34)

PANIC (from the French *panique,* which was taken from the Latin *pānicus,* which in turn was taken from the Greek *Panikōs,* meaning "pertaining to or caused by Pan")

Number of items: 33
Range of agreement: 34–60%
Number of items at least 50% agreement: 7
Adequacy rating: 1.0

DEFINITION

there is a sense of being gripped by the situation (58), I seem to be caught up and overwhelmed by the feeling (48); I feel vulnerable and totally helpless (46); there is a sense that I have no control over the situation (42), a sense of being totally unable to cope with the situation (42), not knowing where to go, what to do (42); thoughts just race through my head without control (38); everything seems chaotic (38)

there is a quickening of heartbeat (60), my pulse quickens (54), my blood pressure goes up; blood seems to rush through my body (52); there is absolute physical turmoil (46); I'm stunned (42); my heart pounds (40), my body seems to speed up (38); there is an excitement, a sense of being keyed up, overstimulated, supercharged (36)

my whole body is tense (52); my hands are shaky (44); there is a tight knotted feeling in my stomach (40); I'm jumpy, jittery (36); I want to do something, anything, to change the situation and relieve the tension (34)

there is a clutching, sinking feeling in the middle of my chest (46); there is a narrowing of my senses, my attention becomes riveted on one thing (42); there is a sense of aloneness, being cut off, completely by myself (42); I sweat (38); I'm afraid of the feeling (38); there is an intense concern for what will happen next (36); I seem to act on reflex, without thinking (36); I want to be comforted, helped by someone (36); I'm intensely here and now (34)

the feeling begins with a sharp sudden onset (54), it comes without warning (50); the feeling is only brief in time; it's over quickly (40)

PASSION (from the Latin *passio,* meaning *"suffering"*)
>   Number of items: 59
>   Range of agreement: 34–76%
>   Number of items at least 50% agreement: 24
>   Adequacy rating: 1.0

DEFINITION

I want to touch, hold, be close physically to the other person (76); there is a desire to give of myself to another person (64); there is a sense of empathic harmony with another person; in tune, sharing and experiencing the same feelings and thoughts (64); I want to be tender and gentle with another person (60); there is a total concentration on another person, an intense awareness of the other person (60); I want to feel with the other person, experience with the other person with every sense; to be psychologically in touch with another person (58); there is a sense of belonging with another person, a belonging from which other people are excluded (50); there is a sense of confidence in being with another person (46), an intense positive relationship with another person or with other people; a communion, a unity, a closeness, friendliness and freedom, mutual respect and interdependence (42); there is a sense of being wanted, needed (40); I want others (or the other person) to feel the same as I do (38); there is a sense of trust and appreciation of another person (36); I want to help, protect, please another person (34); there is a realization that someone else is more important to me than I am to myself (34); there is a sense of giving, doing something for another person (34)

there is a warm excitement (72); there is an intensified focus to my sensations (66); I have a sense of vitality, aliveness, vibrancy, an extra spurt of energy or drive (60); I seem to be immediately in touch and appreciative of immediate physical sensations (58), a sense that I'm experiencing everything fully, completely, thoroughly; that I'm feeling all the way (56); there is a sense of being more alive (48); I seem to sense everything and experience everything immediately (36); another dimension has been added and everything has a greater intensity (36); I have a floating, soaring sensation (36); all my senses seem to be completely open (34)

there is an excitement, a sense of being keyed up, overstimulated, supercharged (74); there is a quickening of heartbeat (64), my blood pressure goes up; blood seems to rush through my body

(52), my body seems to speed up (42), my heart pounds (42), my pulse quickens (42), my body tingles (36), my breathing becomes faster (34)

my muscle tone is suddenly enhanced (36), I feel strong inside (36); there is a sense of being more substantial, of existing, of being real (36)

I seem to be caught up and overwhelmed by the feeling (60), gripped by the situation (46)

there is a feeling of warmth all over (56), an inner warm glow, a radiant sensation (50)

I feel sexually excited (70); I'm intensely here and now (60); I'm completely focused on the feeling; nothing intrudes; all other feelings cut out; it fills my whole being, spreading over everyone and everything; I lose myself completely in the feeling and experience (56); I seem to nurture the feeling within myself; I want the feeling to continue, to keep going (52); I'm completely wrapped up in the moment, the present, the here and now, with no thought of past or future (46); there is a sense of longing (40); there is a narrowing of my senses, my attention becomes riveted on one thing (40); there is no thinking, just feeling (38); there is a great desire to let myself go completely (36); I breathe more deeply (34); I'm less aware of time (34)

it's a very personal feeling (60); it fills me completely (52); the feeling is very deep inside; I seem to feel it at the pit of my being (44); it seems to build up more and more (44), there is a slow gradual swelling intensity of feeling, until a peak is reached (44); the feeling seems to be all over, nowhere special, just not localized (42); there is a throbbing swell of intensity of feeling (40); the feeling flows from the inside outwards (36)

PITY (from the Latin *pietas, meaning "piety"*)
Number of items: 22
Range of agreement: 34–78%
Number of items at least 50% agreement: 4
Adequacy rating: 1.5

DEFINITION
there is a lump in my throat (50); a heavy feeling in my stomach (44); there is an inner ache you can't locate (42), a sensation of my heart sinking (38); I can't smile or laugh (34); my heart seems to ache (34)

I feel more understanding of others (42); I want to help, protect, please another person (38); there is a sense of giving, doing something for another person (34); there is a total concentration on another person, an intense awareness of the other person (34)

there is a sense of regret (52); I begin to think about what I can do to change the situation (34)

there is a sense that I have no control over the situation (38), I seem to be caught up and overwhelmed by the feeling (36)

I keep thinking about how bad it is for the other person (78); I feel choked up (50); I keep thinking how lucky I am (42); I keep searching for an explanation, for some understanding; I keep thinking, "why?" (36); I want to look away but somehow I'm fascinated (36)

the feeling is all involuntary, there is no anticipation on my part, it all just comes (46); it's a very personal feeling (40); it's involved with other feelings (36)

PRIDE (in Old English, *pryde,* derived from *prūd,* meaning "proud")
Number of items: 43
Range of agreement: 34–74%
Number of items at least 50% agreement: 19
Adequacy rating: 1.0

DEFINITION

there is an inner buoyancy (66); I'm excited in a calm way (62); there is a warm excitement (58), a sense of vitality, aliveness, vibrancy, an extra spurt of energy or drive (56), a sense of being more alive (52), a special lift in everything I do and say; I feel bouncy, springy (52); I have a strong sense of interest and involvement in things around me (48); I feel effervescent, bubbly (46), more alert (42), wide awake (42), with a sense of lightness, buoyance and upsurge of the body (42); my senses are perfectly focused (42)

there is an inner warm glow, a radiant sensation (74); there is a renewed appreciation of life (64); there is a sense of well-being (56); I feel like smiling (56); I'm optimistic about the future; the future seems bright (52); everything is going right for me (52), the world seems basically good and beautiful; men are essentially kind; life is worth living (50); there is a sense of fullness (48); a sense of "rightness" with oneself and the world; nothing can go wrong (44); there is a feeling of warmth all over (38);

a sense of harmony and peace within (34), a sense of smiling at myself (34)

I feel taller, stronger, bigger (60), strong inside (58); I have a sense of sureness (50), a sense of being important and worthwhile (50); I keep thinking how lucky I am (46); I have a sense of being superior (36), a sense of power (34); I feel expansive (34); there is a sense of more confidence in myself; a feeling that I can do anything (34)

I feel outgoing (42), I want to be with friends (34)

there is a sense of accomplishment, fulfillment (60); I want to be noticed, have others pay attention to me (38); there is an excitement, a sense of being keyed up, overstimulated, super-charged (38); I seem to nurture the feeling within myself; I want the feeling to continue, to keep going (36); there is a heightened self-awareness (34)

it's a very personal feeling (60); it's involved with other feelings (40); it's more an "inner" than an "outer" feeling (38)

RELIEF (from the Latin *relevāre,* meaning "raise again" or "assist")
Number of items: 27
Range of agreement: 34–80%
Number of items at least 50% agreement: 6
Adequacy rating: 1.0

DEFINITION

there is a general release, a lessening of tension (80), a state of release (70); I'm loose, relaxed (64); I feel like smiling (58); there is a renewed appreciation of life (54); I have a sense of well-being (48); I'm optimistic about the future; the future seems bright (46); there is a sense of harmony and peace within (44); I feel safe and secure (44), nothing is a burden; problems fade away and I'm free from worry (42); the world seems basically good and beautiful; men are essentially kind; life is worth living (42); I am free of conflict (38), everything is going right for me (36), I'm at peace with the world (36); there is a mellow comfort (36); everything—breathing, moving, thinking—seems easier (34); I'm completely free from worry (34)

there is a sense of lightness, buoyancy and upsurge of the body (46); I'm excited in a calm way (40); there is an inner buoyancy (40), a sense of being more alive (36), a warm excitement (34)

I keep thinking how lucky I am (62); I feel outgoing (42); I breathe more deeply (42); there is a sense of accomplishment, fulfillment (38); the feeling seems to be all over, nowhere special, just not localized (40)

REMORSE (from the Latin *remorsus,* meaning "a biting back")
Number of items: 35
Range of agreement: 34–82%
Number of items at least 50% agreement: 8
Adequacy rating: 1.0

DEFINITION

there is a sense of regret (82); I keep blaming myself for the situation (56); I wish I could go back in time (50); I begin to think about what I can do to change the situation (44); I get mad at myself for my feelings or thoughts or for what I've done (42); there is a sense of weakness (40); I have a feeling that time has passed and it's too late (40); there is a yearning, a desire for change; I want things to hurry up and begin to change (38); it seems that nothing I do is right (36); there is a longing to have things the same as before (34)

there is an inner ache you can't locate (50); I have no appetite; I can't eat (44); there is a clutching, sinking feeling in the middle of my chest (40), a tugging sensation inside (38); there is a heavy feeling in my stomach (36), a heaviness in my chest (34); I can't smile or laugh (34)

I feel empty, drained, hollow (52), all excitement, vitality is gone (36), I feel let down (34)

there is a sense of being gripped by the situation (42), I seem to be caught up and overwhelmed by the feeling (36)

there is a sense of aloneness, being cut off, completely by myself (36); I become introspective, turn inwards (36)

I keep thinking about what happened over and over again (58); my whole existence seems to be changed (42); I keep searching for an explanation, for some understanding; I keep thinking, "why?" (38); there is a tight knotted feeling in my stomach (34)

it's a very personal feeling (58); it's involved with other feelings (52), a confused, mixed-up feeling (46); it's more an "inner" than an "outer" feeling (40); the feeling is very deep inside; I seem to feel it at the pit of my being (36); the feeling goes slowly

(36), it seems to linger; to last a long time, with no immediate release (34)

RESENTMENT (from the French *ressentir;* the prefix *re* indicates withdrawal or backward motion; *sentir* goes back to the Latin *sentīr,* meaning "feel")

Number of items: 22
Range of agreement: 34–68%
Number of items at least 50% agreement: 2
Adequacy rating: 2.0

DEFINITION

I'm easily irritated, ready to snap (68); my whole body is tense (52); there is a tight knotted feeling in my stomach (46), I'm wound up inside (44), my face and mouth are tight, tense, hard (44); I'm hypersensitive (42); there is a tension across my back, my neck, and shoulders (40); I want to do something, anything, to change the situation and relieve the tension (34)

I want to say something nasty, something that will hurt someone (46); I want to strike out, explode, but I hold back, control myself (42); I keep thinking of getting even, of revenge (40)

there is a sense of being gripped by the situation (48), I seem to be caught up and overwhelmed by the feeling (40); I feel sorry for myself (38)

my blood pressure goes up; blood seems to rush through my body (40); I have a sense of being trapped, closed up, boxed, fenced in, tied down, inhibited (38); I can only think of what caused the feeling (36); I feel let down (36); there is a sense of being deserted, betrayed and the world indifferent to me (36); I begin to think about what I can do to change the situation (36)

it's involved with other feelings (40); it's a very personal feeling (34)

REVERENCE (from the Latin *reverentia,* which has essentially the same meaning as *reverence* in English)

Number of items: 36
Range of agreement: 34–72%
Number of items at least 50% agreement: 8
Adequacy rating: 1.5

DEFINITION

there is a sense of harmony and peace within (56); there is an inner warm glow, a radiant sensation (56), I am peaceful, tranquil, quiet (52); there is a renewed appreciation of life (52); there is a sense of fullness (40); I'm at peace with the world (38); there is a feeling of warmth all over (38), a sense of well-being (36); everything seems quiet (36); I think about beautiful things (34); it's as if God is in his heaven and all is right with the world (34)

I seem to be immediately in touch and appreciative of immediate physical sensations (72), my senses are perfectly focused (40); I'm excited in a calm way (40); there is an intense awareness of everything; I seem to experience things with greater clarity; colors seem brighter, sounds clearer, movements more vivid (36); I have a strong sense of interest and involvement in things around me (34), all my senses seem to be completely open (34); there is a warm excitement (34), a floating, soaring sensation (34)

there is a sense of being gripped by the situation (38), I seem to be caught up and overwhelmed by the feeling (38)

I feel strong inside (38); there are moments of tremendous strength (34)

there seems to be religious overtones (64); there is a sense of being close to something unknown (42); I feel close to God (38); I have a sense of strangeness, unreality, as if I'm temporarily in another world (36); I feel choked up (36); there is a state of timelessness (34); there is a sense of the unknown (34); I become introspective, turn inwards (34); there is a quickening of heartbeat (34)

it's a very personal feeling (58); it's more an "inner" than an "outer" feeling (56); the feeling is very deep inside; I seem to feel it at the pit of my being (38); it's involved with other feelings (34)

SADNESS (in Old English, *sæd,* which has essentially the same meaning as *sad* in current English)

Number of items: 35
Range of agreement: 34–66%
Number of items at least 50% agreement: 7
Adequacy rating: 1.0

DEFINITION

there is a lump in my throat (66); there is a sense of loss, of deprivation (64); there is a clutching, sinking feeling in the middle of my chest (46); there is an inner ache you can't locate (46); I have no appetite; I can't eat (46); there is a heavy feeling in my stomach (42); my heart seems to ache (40); I can't smile or laugh (38); there is a gnawing feeling in the pit of my stomach (36); there is a heaviness in my chest (34)

I feel empty, drained, hollow (52), let down (48), all excitement, vitality is gone (38)

there is a sense of regret (60); a sense of longing (44), a longing to have things the same as before (34)

I seem to be caught up and overwhelmed by the feeling (38), there is a sense of being gripped by the situation (36)

I feel choked up (58); there is a sense of nostalgia as old memories crop up and I think of the past (54); there is a sense of disbelief (46); tears well up (46), I cry (42), tears come to my eyes, the sort of tears not just from the eyes, but my whole self is crying (34); I keep thinking about what happened over and over again (40); I keep searching for an explanation, for some understanding; I keep thinking, "why?" (36); there is a throbbing in my throat (36); I become introspective, turn inwards (36)

it's a very personal feeling (60); it's involved with other feelings (44); the feeling is very deep inside; I seem to feel it at the very pit of my being (42); it's more an "inner" than an "outer" feeling (40); the feeling fills me completely (36); it goes slowly (36), it seems to linger, to last a long time, with no immediate release (36)

SERENITY (from the Latin *serēnus,* which has essentially the same meaning as *serene* in English)
    Number of items: 50
    Range of agreement: 34–84%
    Number of items at least 50% agreement: 21
    Adequacy rating: 1.0

DEFINITION

I am peaceful, tranquil, quiet (84); there is a sense of harmony and peace within (80), a sense of well-being (78); I'm loose, relaxed (76), completely free from worry (70); there is a renewed appreciation of life (66); I'm at peace with the world (62), I feel safe and secure (60), everything seems quiet (58); there is a sense of being very integrated and at ease with myself, in harmony with myself (56); there is a general release, a lessening of tension (54); I'm optimistic and cheerful; the world seems basically good and beautiful; men are essentially kind; life is worth living (54); I think about beautiful things (54); there is an inner warm glow, a radiant sensation (54), a sense of "rightness" with oneself and the world; nothing can go wrong (52); I am free of conflict (52); there is a mellow comfort (50); I feel like smiling (48), everything is going right for me (42); nothing is a burden; problems fade away and I'm free from worry (42), everything seems in place, ordered, organized (42); there is a feeling of warmth all over (42); there is a sense of fullness (40); my body seems to soften (40); I'm in tune with the world (40); my movements are graceful and easy, I feel especially well coordinated (36)

there is a particularly acute awareness of pleasurable things, their sounds, their colors, and textures—everything seems more beautiful, natural, and desirable (52); there is an inner buoyancy (46); my senses are perfectly focused (42); there is an intense awareness of everything; I seem to experience things with greater clarity; colors seem brighter, sounds clearer, movements more vivid (42); there is a sense that I'm experiencing everything fully, completely, thoroughly; that I'm feeling all the way (38); there is a sense of being more alive (38), a sense of lightness, buoyancy and upsurge of the body (36); I seem to be immediately in touch with the world; a sense of being very open, receptive, with no separation between me and the world (34)

I'm less aware of time (46), it's a state of timelessness (46); I seem to nurture the feeling within myself; I want the feeling to continue, to keep going (46); I don't want anything changed (44); I feel strong inside (42); I want others (or the other person) to feel the same as I do (40); I have a sense of being removed from daily chores (38); I want to hold back time, capture the moment (36); I breathe more deeply (36); my body seems to slow down (36)

it's a simple, pure feeling (56); a very personal feeling (54); the feeling fills me completely (50); it's more an "inner" than an "outer" feeling (44); there doesn't seem to be much change in the intensity of the feeling; it pretty much stays at one level (44); the feeling seems to be all over, nowhere special, just not localized (42)

SHAME (in Old English, *sc(e)amu,* which has essentially the same meaning as *shame* in current English)
>Number of items: 28
>Range of agreement: 34–70%
>Number of items at least 50% agreement: 4
>Adequacy rating: 1.0

DEFINITION

>there is a sense of regret (70); I keep blaming myself for the situation (62), I get mad at myself for my feelings or thoughts or for what I've done (60); I begin to think about what I can do to change the situation (42); there is a sense of weakness (40); I want to hide my feeling (40); I have a sense of being no good, worthless (40); there is a yearning, a desire for change; I want things to hurry up and begin to change (38); it seems that nothing I do is right (34); there is a longing to have things the same as before (34)

>I feel as if I'm under a heavy burden (44); I can't smile or laugh (38); there is a clutching, sinking feeling in the middle of my chest (38), a gnawing feeling in the pit of my stomach (38), an inner ache you can't locate (36)

>I want to withdraw, disappear, draw back, be alone, away from others, crawl into myself (52); there is an impulse to hide, to escape, to run, to get away (38)

>I keep thinking about what happened over and over again (48); I want to do something, anything, to change the situation and relieve the tension (40); I feel vulnerable and totally helpless (36); I feel empty, drained, hollow (34)

>it's a confused, mixed-up feeling (46), it's involved with other feelings (44); it's a very personal feeling (44); it all seems bottled up inside of me (38); it's more an "inner" than an "outer" feeling (38); there is a sense that the feeling will never end (36), it seems to linger; to last a long time, with no immediate release (34)

SOLEMNITY (from the Latin *sōlemnitas,* which has essentially the same meaning as *solemnity* in English)
>Number of items: 13
>Range of agreement: 34–66%
>Number of items at least 50% agreement: 2
>Adequacy rating: 2.5

DEFINITION

everything seems quiet (42); there is a renewed appreciation of life (38); I am peaceful, tranquil, quiet (36); there's a sense of harmony and peace within (34)

there seems to be religious overtones (66); there is a sense of being gripped by the situation (40); I become introspective, turn inwards (40); there is a narrowing of my senses, my attention becomes riveted on one thing (38); my senses are perfectly focused (36)

it's more an "inner" than an "outer" feeling (50); it's involved with other feelings (38); it's a very personal feeling (36); the feeling goes slowly (34)

SURPRISE (from the French *surprendre;* the prefix *sur* corresponds to "super"; *prendre* means "take")
Number of items: 23
Range of agreement: 34–54%
Number of items at least 50% agreement: 7
Adequacy rating: 1.0

DEFINITION

there is a warm excitement (54); I feel wide awake (48), more alert (46), with a sense of vitality, aliveness, vibrancy, an extra spurt of energy or drive (46), a sense of being more alive (38); I'm excited in a calm way (36)

there is a quickening of heartbeat (54), my pulse quickens (52); there is an excitement, a sense of being keyed up, overstimulated, supercharged (52)

there is a feeling of warmth all over (42), an inner warm glow, a radiant sensation (38); there is a renewed appreciation of life (34)

there is a sense of disbelief (52), I can't believe what's happening is true (52); I keep thinking how lucky I am (46); I feel outgoing (44); I'm breathless (42); I feel like laughing (36)

it's a feeling that comes without warning (50); it is only brief in time; it's over quickly (44); it begins with a sharp sudden onset (40); the feeling is all involuntary, there is no anticipation on my part, it all just comes (40); the feeling fills me completely (34)

CHAPTER 3

Comments on the Dictionary, the Model, and the Method

The dictionary presented in Chapter 2 represents a summary of statements used by over one-third of a sample of 50 American-English speaking persons in describing experiences associated with each of 50 emotional terms. Thus, the definitions reflect commonalities of reported experiences for each term. There were, of course, individual differences among subjects in describing experiences for each term, but at this point the emphasis is on commonalities rather than differences—a consideration of individual differences in report will be presented in a subsequent chapter.

It is unlikely that any particular experience of an emotional state for a single subject is wholly covered by the dictionary definition. In some respects, the experiences of each subject are undoubtedly unique. In fact, for any one person, even though experiences at different times are labeled by the same term, these experiences are likely to differ somewhat from one another. That is, anger at one time is probably somewhat different from anger at another time, even though both experiences are labeled "anger."

But at a more abstract level of description, for a given individual anger at one time has certain common elements with anger at another time, and similarly from individual to individual there apparently are certain common elements in emotional experiences given the same label. The definitions contained in the dictionary of emotional meaning reflect these common elements at a level of abstraction which permits people to use the same term to label concretely diverse experiences. There can be no doubt, however, that the definitions of each term are only rough and to some degree abstract approximations of the description of any single experience.

It is all the more surprising, therefore, that this effort to develop a dictionary of emotional meaning met with as much success as the adequacy ratings apparently suggest. In fact, the results are more promising than were initial expectations in this direction. As shown in Table 3-1, of the 50 terms considered in the dictionary, 31 received a median rating of *1*, indicating that over half the judges viewed the definitions of these terms as comprehensive and accurate. Eight other terms were rated *1.5*, indicating somewhat less adequacy for these definitions but still at a fairly high level of accuracy and comprehensiveness. While it is difficult to establish an acceptable lower limit for these ratings, it is reasonable to suggest that considerable success was achieved in defining at least 39 of the 50. terms. This seems to be the case despite the fact that the definitions are necessarily approximations of any single experience and represent a somewhat abstract level of description.

On the other hand, it also must be noted that 11 of the 50 terms, which is over 20% of the sample of words studied, did not achieve adequacy ratings indicative of comprehensive and accurate definitions (see Table 3-1). Nine of these words were rated *2*, and two were rated *2.5*, suggesting that the definitions of these words, while judged to be "fairly accurate and comprehensive," either omitted or inaccurately described a significant aspect of the experiences associated with each term.

TABLE 3-1

Median Adequacy Ratings of Each Term in The Dictionary of Emotional Meaning

1.0		1.5	2.0	2.5
Anger	Guilt	Affection	Admiration	Dislike
Anxiety	Happiness	Boredom	Amusement	Solemnity
Apathy	Impatience	Confidence	Awe	
Cheerfulness	Jealousy	Determination	Contempt	
Contentment	Love	Disgust	Gratitude	
Delight	Nervousness	Inspiration	Hate	
Depression	Panic	Pity	Hope	
Elation	Passion	Reverence	Irritation	
Embarrassment	Pride		Resentment	
Enjoyment	Relief			
Excitement	Remorse			
Fear	Sadness			
Friendliness	Serenity			
Frustration	Shame			
Gaiety	Surprise			
Grief				

There seems to be no obvious characteristic common to all 11 of these terms, such as etymological background, valence, or frequency of usage as indicated by the Lorge-Thorndike Word Count. However, of the 11 less adequately defined terms, 5 have similar meanings, including Contempt, Hate, Irritation, Resentment, and Dislike. It is conceivable that these five terms, as well as the other six perhaps, involve historical or situational cues which serve as the principal basis for discriminating between one emotional state and another. Without knowing the historical background of events or the specific situation in which the emotional experience occurs, it may not be possible to discriminate, for example, among feelings of Contempt, Irritation, or Resentment.

A more likely possibility, however, lies in the inadequacy of the check list used to obtain the descriptions of each emotional state. This is supported by the observation that definitions of the 11 less adequately defined terms contain relatively fewer items than the definitions of other terms in the dictionary. For example, Dislike is defined by only 10 items, Hope by 12 items, Contempt by 14 items. Contrast these with terms such as Affection defined by 45 items. Depression defined by 83 items, and Happiness defined by 66 items. Even though considerable effort was made to obtain a comprehensive range of items, and a large number of items were finally used in collecting the data, it is likely that the check list did not contain items specific enough to the 11 terms whose adequacy ratings were relatively low. As the most tenable hypothesis, therefore, the faulty definitions contained in the dictionary are probably a function of shortcomings in the basic check list of descriptive items.

Overlap and Specificity of Definitions

Notwithstanding the rather high adequacy ratings of the vast majority of definitions in the dictionary, inspection of the results reveals a good deal of overlap among many of the terms. Although the definition of terms such as Happiness, Joy, Love, or Affection were judged to be accurate and comprehensive, their definitions obviously contain many of the same descriptive items.

Terms that have largely overlapping definitions also are defined by some distinctive items usually not found in the definitions of other similar words. Nevertheless, there are certain realistic limits to the specificity of the definitions presented. Regardless of the adequacy ratings obtained, it is unreasonable to expect that every definition is consistent with one and only one emotional term. The overlap among definitions suggested a cluster analysis of items, and on the basis of these results the emotional terms were classified into a number of groups. This treatment of the data will be discussed in the following chapter dealing with the structure of emotional meaning. At this point the data suggest that reliable distinctions can most likely be made between groups of emotions (as described in Chapter 4), but distinctions between two emotional terms within the same group may be a good deal more tenuous.

The Model and the Method

THE MODEL

The general model underlying this research derived from an atomistic metaphor, which suggested that experiences might profitably be described in terms of patterned bits of information, not unlike the way in which information is conveyed on a television screen or radar scope. Obviously this research used gross approximations in contrast to the precision of electronic techniques, and it would probably be unwise to use the atomistic metaphor other than to suggest a general point of departure for this line of inquiry. The important point to be noted is that the moderate success of this research lends support to further investigation in this area using a similar model of attack.

The undeniable complexity of emotional phenomena has certainly been one of the major stumbling blocks in this area of research. Poets and novelists have tried to capture and convey the meaning of emotional experience by a variety of linguistic devices, and of course there have been many instances of successful communication within a literary framework. By and large, psychologists have not been nearly as successful, though occasionally writers like James and Freud break through the bounds of conventional psychology and indeed convey what seem to be rich and valid descriptions of emotional experiences. But academically oriented research psychologists have contributed little to this field, and many have taken refuge in the argument that an explication of emotional experience is outside the legitimate realm of scientific psychology. If one wants to learn something about the experience of guilt, anxiety, or joy one might perhaps turn to Dostoyevsky, Kierkegaard, or Wordsworth, but certainly little is to be learned in this area from even the most careful study of Thorndike, Hull, Skinner, or any of the other major figures of academic psychology. None of these psychologists suggests that people do not *experience* emotion; but from the viewpoint of neobehaviorism that has characterized most of American academic psychology, problems concerned with emotional experience are simply outside the proper range of psychological investigation.

There is probably little to be gained from reviewing the old arguments about this and related issues. These kinds of philosophical battles have usually hindered rather than helped us get on with the tasks of psychological inquiry. The tasks, frankly, often seem obvious enough, and if less attention were paid to the more formal philosophies of psychology which state what "thou shalt not study," probably a good deal more knowledge about significant problems would be acquired. But it is hardly original or profound to suggest that a psychology that tells us nothing about the experience of love and hate, joy or sadness, is omitting a vast and significant realm of psychological phenomena.

From this point of view, the issue of complexity in describing emotional phenomena is a central problem for any research in this area, and the atomistic model used in the present study is a promising way of at least beginning to deal with this problem. By breaking down the descriptive procedure into atomistic units, the task of describing complex phenomena becomes manageable, because for each unit of the description, a subject is required only to make the relatively simple decision that the unit *does* or *does not* apply to a given experience. Then, on the basis of a series of such decisions, a first approximation can be made in the descriptive task.

However, the simple accumulation of bits of descriptive information can only be considered a beginning in the overall descriptive enterprise. The next step is to arrange these bits into appropriate patterns that presumably reflect the pattern of the referential experience. Thus, having described each emotional term at a relatively atomistic level in the dictionary presented in Chapter 2, we shall consider the pattern or structure of emotional meaning in the next chapter. The atomistic model at least provided a feasible basis for initiating this line of inquiry, and the results derived from this model serve as a basis for moving to the next level of analysis in our efforts to understand the language of emotional experience.

The Method

One of the major barriers to the study of emotional experience has been the limitations of the language readily available to an observer. Mandler, for example, in discussing the difficulties of investigating the private experience of emotion says, "I cannot possibly use the rather crude instrument of language to express the myriad impressions, feelings, ideas, notions, and emotions that flood my private screen. I can attempt to approach it, but will forever feel frustrated in trying to do these feelings full justice" (Mandler, 1962, p. 303).

Mandler's statement is undeniably consistent with observations made during the initial interviews conducted at the beginning of this research. There were indeed a few subjects who demonstrated rather remarkable verbal skills in their descriptions of emotional experiences, but by and large most people had to do a good deal of groping to find the words they felt were appropriate. Even with plenty of time, encouragement, and a sympathetic and patient listener, the task for the subjects was not an easy one. On many occasions people were frustrated because they felt their words didn't adequately capture the experiences they were trying to describe.

But these observations do not necessarily imply that a given language, in this case American English, lacks potential resources that make possible an approximate description of particular experiences. Although instances may not be frequent in which the language is used with sufficient skill and flexibility to provide descriptions that convey the experience adequately, even one instance of such a description supports the assumption that American English is indeed a potentially useful tool for obtaining experiential reports. The problem, in part, is to make the potential resources of the language readily available to an observer.

Thus, the check list was developed as a means of pooling relevant descriptive statements made by a large number of people, combining these verbal resources so that an individual might be able to use more fully the potential richness of the language. In this sense then the check list provides a basic vocabulary for verbal reports of emotional experiences in much the same way that the MMPI provides a basic vocabulary for verbal reports of experiences relevant to psychopathology.

The results of this investigation suggest that at least some success was achieved in developing this vocabulary; however, like any other similar instrument, using a check list such as the one used to collect data for the dictionary of emotional meaning raises a number of problems. The limited range of content covered by the check list has been discussed in a preceding section of this chapter. At this point it will suffice to note that in dealing with phenomena as complex and varied as emotional experiences, one can hardly hope, even with 556 statements, to cover all of the events, the nuances, and subtle details of different emotions as experienced by different people. In fact, within the practical limits that we are bound to work in, every investigator will inevitably encounter a certain degree of the frustration mentioned by Mandler. We can probably never capture verbally the entire scope of any single experience; our results are bound to be imperfect and limited. But this inevitable limit of our knowledge is hardly a legitimate basis for curtailing investigation that might be expected to decrease the extent of our ignorance. To use a somewhat awkward quantitative metaphor, systematic knowledge in this area before the present study might be said to have been at about 5% of some theoretical potential. This research possibly raises that level to something closer to 6%, and perhaps we shall never move much beyond 30 or 40%. But there obviously is still a great deal of work to be done in *decreasing our ignorance* before reaching the limit of achievement. In any event, whether or not one selectively inattends or one chooses to work along this line of inquiry is probably more a matter of personal taste than reasoned argument, and if the choice is along the line represented by this research, limited goals must be accepted as legitimate and satisfying. Various methods might be developed to extend these limits, just as the check list extends the limited vocabulary immediately available to a person describing his experiences, but every method will entail certain shortcomings.

For example, even if one were to devise a thoroughly comprehensive check list of relevant descriptive statements, factors other than those immediately concerned with the language of emotional experience will influence one's results. Subjects differ in their "checking tendencies," in the likelihood that they will or will not check a given item, regardless of its content. In the present sample, one subject made a total of only 338 checks in describing all 50 emotional experiences, while at the other extreme, another subject made a total of 7787 checks. It is conceivable, of course, that this difference validly represents a difference in the richness of their emotional experiences or in the richness of the language they use to describe their emotional experiences. But it seems more likely that a certain amount of the variance in these individual differences can be accounted for on the basis of a response bias related to check list behavior, perhaps as a function of the specific instrument used, the instructions, or the situation in which the data were obtained. In addition, as indicated earlier, using the check list to describe an experience requires recall of previous events which may, in the present study, have occurred a considerable period of time before the description is obtained. The lapse of time between the actual experience and the reported description undoubtedly gives rise to some degree of distortion, probably some leveling and sharpening characteristic of most tasks that depend upon long-term memory. Further distortion may also occur during the data collection procedure, as the subject is reading through the many items, presumably trying to match the verbal statements with his recalled experience. Moreover, in using an instrument such as the check list, some degree of abstraction is involved. Each individual's emotional experience and the language he uses to describe this experience is in some respects unique, and the results obtained are necessarily abstractions from the concrete level of individual experience and language.

The check list technique, therefore, has the advantage of providing the subject with a ready-made vocabulary which he can use in a relatively simple way to describe complex phenomena. It also has clear-cut weaknesses which restrict its usefulness. As a technique for investigating the language of emotional experience of a single subject or for establishing subtle individual differences among subjects, it is probably too gross, too abstract, and influenced too much by variables such as response bias to be the method of choice. However, at the early stages of investigation in this line of inquiry, as we move from the initial step of natural observation to a more systematic exploration of this area, the check list technique as used in this study seems adequate and appropriate. Notwithstanding the effects of individual differences in response sets and other sources of distortion, the check list does provide a useful means of identifying some commonalities among people in their verbal descriptions of experiences associated with labels of emotional states.

A REVISED CHECK LIST

One of the obvious problems in the check list used to compile the dictionary is its length—556 items, some of which are three or four lines long. Careful reading of each item and deciding whether or not it described a given experience may not have been an overly complex task, but it certainly required a high degree of motivation and diligence.

Although the use of an extensive list of statements seemed warranted in the initial descriptive phase of this line of inquiry, subsequent research might well benefit from this experience by using shortened versions of the check list. One such version has been prepared and is presented at the end of this chapter. Comprised of 382 items, it was constructed by eliminating items that occurred with frequencies less than 100 in the data obtained for the dictionary and that were not contained in the definition of at least one term. In addition, a few items that appeared to be nearly synonymous and which had a very high rate of cooccurrence in the cluster analysis discussed in the next chapter were combined and slightly rewritten for purposes of clarity.

There are of course a variety of uses to which such a check list might be put. For example, although a good deal of psychological research has focused on manifest anxiety, less attention has been devoted to reported anger or depression—and certainly even less work has been done on the emotional states of happiness and love. The dictionary of emotional meaning tells us the ways in which people report experiences associated with the words, but it also provides a basis for developing measures relevant to each of these emotional states. Thus, paralleling the various manifest anxiety scales, one might develop scales of manifest anger, depression, happiness, or love using the dictionary definitions of these terms. It is perhaps unnecessary at this point to emphasize that such scales would not "measure anger" or "measure love"; they would simply provide a quantifiable means for people to report feelings associated with a given event or situation. Nevertheless, just as the manifest anxiety scales have been of some use in psychological research, perhaps similar scales for other emotional states might be of some use.

To this end, four such scales have been prepared using the definitions contained in the dictionary and the short form of the check list. Each investigator would have to decide how these scales are to be presented, such as whether the items in a given scale are presented alone or embedded in a larger list. He would also have to determine the specific nature of the instructions given to a subject—using a critical incident technique as in the present research or some other means of eliciting responses. These kinds of decisions depend upon the particular task for which a scale might be used, and the results of the present investigation can perhaps serve best as a pool of items to be used in various ways for a variety of tasks. The items contained in each of the scales of manifest anger, depression, happiness, and love are listed in Table 3-2. The numbers listed refer to the numbered items in the short form of the check list. Although these scales represent an incidental side result of this research, the entire project might have some value if it gives some impetus to psychological investigation of emotional states other than fear and anxiety. Surely manifest happiness and manifest love are as intrinsically worth investigating as manifest anxiety.

OTHER METHODS

Although the dictionary of emotional meaning is based on data collected by means of a check list, this technique, as indicated in preceding sections of this chapter, has distinct limitations for certain other kinds of research. In Chapter 6 a series of studies dealing with individual and cultural differences and the development of emotional meaning will be presented, and a content analysis system will be discussed. These more open-ended techniques of course involve certain methodological problems, but as indicated in Chapter 6 the advantages of these techniques for certain research purposes sometimes outweigh those associated with a check list or questionnaire form.

TABLE 3-2

Scales of Manifest Emotions: Key Items for Anger, Depression, Happiness, and Love Based on Short Form of the Check List

Anger		Depression				Happiness			Love			
9	77	83	167	252	302	8	111	264	2	91	224	289
21	101	96	168	253	305	12	122	274	12	92	225	309
24	105	100	169	259	312	28	126	275	23	99	227	310
29	150	104	183	262	323	33	132	277	24	106	229	335
31	163	105	187	265	333	38	136	287	33	111	232	337
36	169	107	192	266	341	46	143	310	34	126	234	344
45	175	108	195	267	346	47	146	317	38	132	236	346
46	183	120	201	270	347	51	189	335	46	143	242	347
61	212	124	214	273	350	59	194	337	47	146	250	354
62	328	130	221	276	359	63	218	347	51	163	254	360
67	340	134	233	280	361	84	224	354	59	194	263	361
68	342	157	237	288	366	85	229	360	63	216	264	363
71	350	162	246	292	374	92	236	368	65	217	285	372
72	363	163	249	298	378	97	250	380	84	218	286	374
	374				379	99	254	386	85	219	287	379
						106	258					

A Short Form of the Check List

_____ 1. weakness across my chest

_____ 2. I feel soft and firm

_____ 3. as if I'm suffocating or smothering

_____ 4. there is a heavy feeling in my stomach

_____ 5. I'm not aware of what's going on inside

_____ 6. there is a clutching, sinking feeling in the middle of my chest

_____ 7. a gnawing feeling in the pit of my stomach

_____ 8. all my senses seem completely open; I seem to sense everything immediately, completely, fully, with no separation between me and the world

_____ 9. my blood pressure goes up; blood seems to rush through my body

_____10. I.feel empty, drained, hollow, dead inside

_____11. I'm more aware of what's going on inside of me

_____12. I feel taller, stronger, bigger

_____13. there's a lump in my throat

_____14. there's a combination of pain and pleasure

_____15. my stomach shivers and trembles; I'm jumpy inside

_____16. there is no sensation; I'm numb, desensitized

_____17. as if I'm out of touch, seeing things from far away

_____18. my hands are shaky

_____19. I'm cold, yet perspiration pours out of me

_____20. I sweat

_____21. muscular rigidity

_____22. my body seems to soften

_____23. breathing becomes shallower

_____24. my pulse and heartbeat quicken

_____25. Slightly headachy, as if my brain were tired

_____26. clammy hands

_____27. I'm shivery

_____28. I'm really functioning as a unit

_____29. as if everything inside, my stomach, my throat, my head is expanding to the utmost, almost bursting, as if I'll explode

_____30. blood rushes to my head as if I'm intoxicated

_____31. my body seems to speed up

_____32. muscle tone is suddenly enhanced

_____33. there's a sense of vitality, vibrancy, an extra spurt of energy or drive, a special lift in everything I do and say; I feel bouncy, springy

_____34. I feel sexually excited

_____35. I feel nauseated, sick to my stomach

_____36. a narrowing of my senses, my attention becomes riveted on one thing

_____37. I breathe more deeply

_____38. I feel strong inside

Check List (*continued*)

____ 39. there are moments of tremendous strength	____ 57. feeling of suspension in my stomach
____ 40. an inner ache you can't locate	____ 58. there is a tightness, a constriction across my chest
____ 41. my arms and legs feel heavy	
____ 42. there's absolute physical turmoil	____ 59. I feel effervescent, bubbly
____ 43. I'm breathless	____ 60. my head aches, throbs
____ 44. warmth in the pit of my stomach	____ 61. fists are clenched
____ 45. a tight knotted feeling in my stomach	____ 62. my senses are perfectly focused; there's an intensified focus to my sensations
____ 46. there's an excitement, a sense of being keyed up, overstimulated, supercharged	____ 63. I'm excited in a calm way; a warm excitement
____ 47. there's an intense awareness of everything; I seem to experience things with greater clarity; colors seem brighter, sounds clearer, movements more vivid	____ 64. I have no appetite; I can't eat
	____ 65. a floating, soaring sensation
	____ 66. like a gnawing inside without pangs
____ 48. I stop breathing for a moment	____ 67. my face and mouth are tight, tense, hard
____ 49. there's a throbbing in my throat	
____ 50. there is a dull sensation of pain in my chest	____ 68. my whole body is tense
	____ 69. there's a deep, intense pain
____ 51. I'm peaceful, tranquil, quiet, in tune with the world	____ 70. I feel choked up
____ 52. everything seems out of proportion	____ 71. there is a churning inside
	____ 72. my heart pounds
____ 53. I feel understimulated, undercharged; all excitement, vitality is gone; I'm heavy, logy, sluggish, less responsive	____ 73. my mouth gets dry
	____ 74. I feel tired, sleepy
____ 54. there's an increased awareness of essential things like hot and cold, texture and smell	____ 75. something inside seems to go, seems cut loose
	____ 76. my heart seems to ache
____ 55. there's tension across my back, my neck, and shoulders	____ 77. my teeth are clenched
____ 56. my teeth grind against each other	____ 78. my throat is tight, constricted

Check List (*continued*)

____ 79. tension in my arms and legs

____ 80. a shiver goes up my spine

____ 81. there's an inner imbalance

____ 82. I have to urinate

____ 83. I'm wound up inside

____ 84. a sense of harmony and peace within

____ 85. there is an inner warm glow, a radiant sensation, a feeling of warmth all over

____ 86. I'm all loose inside, like a mess of jelly inside

____ 87. my senses aren't working quite right

____ 88. I become conscious of my breathing

____ 89. hands are moist

____ 90. my body tingles

____ 91. I feel wide awake, more alert, more alive

____ 92. a sense of lightness, buoyancy and upsurge of the body, an inner buoyancy

____ 93. there is a queasy feeling in my stomach

____ 94. I need to take a deep breath

____ 95. I'm unfocused and I can't focus; my sensations are blurred

____ 96. as if everything inside has stopped

____ 97. I am free of conflict, in harmony and at ease with myself; my mind and body seem totally unified

____ 98. as if there were a tight, cold fist inside

____ 99. there is a general release, a lessening of tension; I'm loose and relaxed

____ 100. my body seems to slow down

____ 101. my reactions seem to be exaggerated

____ 102. my temples throb

____ 103. I'm hypersensitive

____ 104. a sense that somehow I can't experience things wholly; as if there is a lid or some sort of clamp which keeps me from perceiving; sounds and sights are muted, dulled, as if there were a veil over me, over everything; my feelings are dulled

____ 105. I'm jumpy, jittery, ready to snap

____ 106. a sense of well-being

____ 107. there's a sense of weakness

____ 108. I feel off balance

____ 109. I'm chilled, cold all over

____ 110. I feel hot and flushed

____ 111. a sense that I'm experiencing everything fully, completely, thoroughly; that I'm feeling all the way

____ 112. a tugging sensation inside

____ 113. a sense of fullness

____ 114. there seems to be a lack of feeling inside

____ 115. a sense of being exceptionally strong or energetic

Check List (*continued*)

_____ 116. there's some difficulty in breathing; I can't take a full breath

_____ 117. I can hear my heart beat

_____ 118; there's no thinking, just feeling

_____ 119. my diaphragm feels constricted

_____ 120. there's a sensation of my heart sinking

_____ 121. my breathing becomes faster

_____ 122. my movements are graceful and easy, I feel especially well coordinated

_____ 123. my senses are sharp but can't be focused on anything for any length of time; as though I'm flitting from thing to thing

_____ 124. there's a heaviness in my chest

_____ 125. my throat aches

_____ 126. there's a mellow comfort

_____ 127. I can't sleep

_____ 128. everything—breathing, moving, thinking—seems easier

_____ 129. I have to swallow frequently

_____ 130. a sense of wandering, lost in space with nothing solid to grab onto

_____ 131. I'm very aware of my surroundings, especially sensitive to everything around me

_____ 132. a sense of "rightness" with myself and the world; everything is going right for me, nothing can go wrong

_____ 133. the world seems a vast panorama I'm viewing from outside

_____ 134. everything seems unimportant, useless, absurd, meaningless, trivial

_____ 135. I'm alternately detached and then keenly aware of my surroundings

_____ 136. a strong sense of interest and involvement in things around me

_____ 137. there's a sense of disbelief; I can't believe what's happening is true

_____ 138. there seems to be religious overtones

_____ 139. I have a sense of strangeness, unreality, as if I'm temporarily in another world

_____ 140. a sense of the unknown, of being close to something unknown

_____ 141. a sense of being removed from daily chores

_____ 142. I'm just carried along by what is happening—adrift without an anchor

_____ 143. there's a renewed appreciation of life

_____ 144. there's a sense of tenuousness or disintegration of the world

_____ 145. things seem to be out of time, out of space, eternal, just there

_____ 146. I'm optimistic and cheerful; the world seems basically good and beautiful; men are essentially kind; life is worth living; the future seems bright

_____ 147. the world seems no good, hostile, unfair

_____ 148; everything seems chaotic

_____ 149. the air seems heavy

Check List (*continued*)

____150. sense of being gripped by the situation

____151. I want to give thanks to God

____152. a sense that another dimension has been added and everything has a greater intensity

____153. I want to look away but somehow I'm fascinated

____154. I feel a need to pray

____155. everything seems quiet

____156. I have a sense of running endlessly, not knowing where to turn next, getting nowhere

____157. I feel as if I am in a vacuum

____158. nothing is a burden; problems fade away and I'm free from worry

____159. I feel close to God

____160. the world seems to be characterized by an ebbing and flowing fullness

____161. I become aware of the vastness and spaciousness of the world around me

____162. there's a lack of involvement and not caring about anything that goes on around me

____163. I seem to be caught up and overwhelmed by the feeling

____164. everything seems in place, ordered, organized

____165. a sense of anticipation, waiting for something to happen

____166. there is a sense of regret

____167. there is a sense of longing

____168. there is a sense of loss, of deprivation

____169. I can only think of what caused the feeling

____170. I keep wondering if I'm doing the right thing

____171. I'm stunned

____172. I think of death

____173. I feel disoriented

____174. I try to escape into dreams and fantasies

____175. I keep thinking about what happened over and over again

____176. Thoughts race through my head without control, never getting anywhere, thinking the same things over and over again

____177. I try to stop thinking of the situation and try to think of other things

____178. I want to understand but I can't

____179. I seem to be going around in a daze

____180. I can't control my thinking rationally; unable to think or reason correctly

____181. I have many different thoughts going through my head

____182. all sensations, sounds, images, ideas crowd together, overlap

____183. I keep searching for an explanation, for some understanding; I keep thinking, "why?"

____184. there is a sense of nostalgia as old memories crop up and I think of the past

Check List (*continued*)

_____185. I keep blaming myself for the situation

_____186. I seem to be functioning intellectually at a higher level; able to think clearly, understand everything

_____187. I begin to think about what I can do to change the situation

_____188. I'm extremely distractable, unable to concentrate

_____189. I'm completely free from worry

_____190. my mind goes blank and I can't think

_____191. I wish I could go back in time

_____192. I become introspective, turn inwards

_____193. my thinking is rapid

_____194. I think about beautiful things

_____195. I'm completely uncertain of everything

_____196. I'm haunted by terrible thoughts that I cant't stop

_____197. I keep thinking of past successes

_____198. my mind wanders

_____199. I'm not too alert

_____200. I keep asking myself a thousand questions

_____201. I feel mentally dull

_____202. I keep thinking of getting even, of revenge

_____203. as if everything has stopped, is standing still; time seems to stand still

_____204. somehow my sense of time is disturbed, disrupted

_____205. a sense that this is the end; there is no future in sight

_____206. as if there is a great dividing line between the time before and what's happened now

_____207. there's an intense concern for what will happen next

_____208. a feeling that time has passed and its too late

_____209. there is a very strong sense that time seems to slow down, to drag

_____210. I'm less aware of time

_____211. a sense of eternity or permanency

_____212. I'm completely wrapped up in the moment, the present, the here and now, with no thought of past or future

_____213. time seems to speed up, to rush by

_____214. a sense of uncertainty about the future

_____215. there is no sense of the past, no present, no future; I'm suspended in time; in a state of timelessness

_____216. I want to hold back time, capture the moment

_____217. there's a desire to give of myself to another person

_____218. a sense of trust and appreciation of another person

_____219. sense of confidence in being with another person

_____220. I want to be noticed, have others pay attention to me

Check List (*continued*)

_____ 221. a sense of being deserted, betrayed and the world indifferent to me

_____ 222. a sense of being a stranger in the world

_____ 223. I want to talk to someone

_____ 224. I want others (or the other person) to feel the same as I do

_____ 225. I want to touch, hold, be close physically to the other person

_____ 226. I want to talk to someone about my feelings

_____ 227. a sense of being wanted, needed

_____ 228. I want to be with friends

_____ 229. a sense of loving everyone, everything

_____ 230. I keep thinking of what the other person has, how successful or how lucky he is

_____ 231. realization that someone else is more important to me than I am to myself

_____ 232. I want to feel with the other person, experience with the other person with every sense; to be psychologically in touch with another person

_____ 233. I want to be comforted, helped by someone

_____ 234. a sense of belonging with another person, a belonging from which other people are excluded

_____ 235. I am very aware of myself in relation to others

_____ 236. I want to make others happy

_____ 237. a feeling of a certain distance from others; everyone seems far away

_____ 238. I'm just out of contact with the other person; I can't reach him, can't communicate with him

_____ 239. a sense of belonging with others

_____ 240. I want to communicate freely, share my thoughts and feelings with everyone around

_____ 241. I keep thinking about how bad it is for the other person

_____ 242. I want to be tender and gentle with another person

_____ 243. I don't care what anyone else thinks

_____ 244. there is a heightened self awareness

_____ 245. a sense of selflessness or surrender of myself; absolutely no self-consciousness, I completely lose myself

_____ 246. I have a sense of not knowing where to go, what to do; there is no way of ever getting out

_____ 247. a sense of not feeling or being me, of being unreal

_____ 248. I feel invulnerable

_____ 249. I feel insignificant

_____ 250. a sense of being important and worthwhile

_____ 251. I have a sense of innocence

_____ 252. seems that nothing I do is right

_____ 253. I feel vulnerable and totally helpless

_____ 254. I feel safe and secure

Check List (*continued*)

_____ 255. a sense of being a bit ajar within myself

_____ 256. I forget my physical self; I don't care how I look

_____ 257. I have a tremendous sense of being in a hurry, in a rush

_____ 258. a sense of smiling at myself

_____ 259. I feel aimless

_____ 260. I'm intensely here and now

_____ 261. as if I'm standing outside of myself as an observer

_____ 262. a sense of being incomplete; as if part of me is missing

_____ 263. there is something complete within me

_____ 264. I have a sense of sureness, that I can do anything, that no obstacle is too great for me

_____ 265. it hurts to be alive

_____ 266. I feel lost

_____ 267. I feel as if I'm under a heavy burden

_____ 268. my whole existence seems to be changed

_____ 269. a sense of being superior

_____ 270. I lose all confidence in myself and doubt myself

_____ 271. I feel mechanical, like a robot, an automaton

_____ 272. sense of being split, disintegrated, fragmented

_____ 273. my attention is completely focused on myself, I'm preoccupied with myself

_____ 274. I feel clean

_____ 275. I feel as if I look especially good

_____ 276. a sense of being totally unable to cope with, to control the situation

_____ 277. there is a sense of accomplishment, fulfillment

_____ 278. I get mad at myself for my feelings or thoughts or for what I've done

_____ 279. I have a sense of being no good, worthless

_____ 280. I feel let down

_____ 281. I have a sense of power

_____ 282. I have a feeling of being here, but not here

_____ 283. sense of being low, close to the ground

_____ 284. I feel expansive

_____ 285. I feel I can really be myself

_____ 286. there's a sense of being more substantial, of existing, of being real

_____ 287. I keep thinking how lucky I am

_____ 288. I feel sorry for myself

_____ 289. a sense of being carefree but within balance

_____ 290. I seem to be acting without effort or compulsion, just going along with things as they come, in no hurry

_____ 291. I seem to be fighting myself

_____ 292. I can't smile or laugh

_____ 293. I'm afraid of expressing, releasing the feeling; I want to hide my feeling

Check List (*continued*)

_____ 294. I have trouble talking; my voice gets more or less unsteady; I stutter, stammer, hesitate

_____ 295. tears come to my eyes, the sort of tears not just from my eyes, but my whole self is crying

_____ 296. I'm torn between acting and not acting

_____ 297. there is a lot of aimless physical activity, lots of insignificant, unnecessary little things

_____ 298. there is a yearning, a desire for change; I want things to hurry up and begin to change

_____ 299. I seem to act on reflex, without thinking

_____ 300. I want to act, but I can't

_____ 301. I feel like laughing

_____ 302. I have a sense of being trapped, closed up, boxed, fenced in, tied down, inhibited

_____ 303. I can't express my feelings

_____ 304. I don't want to move; I just want to stay motionless, immobile

_____ 305. it's an effort to do anything

_____ 306. the pitch of my voice goes up

_____ 307. I get giggly

_____ 308. I want to put things in order

_____ 309. my speech gets softer

_____ 310. I feel like singing

_____ 311. my speech becomes very rapid

_____ 312. my body wants to contract, draw closer to myself, avoid all stimulation

_____ 313. there is a great desire to let myself go completely

_____ 314. I am greatly concerned about doing the wrong thing

_____ 315. a longing to have things the same as before

_____ 316. I feel driven to move, be active, do something, anything, dance, jump, run, move—anything but sitting or standing still

_____ 317. I feel outgoing; I want to reach out to everyone I meet

_____ 318. I don't want anything changed

_____ 319. tears well up

_____ 320. I'm momentarily immobilized; paralyzed; unable to act or move

_____ 321. I have a sense of being free, uninhibited, open, no longer blocked. I feel uninhibited and spontaneous—anything goes

_____ 322. I feel more tolerant, accepting, understanding of others

_____ 323. I want to withdraw, disappear, draw back, hide, escape, be alone, away from others, crawl into myself

_____ 324. there is nothing spontaneous, only deliberately, carefully controlled action

_____ 325. I want to do something, anything, to change the situation and relieve the tension

_____ 326. I want to try new things

_____ 327. I cry

_____ 328. there's an impulse to strike out, to do something that will hurt

Check List (*continued*)

_____ 329. I want something but I don't know what

_____ 330. I've got to do something with my hands

_____ 331. the feeling seizes me and takes over. I feel totally incapable of controlling, handling, or stopping it

_____ 332. I want to clap my hands

_____ 333. there's a sense of aloneness, being cut off, completely by myself; everyone seems far away, out of contact

_____ 334. my movements are sharper and quicker

_____ 335. I feel like smiling

_____ 336. a sense of being passive together with a desire to be active

_____ 337. a sense of empathic harmony with another person; a total concentration on another person; a complete understanding; a communion, a unity, a closeness

_____ 338. I feel like slouching, just being limp, completely relaxed

_____ 339. I am completely silent as if I'm mute

_____ 340. I want to strike out, explode, but I hold back, control myself

_____ 341. I have no desire, no motivation, no interest; wants, needs, drives are gone

_____ 342. I want to say something nasty, something that will hurt someone

_____ 343. the feeling seizes me, takes over; I don't know how to stop, overcome the feeling

_____ 344. I want to help, protect, please, do something for another person

_____ 345. it's an erratic, changing, irregular, disorganized feeling

_____ 346. the feeling seems to linger, to go on and on, boundless, endless, limitless

_____ 347. it's more an "inner" than an "outer" feeling; a very personal feeling

_____ 348. it's an almost intangible sort of feeling

_____ 349. there doesn't seem to be much change in the intensity of the feeling; it pretty much stays at one level

_____ 350. it's a confused, mixed-up feeling, involved with other feelings

_____ 351. it seems to be a clearly formed tangible sort of feeling

_____ 352. the feeling is all involuntary, there is no anticipation on my part, it all just comes without warning

_____ 353. it just seems to peter out, to ebb away gradually

_____ 354. the feeling seems to be all over, nowhere special, just not localized

_____ 355. there is a steady, organized, regular, rhythm to the feeling

_____ 356. the feeling is on the surface

_____ 357. a sense that I'll never get over the feeling

_____ 358. the feeling is only brief in time; it's over quickly

_____ 359. the feeling goes slowly

Check List (*continued*)

____ 360. the feeling flows from the inside outwards

____ 361. the feeling is very deep inside; I seem to feel it at the pit of my being

____ 362. there is a slow rhythm to the feeling

____ 363. the feeling begins with a sharp sudden onset

____ 364. it's a very bland sort of feeling

____ 365. the feeling starts somewhere in middle and then fills my whole body

____ 366. it's a bottomless feeling

____ 367. there is a slow gradual swelling intensity of feeling, until a peak is reached

____ 368. I seem to nurture the feeling within myself; I want the feeling to continue, to keep going

____ 369. I'm completely focused on the feeling; nothing intrudes; all other feelings cut out; it fills my whole being, spreading over everyone and everything. I lose myself completely in the feeling and experience

____ 370. I'm afraid of the feeling

____ 371. the feeling seems to come over me gradually, without my being aware of when it starts

____ 372. it's a steady, ongoing feeling

____ 373. there is this throbbing swell of intensity of feeling

____ 374. it's involved with other feelings

____ 375. it's a very complex sort of feeling

____ 376. want to fight against it, not let the feeling overcome me

____ 377. the feeling recurs again and again, in cycles

____ 378. it all seems bottled up inside of me

____ 379. the feeling fills me completely

____ 380. it's simple, pure feeling

____ 381. there is a fast, rapid rhythm to the feeling

____ 382. it seems to build up more and more

CHAPTER 4

The Structure of Emotional Meaning

The preceding chapters are based on an atomistic analysis of the data, treating the definition of each emotional term as a composite of many bits of relatively discrete information. This approach has distinct advantages, particularly at the initial stage of defining terms that refer to extraordinarily complex, subjective phenomena. Following the lead of the atomistic metaphor, as discussed in Chapter 1, this view provided a way of describing the language of emotion with a certain rigor and objectivity, in the sense that the resulting dictionary reflects at least those aspects of emotional meaning for which there is some degree of consensus among members of a particular language community. Moreover, the atomistic view suggested a feasible technical means of investigating phenomena about which any single person might have only a limited vocabulary readily available. And the final result, the dictionary of emotional meaning, apparently achieved some success, as indicated by the adequacy ratings of the majority of definitions. The general atomistic point of view upon which the first part of this investigation was based thus seems promising as a way of conceptualizing further work along this line.

Nevertheless, inspection of the definitions contained in the dictionary revealed a number of items in the check list that occur together in several definitions. This observation suggested that an underlying structure might be found in the definitions, a grammar of emotional meaning reflected by the interrelationships among specific items. Having first delineated each emotional state by individual items, a consideration of the definitions at a somewhat more abstract level seemed appropriate. This led to a cluster analysis of the items in the definitions, with the aim of discovering any consistent patterns among the items defining the various emotional states.

Cluster Analysis of Items

Since the aim of this cluster analysis was to discover the underlying pattern with which the items were used in the definitions of the 50 terms rather than to classify all of the items, fairly stringent criteria for clustering were established. To a certain extent, of course, the criteria for any cluster analysis are more or less arbitrary—and the broader the criteria, the more inclusive is each cluster. Having taken the first step in defining each term at a relatively atomistic level, there seemed to be some promise in moving towards a somewhat more abstract level without aiming for global constructs that might well obscure potentially useful distinctions among the definitions of the various emotional states. It was assumed that the next step in organizing the data could be taken on the basis of a first cluster analysis—which in a sense might reveal the skeleton of interrelationships among the 556 items—with subsequent efforts devoted to the development of more global constructs.

As a first step in the cluster analysis, those items which appeared in the definitions of at least three terms were identified. This step was obviously necessary because an item had to occur in the definitions at least several times in order to obtain some estimate of the frequency with which it occurred with other items. If an item never appeared in the dictionary or appeared only rarely, there was little or no basis for determining whether or not it clustered with other items. Thus, a minimum criterion of appearing in the definitions of three terms was established.

Two hundred and fifteen items met this criterion. To obtain an estimate of the degree to which items followed similar patterns of presence and absence throughout the 50 definitions, a *phi* coefficient was computed between each item and every one of the 214 other items. For example, item 15 in the check list ("there's a lump in my throat") occurred in the definitions of four emotions; item 115 ("I feel choked up") occurred in the definitions of seven emotions. They occurred together in four definitions (i.e., all those in which item 15 appeared), and item 115 appeared three times without item 15. Moreover, they were *both* absent in 43 definitions. The *phi* coefficient of .73 indicates a relatively high degree of similarity in the patterns of these two items, the *phi* coefficient reflecting intersections of both presence and absence of the two items over the 50 definitions.

Then, following the general logic developed by Tryon (1939) and others, this 215×215 matrix of *phi* coefficients was subjected to a cluster analysis such that, in a given cluster, the *phi* coefficient between each item and every item in the cluster was at least .27 ($p < .05$).* Thus, over the 50 definitions in the dictionary, if a particular item in a given cluster appears in the definition of an emotional state, other items in that cluster

* I would like to express my particular appreciation to Rosedith Sitgreaves, Professor of Statistics at Teachers College, and Victor Diamond of the Teachers College Computer Center for their valuable help in dealing with the cluster analysis.

also tend to appear in that definition. Similarly, if the item is absent from the definition, other items in the cluster tend to be absent from that definition. The cluster analysis, therefore, groups items that have similar patterns of presence and absence in the definitions of the 50 emotional states considered in Chapter 2.

THE CLUSTERS

Twelve clusters were identified, and the items in each cluster are listed in Table 4-1. The naming of clusters or factors derived from statistical analyses always involves some projection on the part of the researcher who assigns the labels, and there is always danger that the assigned labels carry "extra" meaning beyond that which can reasonably be supported by the data. Nevertheless, recognizing these dangers, I would suggest that in most cases in the present analysis, the name of the cluster is derived quite obviously and directly from the content of the items in that cluster. Granted, of course, that assigning one label to cover a number of items necessarily involves some abstraction, and inevitably loses specificity of distinctions among particular items, it should be remembered that the aim of this analysis was to establish a structure of emotional meaning at a more general or abstract level than that represented by the atomistic analysis of the dictionary definitions.

In any event, names for the 12 clusters were chosen on the basis of the manifest content of the items, with an effort to select a name that seems best to reflect the commonality among items in each cluster. For example, *Activation* would seem to reflect the central meaning of items such as, "sense of vitality, aliveness, vibrancy, an extra spurt of energy or drive," and "a special lift in everything I do and say; I feel bouncy, springy."

In contrast, the term *Hypoactivation* reflects items such as, "I feel empty, drained, hollow; I feel heavy, logy, sluggish; I feel understimulated, undercharged." And for Cluster 3, items such as, "my blood pressure goes up; blood seems to rush through my body; my body seems to speed up; there's an excitement, a sense of being keyed up, overstimulated, supercharged" would seem to be reflected validly by the label *Hyperactivation*.

In similar ways, the items in Clusters 4, 5, and 6 suggest the obvious labels applied to these clusters. For example, items in Cluster 4 such as, "there is an intense positive relationship with another person or with other people; a communion, a unity, a closeness, friendliness and freedom, mutual respect and interdependence; I want to help, protect, please another person" clearly indicate *Moving Toward* others.

Just as clearly, "I want to withdraw, disappear, draw back, be alone, away from others, crawl into myself; a sense of unrelatedness to others; everyone seems far away; I am out of contact, can't reach others" suggests the general label *Moving Away*. And the term *Moving Against* is an obvious summary phrase for items such as, "there is an impulse to strike out, to pound, or smash, or kick, or bite; to do something that will hurt; I want to strike out, explode, but I hold back, control myself; I want to say something nasty, something that will hurt someone."

Items in Clusters 7, 8, and 9 perhaps require a somewhat greater abstraction from the immediate content, probably as a consequence of the greater range of concrete phenomena covered in each cluster. In Cluster 7, a large number of items deal with a state of relaxed, tension-free comfort, illustrated by "there's a mellow comfort; a sense of well-being; a feeling of warmth all over; I am peaceful, tranquil, quiet." In addition, other items refer to a sense of optimistic harmonious integration both within oneself and in relation to the world. "I'm in tune with the world; everything is going right for me; a sense of being very integrated and at ease with myself, in harmony with myself; I feel I can really be myself." From the point of view of personality theory, these items seem to deal with various aspects of what previous writers have called "adjustment" or "integration," and either of these terms might serve as an appropriate label for this cluster. However, in an effort to convey the more experiential flavor of many of the items, the more general term *Comfort* was chosen, and while it does not cover all aspects of emotional experience described by the statements in the cluster, it would seem to focus on the meaning central to the majority of items.

Paralleling the range of phenomena covered in Cluster 7, the items in Cluster 8 refer to various kinds of *Discomfort*. "There is a clutching, sinking feeling in the middle of my chest; a gnawing feeling in the pit of my stomach; an inner ache you can't locate."

In contrast to the range covered in the two preceding clusters, Cluster 9 clearly and directly deals with *Tension*, reflected by items such as, "my whole body is tense; there's tension across my back, my neck, and shoulders; I'm wound up inside; my face and mouth are tight, tense, hard."

Cluster 10 also offers relatively little difficulty in labeling in that all of the items in one way or another refer to *Enhancement* of oneself. "I feel taller, stronger, bigger; I have a sense of sureness; a sense of being exceptionally strong or energetic; a sense of more confidence in myself; a feeling that I can do anything."

Clusters 11 and 12 present the most difficult problems in assigning a single label to each cluster that reasonably reflects the variety of meanings

TABLE 4-1

Clusters of Items Appearing in the Definitions of 50 Emotional States

CLUSTER 1: ACTIVATION

Sense of vitality, aliveness, vibrancy, an extra spurt of energy or drive
A special lift in everything I do and say; I feel bouncy, springy
I'm excited in a calm way
There's an inner buoyancy
I feel effervescent, bubbly
Warm excitement
I seem more alert
A sense of being more alive
I feel wide awake
A sense of lightness, buoyancy and upsurge of the body
I seem to be immediately in touch with the world; a sense of being very open, receptive,
    with no separation between me and the world
Particularly acute awareness of pleasurable things, their sounds, their colors, and textures—
    everything seems more beautiful, natural, and desirable
There's an intense awareness of everything; I seem to experience things with greater clarity;
    colors seem brighter, sounds clearer, movements more vivid
I seem to sense everything and experience everything immediately
A sense that I'm experiencing everything fully, completely, thoroughly; that I'm feeling all
    the way
A strong sense of interest and involvement in things around me
I feel like singing

CLUSTER 2: HYPOACTIVATION

I feel empty, drained, hollow
I feel heavy, logy, sluggish
I feel understimulated, undercharged
All excitement, vitality is gone
I feel tired, sleepy
My feelings seem dulled
My body seems to slow down
A sense of being dead inside
I feel let down
I feel mentally dull

CLUSTER 3: HYPERACTIVATION

My blood pressure goes up; blood seems to rush through my body
My body seems to speed up
There's an excitement, a sense of being keyed up, overstimulated, supercharged
There's a quickening of heartbeat
My heart pounds
My pulse quickens
The feeling begins with a sharp sudden onset

TABLE 4-1 (*continued*)

CLUSTER 4: MOVING TOWARD

There is an intense positive relationship with another person or with other people; a communion, a unity, a closeness, friendliness and freedom, mutual respect and interdependence

I want to help, protect, please another person

A sense of empathic harmony with another person; in tune, sharing and experiencing the same feelings and thoughts

There's a sense of complete understanding of the other person

I want to feel with the other person, experience with the other person with every sense; to be psychologically in touch with another person

Realization that someone else is more important to me than I am to myself

I want to touch, hold, be close physically to the other person

I want to be tender and gentle with another person

I want to communicate freely, share my thoughts and feelings with everyone around

A sense of giving, doing something for another person

I want to make others happy

A sense of being wanted, needed

I feel soft and firm

A sense of trust and appreciation of another person

Sense of confidence in being with another person

There's a desire to give of myself to another person

CLUSTER 5: MOVING AWAY

I want to withdraw, disappear, draw back, be alone, away from others, crawl into myself

A sense of unrelatedness to others; everyone seems far away; I am out of contact, can't reach others

There's a lack of involvement and not caring about anything that goes on around me

A feeling of a certain distance from others; everyone seems far away

There is a sense of aloneness, being cut off, completely by myself

I feel aimless

As if I'm out of touch, seeing things from far away

A sense of wandering, lost in space with nothing solid to grab onto

A sense of being incomplete; as if part of me is missing

CLUSTER 6: MOVING AGAINST

There is an impulse to strike out, to pound, or smash, or kick, or bite; to do something that will hurt

I want to strike out, explode, but I hold back, control myself

I want to say something nasty, something that will hurt someone

Fists are clenched

I keep thinking of getting even, of revenge

conveyed by the items. In Cluster 11, a number of the items seem to have a retrospective temporal perspective, and refer to the individual's own thoughts, feelings, or behaviors that he regrets. "Seems that nothing I do is right; I get mad at myself for my feelings or thoughts or for what I've done; I keep blaming myself for the situation." Other items,

TABLE 4-1 (*continued*)

CLUSTER 7: COMFORT

There's a mellow comfort
A sense of well-being
A sense of harmony and peace within
I am free of conflict
A feeling of warmth all over
I am peaceful, tranquil, quiet
There is an inner warm glow, a radiant sensation
Sense of "rightness" with oneself and the world; nothing can go wrong
A sense of being very integrated and at ease with myself, in harmony with myself
I'm loose, relaxed
There is a general release, a lessening of tension
Everything—breathing, moving, thinking—seems easier
A sense of being carefree but within balance
I'm optimistic and cheerful; the world seems basically good and beautiful; men are essentially kind; life is worth living
I'm optimistic about the future; the future seems bright
I'm in tune with the world
My movements are graceful and easy, I feel especially well coordinated
I feel I can really be myself
Everything is going right for me
A sense of smiling at myself
Nothing is a burden; problems fade away and I'm free from worry
I think about beautiful things
There's a renewed appreciation of life
I'm completely free from worry
I feel like smiling
I feel safe and secure
I'm at peace with the world
It's a state of release

CLUSTER 8: DISCOMFORT

There is a clutching, sinking feeling in the middle of my chest
There's a lump in my throat
A gnawing feeling in the pit of my stomach
An inner ache you can't locate
My heart seems to ache
There is a heavy feeling in my stomach
There's a heaviness in my chest
I have no appetite; I can't eat
There is a sense of loss, of deprivation
I can't smile or laugh
I feel as if I'm under a heavy burden

however, refer to a dissatisfaction with the current situation. "There is a yearning, a desire for change; I want things to hurry up and begin to change; a longing to have things the same as before; I begin to think about what I can do to change the situation." Thus, unable to devise a single term that would capture the somewhat different meanings of items

TABLE 4-1 *(continued)*

CLUSTER 9: TENSION

My whole body is tense
There's tension across my back, my neck, and shoulders
I'm wound up inside
My face and mouth are tight, tense, hard
A tight knotted feeling in my stomach
I'm hypersensitive
I'm easily irritated, ready to snap
I have a sense of being trapped, closed up, boxed, fenced in, tied down, inhibited

CLUSTER 10: ENHANCEMENT

I feel taller, stronger, bigger
I have a sense of sureness
A sense of being exceptionally strong or energetic
I'm really functioning as a unit
Muscle tone is suddenly enhanced
I feel strong inside
A sense of more confidence in myself; a feeling that I can do anything
A sense of being important and worthwhile
I seem to be functioning intellectually at a higher level
There is a sense of accomplishment, fulfillment
There are moments of tremendous strength

CLUSTER 11: INCOMPETENCE:DISSATISFACTION

Seems that nothing I do is right
I get mad at myself for my feelings or thoughts or for what I've done
I keep blaming myself for the situation
There is a yearning, a desire for change; I want things to hurry up and begin to change
A longing to have things the same as before
I begin to think about what I can do to change the situation
There is a sense of regret
There's a sense of weakness

CLUSTER 12: INADEQUACY

A sense of being totally unable to cope with the situation
There's a sense of not knowing where to go, what to do
I feel vulnerable and totally helpless
A sense that I have no control over the situation
I seem to be caught up and overwhelmed by the feeling
Sense of being gripped by the situation
I want to be comforted, helped by someone

---

in this cluster, the phrase *Incompetence:Dissatisfaction* was chosen, sacrificing brevity and elegance in an effort to summarize fairly the manifest content of this cluster.

While items in Cluster 11 refer to responses that have been made and have turned out "wrong," the items in Cluster 12 imply that the individual feels totally incapable of *any* response. "A sense of being totally unable to cope with the situation; there's a sense of not knowing where to go, what to do; I feel vulnerable and totally helpless." It is not that the individual has done something he regrets, as in Cluster 11, but rather, he is overwhelmed, incapable of acting, feels vulnerable and a sense of *Inadequacy*.

SUMMARY OF CLUSTER ANALYSIS

Having noted that certain items occurred together more or less consistently in the definitions of emotional states presented in the dictionary of emotional meaning, the 215 items that appeared in definitions of at least three emotions were cluster analyzed. Twelve clusters were identified, such that items in each cluster showed similar patterns of presence and absence in the definitions of 50 emotions. Recognizing the difficulties and dangers in assigning general labels, obvious similarity of manifest content within most of the clusters appeared to warrant the designation of more abstract terms as summary headings for these clusters. Thus, the 12 clusters were labeled: (1) *Activation;* (2) *Hypoactivation;* (3) *Hyperactivation;* (4) *Moving Toward;* (5) *Moving Away;* (6) *Moving Against;* (7) *Comfort;* (8) *Discomfort;* (9) *Tension;* (10) *Enhancement;* (11) *Incompetence:Dissatisfaction;* (12) *Inadequacy.*

Interrelationships among Clusters

Inspection of the definitions of emotional states suggests that not only do specific items tend to occur together, but also clusters appear to be consistently related to each other. For example, scanning the definitions of emotional states commonly viewed as pleasant indicates that *Activation* and *Comfort* both are present in the definitions of many of these emotions, though with varying degrees of emphasis. The definitions of both Delight and Contentment, for instance, contain items referring to *Activation* and *Comfort;* though *Activation* seems to be emphasized in Delight and *Comfort* in the definition of Contentment. In fact, closer examination of these kinds of differences in emphasis in the patterning of clusters will serve as an important basis for distinguishing similar emotions in later discussion of the data. At this point, however, primary concern is focused on the interrelationships among clusters over all 50 emotional states.

To evaluate the magnitude of these interrelationships, a first necessary step was to devise a system for quantitatively representing the degree to which each cluster is emphasized in the definition of a given emotion.

"Emphasis," of course, is not a term systematically defined in previous theory or research, but at least rough guidelines for establishing reasonable criteria might be gleaned from earlier work. In studies that deal with content analysis of communications, for example, frequency of occurrence of a particular category usually is interpreted in terms of "emphasis" of that category in the communications analyzed. If one wanted to study the relative emphasis of hostility and reverence in current American television programs, a generally acceptable index of each variable would be a frequency count of the number of hostile acts and the number of reverent acts in a sample of such programs.

Frequency, therefore, would seem to be a typical index of "emphasis." In the definitions of emotional states, there are at least two kinds of frequencies relevant to this issue. First is the number of statements in a cluster which appear in a definition, and second is the number of subjects who mentioned each of these statements. In quantitatively evaluating the degree to which each cluster is emphasized, therefore, both of these frequencies were taken into account: Thus, it was assumed that, if 40 of the 50 subjects agreed, on the average, that 15 of the 17 items in the *Activation* cluster describe a given emotional state, that cluster is emphasized relatively more than in another definition for which only 20 subjects agreed that only one *Activation* item described that emotional state.

In brief, each of the 50 emotions was assigned a *cluster score* for each of the 12 clusters. The *cluster score* indicating the relative emphasis of that cluster in a particular definition was computed as a product of the proportion of items in a cluster appearing in a definition and the mean percentage of subjects who checked each item in the cluster. These scores are summarized in Table 4-2.

To investigate the interrelationships among clusters, correlations were computed between *cluster scores* over the 50 emotions (Table 4-3), and this matrix of intercorrelations was submitted to a principal components factor analysis (Table 4-4).

Two factors account for most of the variance. The first factor is bipolar, defined by four clusters at one end (*Activation, Moving Toward, Comfort,* and *Enhancement*) and the other eight clusters at the other end. From an examination of the clusters defining each emotion in Table 4-2, it is clear that this factor involves a pleasant–unpleasant, positive-negative, or, in more general terms, valence dimension of emotional meaning. That is, *Activation, Moving Toward, Comfort,* and *Enhancement* define those emotional states commonly viewed as pleasant or positive, and the other eight clusters define emotional states commonly viewed as unpleasant or negative.

Factor two provides further clarification of the negative end of the

Emotion	Activation	Hypo-activation	Hyper-activation	Moving Toward	Moving Away	Cluster Moving Against
Admiration	14.8	0	0	12.6	0	0
Affection	15.4	0	0	47.0	0	0
Amusement	22.6	0	0	0	0	0
Anger	0	0	53.0	0	0	46.0
Anxiety	0	0	0	0	0	8.0
Apathy	0	36.8	0	0	38.0	0
Awe	14.2	0	12.6	0	0	0
Boredom	0	51.2	0	0	28.0	0
Cheerfulness	46.4	0	0	5.2	0	0
Confidence	23.2	0	0	7.6	0	0
Contempt	0	0	10.6	0	0	26.4
Contentment	6.8	0	0	5.0	0	0
Delight	44.2	0	12.8	5.8	0	0
Depression	0	48.6	0	0	38.0	0
Determination	9.8	0	16.8	0	0	0
Disgust	0	3.4	5.4	0	0	0
Dislike	0	0	0	0	0	14.8
Elation	43.4	0	24.2	0	0	0
Embarrassment	0	0	21.2	0	10.2	0
Enjoyment	48.2	0	0	2.6	0	0
Excitement	28.6	0	31.4	0	0	0
Fear	0	0	44.6	0	5.4	0
Friendliness	23.0	0	0	25.8	0	0
Frustration	0	4.6	4.8	0	0	7.2
Gaiety	50.2	0	14.6	10.2	0	0
Gratitude	5.6	0	0	7.8	0	0
Grief	0	14.2	0	0	8.2	0
Guilt	0	3.4	0	0	0	0

4-2

Each Cluster in the Definition of Each Emotional State

Comfort	Discomfort	Tension	Enhancement	Incompetence: Dissatisfaction	Inadequacy
10.2	0	0	3.0	0	0
22.4	0	0	4.0	0	0
21.0	0	0	0	0	0
0	0	19.0	0	0	16.8
0	7.2	18.2	0	4.4	20.2
0	0	0	0	0	0
3.0	0	0	0	0	5.4
0	0	9.0	0	12.0	0
43.6	0	0	24.6	0	0
29.8	0	0	68.2	0	0
0	0	25.2	0	0	4.8
51.0	0	0	13.6	0	0
35.0	0	0	3.0	0	0
0	41.8	5.4	0	19.0	35.2
0	0	5.4	32.6	0	7.4
0	0	9.8	0	0	5.4
0	0	10.4	0	5.0	0
29.6	0	0	28.6	0	5.4
0	3.4	10.4	0	34.2	6.6
44.8	0	0	9.4	0	0
5.8	0	5.0	0	0	11.8
0	0	26.0	0	4.8	45.4
27.6	0	0	10.8	0	0
0	3.8	45.6	0	12.8	21.8
42.6	0	0	17.4	0	0
21.8	0	0	3.4	0	0
0	38.2	4.2	0	10.8	20.0
0	10.2	14.8	0	35.2	4.8

TABLE 4-2

Emotion	Activation	Hypo-activation	Hyper-activation	Cluster Moving Toward	Moving Away	Moving Against
Happiness	56.6	0	5.8	3.6	0	0
Hate	0	0	22.6	0	0	54.0
Hope	4.6	0	0	0	0	0
Impatience	0	0	0	0	0	0
Inspiration	23.0	0	11.4	0	0	0
Irritation	0	0	10.2	0	0	15.6
Jealousy	0	0	7.0	0	0	24.0
Love	29.6	0	12.0	66.0	0	0
Nervousness	0	0	14.2	0	0	0
Panic	0	0	47.6	0	4.6	0
Passion	11.2	0	45.2	38.0	0	0
Pity	0	0	0	5.2	0	0
Pride	27.0	0	5.4	0	0	0
Relief	10.4	0	0	0	0	0
Remorse	0	12.2	0	0	0	0
Resentment	0	3.6	5.8	0	0	25.6
Reverence	7.4	0	4.8	0	0	0
Sadness	0	13.8	0	0	0	0
Serenity	13.0	3.6	0	0	0	0
Shame	0	3.4	0	0	5.8	0
Solemnity	0	0	0	0	0	0
Surprise	11.4	0	28.2	0	0	0

valence factor, in that only those clusters involved in definitions of so-called negative emotions have substantial loadings on this second factor. Specifically, there would seem to be two types of "negative" clusters: Type 1 includes *Hypoactivation, Moving Away, Discomfort* and to some extent, *Incompetence:Dissatisfaction;* Type 2, on the other hand, includes *Hyperactivation, Moving Against, Tension,* and possibly *Inadequacy.*

Thus, there would seem to be essentially three groups of clusters underlying the definitions of emotional states presented in the dictionary. The first group might reasonably be called POSITIVE, and consists of *Activation, Moving Toward, Comfort,* and *Enhancement.* The second group

(*continued*)

Comfort	Discomfort	Tension	Enhancement	Incompetence: Dissatisfaction	Inadequacy
42.8	0	0	26.8	0	0
0	6.8	42.2	0	4.6	14.6
4.0	0	0	0	0	0
0	0	26.0	0	12.0	6.0
10.8	0	0	36.8	0	10.2
0	0	42.0	0	11.2	0
0	11.0	32.2	0	6.0	11.2
32.2	0	0	17.6	0	6.7
0	16.0	33.0	0	5.2	15.4
0	4.2	11.4	0	0	44.8
6.4	0	0	0	0	15.2
0	15.4	0	0	10.8	10.6
18.4	0	0	28.4	0	0
28.8	0	0	3.4	0	0
0	25.4	4.2	0	46.4	11.2
0	0	46.8	0	4.4	12.6
13.6	0	0	6.6	0	10.8
0	35.8	0	0	7.6	10.6
42.0	0	0	7.4	0	0
0	0	0	0	47.6	5.2
3.0	0	0	0	0	5.8
4.2	0	0	0	0	0

might be called NEGATIVE: TYPE 1, and consists of *Hypoactivation, Moving Away, Discomfort,* and *Incompetence:Dissatisfaction.* The third group might be called NEGATIVE: TYPE 2, and consists of *Hyperactivation, Moving Against, Tension,* and *Inadequacy.*

These results are summarized in Table 4-5, in which the three groups of clusters are organized along the vertical axis or columns of the table. Only one further point need be made regarding this aspect of the structural analysis. This concerns the horizontal organization of the clusters in Table 4-5. This phase of the analysis does not derive directly from the correlational treatment of the data, but rather, from inspection of the content

TABLE 4-3

Intercorrelations Among Clusters Over 50 Emotional States

	Activation	Hypoactivation	Hyperactivation	Moving Toward	Moving Away	Moving Against	Comfort	Discomfort	Tension	Enhancement	Incompetence: Dissatisfaction	Inadequacy
Activation	1.00	-.26	-.00	.26	-.24	-.28	.80	-.32	-.46	.56	-.38	-.39
Hypoactivation		1.00	-.23	-.14	.91	-.12	-.25	.46	-.06	-.18	.24	.15
Hyperactivation			1.00	.05	-.11	.30	-.20	-.19	.19	-.08	-.18	.53
Moving Toward				1.00	-.13	-.15	.31	-.15	-.25	.12	-.19	-.13
Moving Away					1.00	-.13	-.24	.32	-.08	-.17	.21	.21
Moving Against						1.00	-.29	-.04	.65	-.20	.06	.13
Comfort							1.00	-.33	-.48	.51	-.38	-.46
Discomfort								1.00	.04	-.23	.40	.42
Tension									1.00	-.32	.14	.37
Enhancement										1.00	-.27	-.26
Incompetence: Dissatisfaction											1.00	.13
Inadequacy												1.00

TABLE 4-4

Factor Loadings for Clusters

Cluster	Factor 1	Factor 2
Activation	−.83	.09
Hypoactivation	.49	.72
Hyperactivation	.14	−.59
Moving Toward	−.40	.01
Moving Away	.47	.66
Moving Against	.35	−.63
Comfort	−.85	.16
Discomfort	.55	.42
Tension	.56	−.58
Enhancement	−.64	.10
Incompetence: Dissatisfaction	.51	.28
Inadequacy	.61	−.21

of the clusters. Specifically, the clusters not only appear to be interrelated in terms of the three groups obtained in the factor analysis, but the *content* of the clusters suggests that they deal with four dimensions of emotional

TABLE 4-5

A Structural Analysis of Emotional Meaning

	Clusters		
Dimension	Positive	Negative: Type 1	Negative: Type 2
ACTIVATION	Activation	Hypoactivation	Hyperactivation
RELATEDNESS	Moving Toward	Moving Away	Moving Against
HEDONIC TONE	Comfort	Discomfort	Tension
COMPETENCE	Enhancement	Incompetence: Dissatisfaction	Inadequacy

meaning. That is, *Activation, Hypoactivation,* and *Hyperactivation* concern various levels of ACTIVATION, *Moving Toward, Moving Away,* annd *Moving Against* concern RELATEDNESS to the environment. *Comfort, Discomfort,* and *Tension* concern the HEDONIC TONE of an emotional state. And *Enhancement, Incompetence:Dissatisfaction,* and *Inadequacy* refer to the individual's sense of COMPETENCE in relating to his environment.

Although this aspect of the analysis does not stem directly from the factor analytic treatment of the data, organization of the clusters in terms of four dimensions of content to supplement the results of the factor analysis would seem to be so compelling as to warrant consideration in the structural analysis of emotional meaning. As in the case of any other aspect of the structural analysis, the usefulness of this particular feature in the organization does not depend on the statistical elegance with which it was derived, but rather, on its heuristic value in dealing conceptually with the structure of emotional meaning. In the following chapter, evidence in support of the usefulness of this dimensional aspect of the analysis will be discussed in relation to a number of diverse theories of emotion, with the aim of integrating these various points of view within the structural framework developed here.

Patterning of Clusters in Emotional States

The cluster scores summarized in Table 4-2 provide an estimate of the degree to which each of the 12 clusters is emphasized in the definition of each emotion. On the basis of these data, intercorrelations among clusters were computed and the resulting matrix factor analyzed. Following a similar procedure, these data may also be viewed in terms of the interrelationships among emotional states.

For this analysis, the correlation between each emotion and every other emotion was computed over the 12 clusters. That is, the correlation between, for example, Admiration and Affection was computed on the basis of scores obtained for the two emotions on each of the 12 clusters. This 50×50 matrix of intercorrelations was then submitted to a principal components factor analysis, and the results are summarized in Table 4-6.

It is not all surprising, of course, that the results of this analysis in terms of emotions parallels the similar analysis by clusters presented in Table 4-4. After all, the two analyses are based on the same data merely viewed from somewhat different points of view.

In any event, as in the analysis by clusters, two factors account for a major part of the variance, and these two factors obviously parallel those found for clusters. Specifically, the first factor distinguishes emotions along a bipolar continuum of valence, ranging from Gaiety and Cheerfulness at one end to Frustration and Jealously at the other. The second factor concerns emotions only at the "negative" or unpleasant end of the valence

TABLE 4-6

Factor Analysis of Emotional States Based on Cluster Scores

Factor 1		Factor 2	
Emotion[a]	Loading	Emotion[a]	Loading
Gaiety	.95	Contempt	.72
Cheerfulness	.94	Anger	.70
Happiness	.93	Hate	.68
Enjoyment	.90	Resentment	.67
Delight	.88	Disgust	.65
Friendliness	.88	Irritation	.65
Elation	.85	Fear	.63
Admiration	.84	Jealousy	.60
Amusement	.84	Frustration	.55
Hope	.84	Nervousness	.55
Pride	.84	Panic	.52
Gratitude	.80	Anxiety	.44
Relief	.80	Impatience	.44
Serenity	.79	Dislike	.43
Contentment	.74	Embarrassment	.08
Reverence	.68	Guilt	-.14
Confidence	.66	Shame	-.32
Love	.66	Pity	-.39
Inspiration	.63	Remorse	-.44
Affection	.57	Grief	-.47
Awe	.46	Sadness	-.49
Excitement	.36	Boredom	-.50
Surprise	.28	Apathy	-.54
Determination	.27	Depression	-.63
Passion	.20		
Solemnity	.11		
Apathy	-.18		
Panic	-.25		
Shame	-.30		

TABLE 4-6 (*continued*)

Factor 1		Factor 2	
Emotion[a]	Loading	Emotion[a]	Loading
Boredom	−.30		
Anger	−.32		
Sadness	−.35		
Fear	−.35		
Pity	−.37		
Embarrassment	−.43		
Remorse	−.44		
Grief	−.46		
Dislike	−.48		
Disgust	−.48		
Depression	−.48		
Contempt	−.48		
Guilt	−.49		
Irritation	−.52		
Impatience	−.52		
Hate	−.53		
Resentment	−.56		
Nervousness	−.57		
Anxiety	−.59		
Frustration	−.60		
Jealousy	−.64		

[a] Listed in order of magnitude of factor loadings.

continuum, distinguishing emotions like Contempt, Anger, and Hate at one end from emotions like Depression, Apathy, and Boredom at the other end. Thus, for the second factor, one end is defined by emotions that primarily involve *Hyperactivation, Moving Against, Tension,* and *Inadequcy,* and the other end is defined by emotions involving *Hypoactivation, Moving Away, Discomfort,* and *Incompetence:Dissatisfaction.*

Within the framework provided by this analysis, emotions may be broadly classified as: POSITIVE (Gaiety, Cheerfulness, Happiness, etc.); NEGATIVE: TYPE 1 (Depression, Apathy, Boredom, etc.); and NEGATIVE: TYPE 2 (Contempt, Anger, Hate, etc.).

TABLE 4-7

Primary Clusters in Definitions of Positive Emotions

Activation	Moving Toward	Comfort	Enhancement
Admiration	Affection	Contentment	Confidence
Amusement	Love	Determination	Inspiration
Awe		Friendliness	Pride
Cheerfulness		Gratitude	
Delight		Reverence	
Elation		Serenity	
Enjoyment			
Gaiety			
Happiness			
Hope			

TABLE 4-8

Primary Clusters in Definitions of Negative: Type 1 Emotions

Hypoactivation	Moving Away	Discomfort	Incompetence: Dissatisfaction
Boredom	Apathy	Grief	Guilt
Depression		Pity	Remorse
		Sadness	Shame

TABLE 4-9

Primary Clusters in Definitions of Negative: Type 2 Emotions

Hyperactivation	Moving Against	Tension	Inadequacy
Anger	Contempt	Disgust	Anxiety
Fear	Dislike	Frustration	
Panic	Hate	Impatience	
		Irritation	
		Jealousy	
		Nervousness	
		Resentment	

Within each of these broad groupings, emotions may be further classified on the basis of the particular cluster that receives greatest emphasis in definitions of the emotions. Table 4-7 summarizes this classification for POSITIVE emotions; Table 4-8 for NEGATIVE: TYPE 1 emotions; and Table 4-9 for NEGATIVE: TYPE 2 emotions.

This line of analysis could be continued along a similar vein, making finer distinctions, for instance, among those emotions listed in Table 4-7 under *Activation* on the basis of the cluster that is second greatest in emphasis in the definitions of the various emotional states. However, there is no need at this point to continue with further refinement of the classification system. In a study of the development of emotional meaning discussed in Chapter 6, the usefulness of a further refinement along this line will be discussed. At this point, it will suffice to indicate that the patterning of clusters in terms of relative emphasis in the definitions may serve as a more or less convenient way of classifying emotional states. Depending upon the purpose for which any classification is made, one may classify emotions into three broad groups derived from the factor analysis, or into the 12 subgroups presented in Tables 4-7, 4-8, and 4-9, or into even narrower and more specific subgroups based on further analysis of cluster patterns.

At this stage, the particular level of classification is not likely to have special significance in clarifying the structure of emotional meaning. Much more important is the structural framework of clusters and patterning of clusters in terms of relative emphasis which provides future researchers an empirically derived basis for organizing emotional states at the level of specificity appropriate to their research.

CHAPTER 5

Comments on the Structure of Emotional Meaning

Having started with an atomistic description of verbally reported experiences associated with each of 50 emotional terms, the analysis has moved to a considerably more abstract level. Twelve clusters of items used in the definitions have been identified, and these clusters have been organized on the basis of both a factor analytic study of their interrelationships and several dimensions of content. Each emotional state was then considered in terms of the relative emphasis of the various clusters in the definition of that emotion, and the 50 emotions were classified into three broad groupings suggested by a factor analysis of the definitions. Finally, to provide a somewhat more refined classification, the three broad groups of emotions were further subdivided on the basis of the particular cluster emphasized in each definition. The aim of this analysis, however, was not to provide a hard and fast classification suitable for all purposes, but rather, to suggest a way of classifying emotions at various levels of specificity on the basis of a structural analysis of emotional meaning.

Thus, the initial atomistic analysis represented by the dictionary of emotional meaning has been supplemented by a structural analysis concerned with the organization of definitions in terms of patterns of clusters. Each step in the analysis has essentially involved description of the data at successively more abstract levels of discourse, relying primarily on descriptive statistical techniques. The organization of clusters into four major dimensions, however, derives from inspection of the content of items in these clusters. Although this aspect of the structural analysis clearly involves a conceptual leap from the data, the four dimensions of emotional meaning—ACTIVATION, RELATEDNESS, HEDONIC TONE, and COMPETENCE—provide a potentially useful way of conceptualizing a variety of emotional phenomena. In fact, the structural analysis of emotional meaning based, in part, on these four major dimensions may be viewed as something of a consolidation of earlier theories of emotion.

It may therefore be of some value to consider these dimensions of emotional meaning in the light of other theoretical viewpoints.

Dimensions of Emotion

Throughout the history of psychology as a formal discipline, beginning with Wundt and continuing through the more recent work of writers such as Arnold and Block, psychologists have proposed a variety of conceptual schemes designed to simplify and organize observations of emotional phenomena. One way of viewing these proposals is in terms of the major descriptive dimensions emphasized by each of the writers, and while there is a certain amount of diversity in the terms they use, one does not distort the various theories a great deal by organizing them within the framework suggested by the present investigation.

Table 5-1 presents a summary of the major dimensions of emotion suggested by a sample of the writers in the field, indicating for each one the principal dimensions emphasized in his analysis of emotion.

ACTIVATION

As indicated in Table 5-1, almost every writer in the sample has in one way or another mentioned level of activation as a central aspect of emotion. Block (1957), on the basis of his factor analytic study of semantic differential ratings of emotional words, identifies one factor as *affective intensity* or *level of activation.* Burt (1950), in another factorial study, labels the first factor he obtained in terms of *emotional energy* or *general emotionality,* and the definition is obviously quite similar to the general notion of *Activation.* Duffy, of course, has developed a comprehensive theory centered around the concept of activation (1962), and even in her earliest writings she discussed activation level as a primary dimension of emotion (1941). Harlow and Stagner (1933) do not mention activation *per se,* but their list of four basic components of emotional experience includes excitement and depression—which may reasonably be interpreted as the extremes of the activation dimension. They say,

The innate components of the emotional experience are the four fundamental feeling-tones, pleasure, unpleasantness, excitement and depression. These feelings represent the only identifiable conscious elements in an emotion, aside from sensations and cognition of the stimulating situation [1933, p. 191].

Similarly, in a later work, Stagner (1948) cites excitement–depression as one of two dimensions characterizing emotion. In their analysis of moods, Nowlis and Nowlis (1956) mention level of activation, and

Schachter in a series of brilliant papers (e.g., Schachter & Wheeler, 1962; Schachter & Singer, 1962) not only specifies activation as a primary dimension of emotional states but also experimentally demonstrates the significance of level of activation in defining an emotional state. Scholsberg's well-known analysis of emotion contains activation as one of his three major dimensions (1954), and Young's more recent statement of his position (1967) also includes activation as a central feature. Finally, Wundt, in his tridimensional theory of feeling (1905), specifies excitement–quiescence as one major dimension.

Of all the writers sampled, only Arnold (1960) does not specifically propose an activational dimension of emotion. However, this does not at all mean that she neglects this concept. In her careful discussion of various points of view, she says,

> There is no doubt that energy mobilization (activation) and direction can be inferred in every emotion. But there is also no doubt that the same can be said of every other psychological activity, not only of so-called "dynamic" processes [1960, Vol. 1, p. 153].

Thus, she recognizes activation as an aspect of emotion, but her aim is to identify those aspects of emotional reactions which are unique to "emotion" and therefore can serve to distinguish emotional phenomena from other psychological events.

In summary, then, activation has been mentioned by almost all writers in this sample who have been concerned with identifying dimensions of emotion. It can hardly be considered astonishing, therefore, to discover in the present research that people describe their emotional experiences in terms of three related clusters—*Hypoactivation, Activation,* and *Hyperactivation*—nor does it seem particularly creative to suggest that these clusters each represent a range of reported experience along an overall dimension of ACTIVATION. The findings are obviously consistent with previous speculations.

RELATEDNESS

Arnold perhaps more than any other major writer in the field has emphasized the individual's relatedness to the environment in defining emotional phenomena. After an extensive review of previous literature, she says,

> Summing up our discussion, we can now define emotion as *the felt tendency toward anything appraised as good (beneficial), or away from anything intuitively appraised as bad (harmful). This attraction or aversion is accompanied by a pattern of physiological changes organized toward approach or withdrawal. The patterns differ for different emotions* [1960, Vol. 1, p. 182].

Thus, in terms of the present analysis, Arnold focuses on two clusters—*Moving Toward* and *Moving Away*—in her central definition of emotion.

Block's factor analytic results are somewhat less clear in regards to the three specific clusters within the dimension of RELATEDNESS, but he interprets his third factor—defined by the emotional terms of sympathy, nostalgia, grief, and to a lesser extent, love—as encompassing emotions relevant to interpersonal relatedness and considerations of impermanence. Duffy in the development of her argument to discard concepts such as drive, motivation, and emotion, proposes two basic categories of conceptualization—energy mobilization and direction (Duffy, 1941). Although most of her work has been concerned with energy moblization or level of activation, Duffy's notion of "direction" comes close to the present concept of RELATEDNESS. That is, energy is expended in the organism's relation to the environment, and while Duffy does not clarify her concept of "direction" with nearly as much detail as she does "mobilization," it seems reasonable to conceptualize "direction" in terms of the three clusters of RELATEDNESS—*Moving Away, Moving Toward,* and *Moving Against.* Admittedly, Duffy herself has not developed her concept of direction along this specific line, but it seems to be a reasonable extension of her views. Even if this extension takes Duffy's theory too far afield, there at least appears to be some parallel between her notion of "direction" and the dimension of RELATEDNESS.

Nowlis and Nowlis (1956) specify "social orientation" as a major dimension in their analysis of moods, and Schlosberg's "attention–rejection" factor is clearly congruent with the clusters of *Moving Toward* and *Moving Away*.

Table 5-1 indicates entries for Schachter's point of view both for RELATEDNESS and COMPETENCE. These entries have been made despite the fact that Schachter does not specify either of these two dimensions in his discussion of emotional states—as in the case of Duffy, these entries represent my interpretation and extension of Schachter's views.* Briefly, he suggests that emotional states are defined by the individual's level of activation and his cognitive interpretation of the situation. An elegant and parsimonious conceptualization, Schachter's theory has considerable predictive power in accounting for emotional phenomena.

As indicated earlier, the first factor in Schachter's theory is consistent with the dimension of ACTIVATION; attention here is focused on the

---

* Although the extension of Schachter's theory presented in this section seems reasonable to me, I doubt that Schachter would entirely accept the particulars of the view presented here. I must therefore accept responsibility for this interpretation and development of Schachter's theory, with due apology for any *mis*interpretation.

second aspect of the theory involving the social variables that define an emotional state. In their experimental work, Schachter and his colleagues have been extraordinarily ingenious in manipulating social variables and studying the effects of these manipulations on the individual's labeling of his emotional state. However, in the theoretical formulation of his views, this aspect of the theory has been presented in rather broad, general terms, and one might use the results of the present structuring of emotional meaning to develop this phase of the theory.

Of the four dimensions specified in the structure of emotional meaning, two of these—ACTIVATION and HEDONIC TONE—refer primarily to internal events. The other two—RELATEDNESS and COMPE-TENCE—refer to the individual's perception of himself in relation to the environment. Thus, Schachter's "cognitive–social" aspect of defining emotional states might be defined further in terms of these two latter dimensions. For example, given a certain level of activation, a person might label his emotional state as Joy or Anger as a function of whether he interpretes the situation so that he moves towards or against others. In another instance, a person might label an emotional state as Frustration or Determination, depending upon whether he sees himself in relation to his environment as being *Inadequate* or *Enhanced.* It is unlikely that these two dimensions alone—RELATEDNESS and COMPETENCE— would cover all possible cognitive interpretations of one's social situation, but in terms of the majority of emotional experiences, they probably ac-count for a good deal of the variance. It would therefore seem useful to extend Schachter's theory in this direction, viewing RELATEDNESS and COMPETENCE as two major dimensions concerned with the indi-vidual's cognitive interpretation of his relationship to the environment in which he experiences an emotional state.

In summary, among the writers sampled, Arnold, Block, Nowlis and Nowlis, Schlosberg, and perhaps also Duffy and Schachter (depending upon one's interpretation of their views), the individual's relation to the environment has been recognized as an important dimension of emotional reactions. Although the literature does not reveal as much consensus in dealing with this dimension as it does in considering ACTIVATION, the present findings represent a reasonable extension of preceding work, supplementing earlier concepts of *Moving Away* and *Moving Toward* the environment with a third aspect of relatedness—*Moving Against* the en-vironment. In view of the clear-cut meaning of the large number of emo-tional words relevant to hostility, this third aspect of relatedness seems an obvious and necessary extension of the simpler bipolar classification proposed by previous writers.

Readers familiar with the psychoanalytic literature will recognize the

TABLE 5-1

Summary of Dimensions of Emotion Proposed by Various Theories

Author	Dimension				
	Activation	Relatedness	Hedonic Tone	Competence	Other
Arnold		X			Specific patterns of physiological change
Block	X	X	X		
Burt	X		X		Demonstrative versus inhibitive behavior
Duffy	X	X (?)[a]			
Harlow and Stagner	X		X		
Nowlis and Nowlis	X	X	X		Level of control
Stagner	X		X		
Schachter	X	X (?)[a]		X (?)[a]	
Schlosberg	X	X	X		
Young	X		X		
Wundt	X		X		

[a] The entries for Duffy and for Schachter that are accompanied by (?) represent the writer's own interpretation and extension of the views presented by these two authors. These interpretations are explicated in the text of this chapter.

parallel between the present proposal and Horney's classification of needs (1945). Horney of course was dealing with a different problem—the analysis of inner conflicts—and she uses the three headings of moving toward, moving away, and moving against others as a way of classifying various neurotic needs. Nevertheless, her views are consistent with the results obtained in the present research, and her three headings seem to convey accurately the three clusters in the dimension of RELATEDNESS.

HEDONIC TONE

Young (1967), perhaps more than any other writer in the field, has emphasized HEDONIC TONE as a central feature of emotion, though most other writers include a relevant dimension in their descriptions of emotion. Block's first factor, for example, is labeled "pleasantness–unpleasantness" (1957); Burt identifies one factor as "pleasurable–unpleasurable" (1950); Harlow and Stagner mention "pleasure" and "unpleasantness" as two of their four basic feelings (1933); and Stagner defines "pleasantness–unpleasantness" as one of two basic dimensions in his later analysis of emotional phenomena (1948). Similarly, Nowlis and Nowlis specify "hedonic tone" as one of four dimensions of mood (1956); and both Schlosberg (1954) and Wundt (1905) discuss "pleasantness–unpleasantness" in each of their tridimensional systems for describing emotion.

Thus, from a variety of points of view, HEDONIC TONE has been recognized as a principal aspect of emotion—and probably one doesn't need a great deal of research to appreciate that emotions vary along a dimension of pleasantness–unpleasantness or HEDONIC TONE. In any event, the clusters obtained in the present research clearly parallel many previous proposals in this area, but also differ somewhat in the way in which this dimension is defined. The *Comfort* cluster obviously refers to the pleasant aspect of emotional experience, but in addition to the usual concept of pleasure, the cluster also contains items that refer to tension reduction and adjustment. Thus, the cluster might well have been labeled "Pleasantness–Comfort," but for the sake of brevity the latter term was selected. At the other extreme, the unpleasant aspects of emotion are described in terms of two clusters—*Discomfort* and *Tension*. Like the other dimensions in this structuring of emotional meaning, a tripolar conceptualization rather than the bipolar dimensions commonly suggested in the past seems to be most appropriate in organizing the data. Both the *Tension* and *Discomfort* clusters are defined by "unpleasant" items, but they do not always occur together in the definitions of emotional states. For example, Anger, Contempt, Impatience, Irritation, Panic, and Resentment involve *Tension* but not *Discomfort;* and Pity, Remorse, and Sadness involve *Discomfort* but not *Tension*. Therefore, the present structrue may be viewed as something of an extension or development of earlier proposals—both in terms of combining a tension–relaxation factor in the overall HEDONIC TONE dimension and in distinguishing *Discomfort* and *Tension* as two separate clusters at the "unpleasant" ends of this dimension.

COMPETENCE

As indicated in Table 5-1, the dimensions of ACTIVATION, RELATEDNESS, and HEDONIC TONE have all been discussed by previous writers dealing with the description of emotional phenomena, and the present proposal for structuring emotional meaning brings these suggestions together on an empirical basis derived from the data obtained in the compilation of the dictionary. The fourth dimension, COMPETENCE, represents something more of a departure from previous ways of describing and defining emotions, though other writers have discussed emotion from the viewpoint of the organism's adaptation to the environment. For example, Cannon (1929) in his well-known "emergency theory" of emotion stresses the role of emotion in the organism's survival; and from a more recent and radically different point of view, Sartre (1948) interprets emotion as a way of "adapting" to the world, of changing the world "magically" when the individual cannot respond adequately to reality in a nonemotional way. Thus, for both Cannon and Sartre, working from vastly different perspectives, emotion in one way or another is a means of achieving competence (or for Sartre, at least a sense of competence) in relation to the world.

But undoubtedly the most comprehensive treatment of emotion in terms of adaptation has been presented by Plutchik (1962), who first defines eight basic patterns of adaptive behavior—destruction, reproduction, incorporation, orientation, protection, deprivation, rejection, exploration— and then organizes a large number of emotional states into families based on these aspects of adaptation. Thus, Rage, Anger, and Annoyance are included under the general heading of DESTRUCTION; Ectasy, Joy, and Happiness under REPRODUCTION; Astonishment, Amazement, and Surprise under ORIENTATION (Plutchik, 1962, p. 114). At this point Plutchik's detailed system of classification is not of primary concern, though as he demonstrates in his excellent and thoughtful review of relevant research, his system has considerable heuristic value. Rather, the important point to note is his conceptualization of emotion in relation to adaptation, for one might view the dimension of COMPETENCE in emotional reactions as reflecting a person's sense of how effectively he is adapting to his environment. When his adaptation is particularly effective, he may label his emotional state in terms of Pride or Confidence; when his adaptive attempts are ineffective, he may label his emotional state as Panic or Frustration; or when he focuses on previous failures in adaptation, he may label his emotional reactions in terms of Guilt, Remorse, or Shame.

The dimension of COMPETENCE, therefore, while not specified as such in previous attempts to delinate emotional reactions, is indeed related to a number of suggestions made by writers from diverse points of view. The clearest, most forceful and persuasive statement in this area has been made by Robert White (1959) in his discussion of the concept of competence. After reviewing a number of recent theoretical and research developments, he concludes:

This survey indicates a certain unanimity as to the kinds of behavior that cannot be successfully conceptualized in terms of primary drives. This behavior includes visual exploration, grasping, crawling and walking, attention and perception, language and thinking, exploring novel objects and places, manipulating the surroundings, and producing effective changes in the environment. The thesis is then proposed that all of these behaviors have a common biological significance: they all form part of the process whereby the animal or child learns to interact effectively with his environment. The word *competence* is chosen as suitable to indicate this common property. Further, it is maintained that competence cannot be fully acquired through behavior instigated by drives. It receives substantial contributions from activities which, though playful and exploratory in character, at the same time show direction, selectivity, and persistence in interacting with the environment. Such activities in the ultimate service of competence must therefore be conceived to be motivated in their own right. It is proposed to designate this motivation by the term effectance, and to characterize the experience produced as a *feeling of efficacy* [White, 1959, p. 329].

Thus, White has anticipated the results of the present research by underscoring competence motivation and feelings of *efficacy* as constructs of major import in psychological theory. From my own point of view, I would suggest that the range of feelings related to efficacy can be described in terms of the three clusters obtained in the present analysis—*Inadequacy, Enhancement,* and *Incompetence:Dissatisfaction*—and I prefer the designation of COMPETENCE to efficacy in labeling the overall dimension.

SUMMARY

The structure of emotional meaning derived from the present research appears to be consistent with a number of previous proposals regarding the description of emotional phenomena. Moreover, the system of 12 clusters organized within four major dimensions provides a means of coordinating earlier work within a single conceptual scheme. Recognizing that all such schemes in psychology have a relatively short life expectancy,* the proposed structure has at least some temporary value in that it brings together a number of apparently diverse lines of speculation, provides a framework within which complex emotional phenomena might be described, and suggests a number of theoretical lines of development upon which future research might be based.

* At the present stage in the development of psychology, if a particular conceptual scheme does not change within a short time, it is likely to be either too boring to be read or not open to empirical checks.

Notes toward a Theory of Emotion

It would be too grandiose to suggest that the following notes present a "theory of emotion," with the implication that anything like a comprehensive view of all relevant phenomena are treated. Perhaps with so many gaps in our knowledge, such a theory is neither feasible nor desirable at the present time. Without an adequate empirical base, a grand theory of emotion would be likely to result in fruitless theoretical disputes, inconsequential research, and ill-conceived practice. Moreover, the kinds of data obtained in the present research are not the sort one would probably use with confidence to establish or test a theory of emotion, though these data are useful in the first steps of developing a systematic point of view. The following sections, therefore, are presented as "notes toward a theory of emotion," and while these notes are presented in a series of propositions, this form of presentation is not meant to imply a formal deductive system.

Some of these propositions merely summarize findings previously reported, while others make explicit certain assumptions that have been useful in this work. Still others represent cognitive leaps from the data in directions that seem warranted to me, but may seem inappropriate to others. In any event, the primary aim of these speculations is to stimulate and guide further research, and studies illustrating several such lines of inquiry will be reviewed in the next chapter.

PROPOSITIONS

1. *Emotion refers, in part, to experienced events.*

The point of view expressed in this proposition is obviously phenomenological, though hopefully it is a phenomenology that provides a basis for resolving some of the difficulties usually entailed in phenomenological theories by focusing in detail on the language of reported experience. In a sense, the research reported in preceding chapters might be interpreted as a "social phenomenology" in that it has dealt with those aspects of reported experience which can be shared with others via language, and about which there is some degree of consensus. Thus, while I might have a relatively low degree of confidence in the reports of a single person, my confidence in making inferences about experience from a consensus of reports obtained from several people is considerably higher.

Emotion defined in terms of experience or conscious states has been criticized both from the point of view of psychoanalytic theory and behaviorism. Psychoanalytic writers frequently use phrases such as "unconscious guilt" or "unconscious hate," and presumably these terms refer to emotional states of which the individual is not aware. However, perhaps the best clarification of this usage has been presented by Freud, who says,

> It is surely of the essence of an emotion that we should feel it, i.e. that it should enter consciousness. So for emotions, feelings and affects to be unconscious would be quite out of the question. But in psycho-analytic practice we are accustomed to speak of unconscious love, hate, anger, etc., and find it impossible to avoid even the strange conjunction, 'unconscious consciousness of guilt,' or a paradoxical 'unconscious anxiety.' Is there more meaning in the use of these terms than there is in speaking of 'unconscious instincts?'
> The two cases are really not on all fours. To begin with it may happen that an affect or an emotion is perceived, but misconstrued. By the repression of its proper presentation it is forced to become connected with another idea, and is now interpreted by consciousness as the expression of this other idea. If we restore the true connection, we call the original affect 'unconscious,' although the affect was never unconscious but its ideational presentation had undergone repression. In any event, the use of such terms as 'unconscious affect and emotion' has reference to the fate undergone, in consequence of repression, by the quantitative factor in the instinctual impulse. We know that an affect may be subjected to three different vicissitudes: either it remains, wholly or in part, as it is; or it is transformed into a qualitatively different charge of affect, above all into anxiety; or it is suppressed, i.e. its development is hindered altogether. (These possibilities may perhaps be studied even more easily in the technique of the dream-work than in the neuroses.) We know, too, that to suppress the development of affect is the true aim of repression and that its work does not terminate if this aim is not achieved. In every instance where repression has succeeded in inhibiting the development of an affect we apply the term 'unconscious' to those affects that are restored when we undo the work of repression. So it cannot be denied that the use of the terms in question is logical; but a comparison of the unconscious affect with the unconscious idea reveals the significant difference that the unconscious idea continues, after repression, as an actual formation in the system Ucs, whilst to the unconscious affect there corresponds in the same system only a potential disposition which is prevented from developing further. So that, strictly speaking, although no fault be found with the mode of expression in question, there are no unconscious affects in the sense in which there are unconscious ideas. But there may very well be in the system Ucs affect-formations which, like others, come into consciousness [Freud, 1949, pp. 109–111].

Thus, within the psychoanalytic framework, Freud specifies the "essence of an emotion" in terms of a conscious state, and discusses "unconscious emotion" as a "potential disposition" rather than emotion itself—a view not inconsistent with that presented here.

The criticisms of "emotion as experience" from the viewpoint of modern behaviorism have been stated forcefully and succinctly by Mandler (1962). He first notes that "nobody in modern psychology denies the facts of private experience [p. 302]," citing Skinner in support of his statement. He then rejects experience as a legitimate focus of psychological interest for the following reasons.

First, it is unreasonable to expect that private experience can ever be anything but that. It becomes public, that is comprehensible to others, only after it has been put into some sort of communicable symbolism, namely language [p. 303].

He then goes on to say that language is too crude an instrument to describe emotional experiences, and therefore he would always be frustrated in trying to capture the "myriad impressions, feelings, ideas, notions, and emotions that flood my private screen [p. 303]."*

Mandler's first two points, in my opinion, are incontrovertible. To study experience, certainly it must be made public, and the process of making it public depends upon some language system. But I do not find the third point entirely persuasive. Of course language for most of us is a "crude instrument," but the work of Shakespeare, Joyce, Conrad, Hemingway, Eliot, and a few others suggests that even this crude instrument can be exquisitely refined. One way of sharpening and expanding the vocabulary of descriptive terms readily available to one person has been developed in this research, based on the notion of pooling the relevant language of many people, and while it would be absurd to compare the check list used in compiling the dictionary with the language of Shakespeare, Joyce, and others, it represents at least a beginning in the direction of refining our instrument of report in a form that lends itself to objective and quantitative analysis. There can be no doubt that frustration will be encountered in this sort of work, but there can also be some satisfaction in the process of decreasing our ignorance.

Mandler's second reason for rejecting experience as a topic of psychological investigation concerns the inferences one makes from language. He says,

I can only make inferences about your private world if I can be fairly certain that its qualities and nuances are similar—nay, identical—to mine under the same circumstances. If this assumption is true a phenomenological psychology is still possible. But common sense argues against it, and Titchener's vain attempts to find the elements common to all human experience (even in rather limited and simple experimental situations) seem to doom it.
The remainder is words [pp. 303–304]."

Mandler's emphasis of individual differences is in sharp contrast to Bakan's currently less fashionable assumption that, "after all, we are all pretty much alike." Bakan goes on to say,

It may be true that one cannot *observe* anything but the manifest behavior of the other person. But this does not prevent one from *studying* many other characteristics of the other person. The fact of the matter is that, except in a limited number of latter-day, die-hard, hyperdisciplined studies, most investigators regard the observa-

---

* It is interesting to note that Mandler, working from a quite different point of view, also seems to be using something like an "electronic metaphor."

tions of their studies only as a basis for inference about other things. Our knowledge is almost always the result of *both observation and inference,* and not of observation alone. And if one has to argue that somehow one knows of the other's experiences by *observation and other processes,* the argument is not unique to the field of psychology [Bakan, 1966, p. 13].

Bakan then poses the logical problem of how one makes inferences about experience from behavior. He says,

The inference may be made, for example, that the individual is experiencing pain from observing him saying 'ouch!' Now this may or may not be a valid inference in any given situation. It is indeed possible that a person will say 'ouch' even if he is not in pain, as, for example, in the case of malingering. Let us examine the conditions of such an inference [Bakan, 1966, p. 15].

He develops his argument on the basis of the principle of inverse probability.

Let us now introduce the word *probability,* to indicate the degree of tenability to be associated with proposition. Immediately it becomes evident that the probability that the man is in pain depends upon the probability that he would say 'ouch' if he were in pain, and inversely dependent on the probability that he would say 'ouch' whether or not he were in pain. It is also evident that the tenability of the proposition that the man is experiencing pain is based on other considerations than whether he does or does not say 'ouch.' If, for example, we could see his wound we would maintain that it was highly probable that he was experiencing pain.
The essence of our judgment concerning the experience of the other person on the basis of his overt behavior is our estimate of the *contingency of the overt behavior on experience.* The logic of the relations among these judgments seem to be most adequately handled by the principle which is the basic one for nonfrequency theories of probability, the so-called principle of inverse probability, or the Rule of Bayes; and, the greatest portion of our understanding of the contingency of overt behavior on experience comes from self-observation. It is in the combination of inference through the use of inverse probability and self-observation that knowledge concerning the experience of the other person in possible [Bakan, 1966, pp. 15–16].

Although a haphazard eclecticism is esthetically unsatisfying, the assumptions of both Mandler and Bakan are currently tenable. At a concrete level, certainly Mandler is right—every experience is somehow different from every other experience. The experience of "my heart pounding" today is concretely different from "my heart pounding" yesterday, and it is probably different from everyone else's experience of a "pounding heart." But at a more abstract level of description, Bakan's assumption also seems legitimate. At this level, one can at least distinguish between the experience of "my heart pounding" and "my head aching"; and it does not seem so unreasonable to assume that at this more abstract level, "my heart pounding" is similar to "your heart pounding." Equating concretely diverse phenomena by treating them at a relatively abstract level is characteristic of all areas of psychological investigation. The way in which a rat presses a bar on one trial is likely to be different from his behavior on another trial if all elements of the behavior are concretely and precisely measured. But for purposes of investigation, one bar press is equated with another, and at the relatively gross level at which the counter operates, the responses are indeed identical. Similarly, in measuring intelligence, one response to a vocabulary item may be concretely different from another, but for purposes of measurement, they may receive equal credit and thus be treated as if they were identical. Thus, the validity of one's assumption that "people are pretty much alike" or that "people are different from each other" depends upon the precision and level of abstraction of one's observations. At a relatively abstract level, all human beings are pretty much alike—all of us are mortal, pay taxes, and have one head. But of course at a more concrete level, each human being is unique—each dies his own way and at his own time, pays his particular taxes, and has his own highly individual head.

From this point of view, then, Mandler's critique of phenomenological investigation is considerably mitigated, and inferences about experience from the language of emotion would seem to be legitimate, though one must also recognize that this language is likely to be less precise and more abstract than the language of behavior. This does not at all imply that focusing on the language itself is not a valuable concern. Certainly this has been the major focus of the present research, and the data can be treated entirely within the framework of a behaviorally oriented communication theory. Moreover, studies of emotional behavior, the physiology of emotion, and relevant social psychological variables must all be considered in developing a comprehensive view of emotional phenomena. Without presuming to develop such a view, I am merely suggesting that experiential events should also be considered.

With regards to the general problem of the discrepancy between abstract generalizations of theory (as presented in this chapter) and the concrete uniqueness of every individual, Pervin's discussion of the existentialists' emphasis of individual differences reflects my own point of view. Pervin says:

This emphasis (*on the uniqueness of individuals*) is worthy in cautioning us against unrealistic generalizations and abstractions. The individual is free and unique. But, does this mean that he behaves unlawfully and unpredictably? There is something common to all these individuals that we are, and this may be the subject of scientific endeavor. The understanding of patterned and lawful aspects of human behavior [*and experience**] is the subject of inquiry for psychology. If in some

---

* Inserted by author.

way all or part of behavior is lawful, then to that extent human behavior can be predicted. While the laws we ultimately arrive at may not lead to a complete understanding and prediction of each and every individual, they may represent a considerable advance beyond the present darkness and mystery [Pervin, 1966, p. 213].

2. *The construct of emotion refers to a class of more specific states identified by labels such as affection, anger, boredom, etc. Each of these labels refers to a range of experiences about which there is more or less consensus among members of the same language group.*

This proposition makes explicit the basis for the dictionary of emotional meaning presented in Chapter 2, and in turn the definitions compiled for the 50 terms in the dictionary illustrate the range of experiences and the degree of consensus found among members of a particular language group. In some instances the consensus is not high, and in all instances there are differences in usage and definition of emotional terms. But the dictionary of emotional meaning confronts essentially the same problem as any other dictionary—that is, there are individual and group differences in the usage and meaning of *all* words in a language, and all that any lexicographer can hope to achieve is a recording of approximate "modal" meanings represented in current usage. As Hall says,

> The linguistician can simply define linguistic forms and their approximate meaning, but he cannot do the work of the chemist, the physicist, the anthropologist, etc., in analyzing and defining further ramifications of ultimate physical and social structure involved. To define meaning completely and exactly, even though of the simplest linguistic form, we should have to have a complete knowledge of the structure of the universe, and also of everything going on inside the body and head of every hearer. This is manifestly impossible. Meaning remains something approximate and indefinite, much more so than linguistic form; and yet we are left with the paradox that meaning, even with the difficulties it presents us (both the analyst and the unreflecting speaker of language), is what makes language effective in human society [Hall, 1950, p. 129].

But while the problem is essentially the same, it must also be recognized that consensus about the meaning of an emotional word like "love" or "hate" is likely to be lower than that for words like "table" and "chair." All the more reason, therefore, that we should devote special attention to words we use to label emotions, particularly in view of the fact that "love" and "hate" probably play a more important part in most people's lives than do "table" and "chair."

3. *The language of emotion reflects, somewhat abstractly and with less than perfect precision, the referent experiences; but it is also influenced by the nature of the language used to report experiences, linguistic habits, and variables related to the reporting process.*

Although I begin with the assumption that, other things being equal, I can trust other people's reports of their experiences, I also realize that these reports are susceptible to all sorts of error—repressions, suppressions, conscious distortions, and omissions. They are also limited by the language of report (though I have suggested earlier that the potential of English as an instrument for reporting experiences is only barely tapped by most of us), and reports made by any individual are influenced by his particular linguistic habits, response sets, motives in reporting his experiences, variables associated with the situation in which reports are obtained, and techniques used in obtaining the reports. Thus, one might reasonably expect differences between free association reports obtained from a patient in a psychoanalytic situation and those obtained from a research subject using a check list of descriptive phrases. These kinds of problems indeed make research in this area difficult, but not impossible. Progress in this line of inquiry will undoubtedly be slow, but frankly, our systematic knowledge in this area is so limited that any rigorous investigation is likely to result in dividends that are substantial in relation to what is already known.

To a certain extent, some distortions contributed by individuals probably tend to be cancelled out when using group data, and the dictionary of course is based on such data. But there are also distortions that cut across all subjects in a particular group and thus influence group data. For example, the particular method used in obtaining reports inevitably determines the results to some extent. Therefore, while there is something to be said for developing more or less standardized techniques for collecting data in a given line of inquiry, it would be unfortunate if all investigators used exactly the same technique. It would seem that we have had enough of a "psychology of one form of the F scale" and a "psychology of a particular manifest anxiety scale," with little generalization even to another scale presumably measuring the same variable. Therefore, while the check list devised in this research might well be useful in other investigations, one would hope for the development of other techniques in future work. A beginning in this direction, using both oral and written reports, will be described in the research presented in the next chapter.

4. *The definitions of emotional states can be structured in terms of 12 clusters of descriptive items that in turn can be fit into four major dimensions of reported emotional experience. This structure of emotional meaning is summarized in Table 5-2.**

This proposition merely summarizes the analysis presented in Chapter 4

---

* The body of Table 4-5 is repeated here for clarity of presentation.

TABLE 5-2

A Structural Analysis of Emotional Meaning

Dimension	Clusters		
	Positive	Negative: Type 1	Negative: Type 2
ACTIVATION	Activation	Hypoactivation	Hyperactivation
RELATEDNESS	Moving Toward	Moving Away	Moving Against
HEDONIC TONE	Comfort	Discomfort	Tension
COMPETENCE	Enhancement	Incompetence: Dissatisfaction	Inadequacy

and discussed in the preceding sections of this chapter. As indicated earlier, this structuring of the definitions obtained does not account for all aspects of every emotional state nor does it presume to identify anything like the "basic and universal" dimensions of human experience. This aim was a fantasy of earlier psychologists that led to meaningless *cul de sacs,* and in a subsequent proposition I shall suggest certain variables that are likely to influence the definitions of emotional states and the underlying structure of emotional meaning. Nonetheless, the proposed structure would seem to have at least temporary heuristic value.

5. *Labeling an emotional state depends upon the individual's pattern of experience, represented verbally by the organization and relative emphasis of the clusters identified in the structural analysis of emotional meaning. Change in either an aspect of the experience represented by a particular cluster or in the pattern of emphasis among the various aspects of experience involves change in the emotional state and the label of that state.*
The reasoning here is similar to that of Schachter, except that a four-dimensional rather than two-dimensional system of analysis is proposed. Whereas Schachter suggests that emotional states are labeled on the basis of an individual's level of activation and cognitive interpretation of the situation, I would suggest that these labels are a function of one's awareness of his level of activation, his relatedness to the environment, the hedonic tone of the experience, and one's sense of competence. Thus, an emotional state—and the label attached to that state as a consequence of language learning—certainly depends on the perception of whether one is hypoactivated, activated, or hyperactivated. But it also depends upon whether one perceives oneself as moving towards or away or against the environment; on whether the experience involves discomfort, comfort,

TABLE 5-3

Dimensions Involved in the Definition of Each Emotion Term

Emotion	Dimension			
	Activation	Relatedness	Hedonic Tone	Competence
Admiration	X	X	X	X
Affection	X	X	X	
Amusement	X		X	
Anger	X	X	X	X
Anxiety			X	X
Apathy	X	X		
Awe	X		X	X
Boredom	X	X		X
Cheerfulness	X	X	X	X
Confidence	X	X	X	X
Contempt	X	X	X	
Contentment	X	X	X	X
Delight	X	X	X	X
Depression	X	X	X	X
Determination	X		X	X
Disgust			X	
Dislike		X	X	X
Elation	X	X	X	X
Embarrassment	X	X	X	X
Enjoyment	X	X	X	X
Excitement	X		X	X
Fear	X		X	X
Friendliness	X	X	X	X
Frustration	X	X	X	X
Gaiety	X	X	X	X
Gratitude	X	X	X	X
Grief	X	X	X	X
Guilt		X	X	X
Happiness	X	X	X	X

TABLE 5-3 (continued)

Emotion	Dimension			
	Activation	Relatedness	Hedonic Tone	Competence
Hate	X	X	X	X
Hope	X		X	
Impatience			X	X
Inspiration	X		X	X
Irritation	X	X	X	X
Jealousy		X	X	X
Love	X	X	X	X
Nervousness	X		X	X
Panic	X		X	X
Passion	X	X	X	X
Pity		X	X	X
Pride	X	X	X	X
Relief	X		X	
Remorse	X	X	X	X
Resentment		X	X	X
Reverence	X		X	X
Sadness	X		X	X
Serenity	X		X	
Shame		X	X	X
Solemnity			X	
Surprise	X		X	

or tension; and whether one feels inadequate, enhanced, or incompetent and dissatisfied. Moreover, the label assigned to a particular state depends upon the specific pattern in which these clusters are perceived.

It is not necessarily true that each dimension of emotional meaning must be represented in every emotional state; an inspection of Table 5-3 indicates that, of the 50 terms treated in the dictionary, the definitions of 22 involve all four dimensions; 18 involve three dimensions; 8 involve two dimensions; and 2 involve only one dimension. Thus, the definitions of a large majority of terms in the present sample include at least three of the four major dimensions of emotional meaning. It should also be noted that the proposition as stated is something of an oversimplification, because the cluster analysis does not include all items in the definitions of all terms. For any term there may be items uniquely descriptive of the experience which are not accounted for in any cluster and are thus not included in the formulation of this proposition. At this point, therefore, the proposition must be interpreted as an approximation of the actual process of labeling emotional states. In addition, of course, there are individual differences in the labels people assign to various experiences, though the data obtained for the dictionary suggest a somewhat higher consensus among members of the language group sampled than I had expected. Nevertheless, labels associated with particular patterns of clusters are a consequence of social learning, and since the history of learning for any two people is somewhat different, we would expect some differences in labeling. This is particularly true for emotional states defined by similar patterns of clusters, so that one would expect, for example, individual differences in use of words like Love and Affection or Confidence and Determination. Schachter has suggested even grosser differences in labeling as a result of early learning (such as learning to label any state involving tension as "hunger"), and certain kinds of pathological behavior might be accounted for in terms of idiosyncratic labeling habits (Schachter, 1964).

The definition of emotional states involves both the clusters referring to certain aspects of experience and the perceived pattern of these clusters. The patterning of experience obviously involves perceptual–cognitive responses like those involved in responding to nonemotional events. There are two major implications of this point of view. First, the distinction between emotion and cognition as referring to two clearly different kinds of processes hardly seems tenable. Cognitive processes are part of any emotional response, though these processes may not follow the conventional rules of rational thought. Second, individual differences in perceptual–cognitive style defined by responses to nonemotional stimuli should also be reflected in the ways in which emotional experiences are organized. Thus, a person who tends to make fine distinctions among stimuli unrelated to emotional phenomena is likely to make fine distinctions in the perceptual–cognitive organization of his emotional experiences. Perls, Hefferline, and Goodman (1965) have explicated this point of view, and a relevant research along this line of inquiry will be reported in Chapter 6.

6. *Emotional states are elicited by stimuli psychologically relevant to the four dimensions of emotional meaning:* ACTIVATION, RELATEDNESS, HEDONIC TONE, *and* COMPETENCE.

Both Proposition 5 and Proposition 6 are based on the structure of emotional meaning derived from the data, but in the preceding proposition, the emphasis is on labeling behavior, while in this section a model for eliciting and predicting emotional states is proposed. Essentially, the proposition suggests a model for either designing stimulus situations likely to elicit a given emotional state or for predicting the emotional state likely to be evoked in a particular situation. The reasoning that leads to this proposition is quite simple and straightforward. On the basis of the reports collected for the dictionary, four major dimensions of emotional experience were identified. In analyzing the antecedents of emotional states, therefore, it seems reasonable to consider the possible effects of each stimulus variable in terms of these four dimensions, assuming there is a lawful relationship between antecedent stimulus events and the individual's subsequent emotional response. The problem may involve, for example, the design of experimental procedures to elicit an emotional state or the prediction of an emotional state on the basis of given situational variables. In either case, the model suggests that stimuli in a given situation be interpreted in terms of probable patterns of reaction along the four major dimensions of emotional meaning, and that these patterns of reaction in turn be interpreted on the basis of both the definitions contained in the dictionary and the analysis of cluster patterns presented in Table 4-2.

For example, if one were to design a situation likely to elicit Apathy, major focus would be on inducing a state of *Hypoactivation* and a sense of *Moving Away* from others. If one were to design a situation likely to elicit Boredom, major focus would also be on inducing a state of *Hypoactivation,* but with some emphasis also on evoking a sense of *Moving Away* from others and *Incompetence: Dissatisfaction.*

In contrast, to elicit Delight, one would focus on establishing a state of *Activation* as well as *Comfort,* with some consideration also for including a sense of *Moving Toward* others and of *Self-Enhancement.* To elicit Fear, one would design a situation which would be likely to arouse a sense of *Inadequacy* and *Hyperactivation,* and also include events likely to elicit *Tension.*

Thus, instead of the rather gross and global assumptions currently made in some psychological work—for example, that threat elicits anxiety or that insult elicits anger—the proposed model suggests a somewhat more specific analysis of the stimulus conditions in terms of probable patterns of reaction along each of the four dimensions of emotional meaning.

As indicated earlier, this model may be a useful conceptual tool either in designing experimental situations to elicit given emotional states or in "understanding" and predicting the likely emotional state elicited in a particular nonexperimental situation. At this stage, of course, the model can provide only a rough guide for eliciting and predicting specific emotional states, because the relation between particular stimuli and particular responses along each dimension of emotional meaning has not been empirically established. A potentially important line of future inquiry, therefore, might well involve describing the relationship between specific stimulus conditions and responses defined in terms of ACTIVATION (see Duffy, 1962, for a beginning in this direction), RELATEDNESS, HEDONIC TONE, and COMPETENCE.

It may be useful to note that two of these dimensions, ACTIVATION and HEDONIC TONE, refer primarily to "internal" variables, while the other two, RELATEDNESS and COMPETENCE, concern the individual's relation to his environment. One would expect, for example, that drugs which influence level of activation or degree of tension would influence, though not completely determine, a person's emotional state—and Schachter's research provides ample support of this hypothesis (Schachter & Singer, 1962; Schachter & Wheeler, 1962). Also, one would expect sociocultural variables concerned with RELATEDNESS and COMPETENCE to influence emotional states, both in terms of the definition of specific emotions and the frequency with which these states occur. From a developmental point of view, Erikson's theory of life stages, for example, would suggest an emphasis on experiences concerned with COMPETENCE during late childhood and a contrasting emphasis on RELATEDNESS during young adult life.

At this point, the proposed structuring of emotional meaning can only serve as a general guide for further inquiry, and the proposition stated in this section merely suggests lines of inquiry that seem to be potentially fruitful. In the next chapter, the results of several such studies concerned with physiological, cultural, and developmental variables will be presented to illustrate the beginnings we have made in these directions.

Before moving on, the problem of individual differences must briefly be considered. In the preceding discussion I have suggested a general framework involving, essentially, correlations between situational events and emotional responses defined in terms of four basic dimensions of emotional meaning. The proposal has been presented as if there were no individual differences in these correlations. That is, for every stimulus event the emotional response is assumed to be the same for everyone. But of course this is patently untrue. While there are likely to be certain consistencies across members of a particular group, undoubtedly there are also individual differences as a function of at least physiological variables, sociocultural factors, and previous learning.

For example, some people probably mobilize energy more rapidly than do others, and thus the level of activation associated with a particular stimulus event is likely to differ among individuals. Some people are more sensitive to pain than are others, and there are likely to be individual differences in the level of discomfort associated with a particular stimulus.

But perhaps the greatest contribution to individual differences is each person's idiosyncratic history of learning. This raises the issue of emotional learning, and while it is not a central concern of the conceptual scheme proposed in this section, it may be useful to consider one point of view in regards to this problem. Recognizing that the present research offers no data directly relevant to this issue, I can only make explicit my own bias—and that briefly—simply to clarify the assumptions underlying the propositions stated in this chapter.

My own view is based on that developed by Harlow and Stagner (1933) and essentially repeated, with some modifications, by others such as Skinner, Estes, Dollard, and Miller, and Mowrer (Beebe-Center, 1951). In short, Harlow and Stagner state that the basis of emotion is innate (i.e., their four fundamental feelings of pleasure, unpleasantness, excitement, and depression are unconditioned responses), but emotion itself is a function of previous conditioning. To rephrase this position within the present framework, I would suggest that the four major dimensions of emotional meaning reflect unlearned, innate responses. The individual doesn't have to learn to be activated, to move towards or away from others, to experience comfort or a sense of inadequacy or enhancement. However, in any given emotional state, the individual's reaction in terms of these four dimensions is undoubtedly influenced by previous learning. Thus, a previously neutral stimulus, as a consequence of learning, may acquire the capacity to elicit hyperactivation, the impulse to move away from others, tension, or a sense of inadequacy, and at the present time, it seems most parsimonious to account for this learning on the basis of classical conditioning.

This is a brief and very general statement about a complex and major problem—the learning of emotion—but within the present context, and in view of the fact that this research does not provide any data that might cast further light on this issue, only this brief statement seems warranted.

A FINAL COMMENT

The preceding propositions certainly do not represent anything like a comprehensive theory of emotion, but they make explicit some of the assumptions underlying the point of view of this research and summarize the major findings of the initial steps in this inquiry. Neither behaviorists nor psychoanalytically oriented investigators are likely to be satisfied with the inferences made from the data, and traditional phenomenologists will probably be uncomfortable with the emphasis on consensus and general trends rather than on the unique individual. But if this perspective is a lonely one, it also has a rich potential for further research. Given the basic findings of the dictionary and the structure of emotional meaning, a variety of researchable questions become apparent, and in the next chapter, investigations along several lines of inquiry suggested by this research will be reported.

CHAPTER 6

Studies of the Language of Emotion

During the course of the main investigation reported in preceding chapters, a number of interrelated studies have been conducted. These include: (a) a developmental study of the language of emotion in children (Farmer, 1967); (b) individual differences in emotional reports as a function of perceptual–cognitive styles (Weinberg, 1967); (c) similarities of emotional descriptions in relation to genetic background (Allerand, 1967); and (d) a cross-cultural comparison of the language of emotion among adolescents in the United States and Uganda.

Before discussing the results of these investigations, the method of analyzing descriptions of emotional experience developed for several of these studies will be considered briefly. In contrast to the check list method used in compiling the dictionary of emotional meaning, the studies reported in this chapter required more open-ended descriptions of emotional experiences obtained either by interviews or written reports. To treat these data, a content analysis system was developed, initially using the interview data and written reports discussed in Chapter 1, and then slightly modifying this system according to the demands of each subsequent study. In general, the data from either interviews or written reports can be treated with a high degree of reliability using this system. For each of the studies reported, well over 90% agreement between independent judges was obtained, and the categories seem comprehensive enough to cover data gathered from a variety of sources.

Rather than repeat the presentation of almost identical systems used in the several studies, one version of the content analysis categories is presented in Table 6-1. The categories are organized in nine sections, with a number of more specific subcategories in each section. These sections cover sensations, physical symptoms, functioning, expressive behavior, interpersonal relations, attitudes, control, sense of time, and arousal of other emotions. The reliability of analysis and the specific application of this system will be considered in discussing each of the following studies.

151

TABLE 6-1

Categories for Content Analysis of Descriptions of Emotional Experiences[a]

SENSATIONS: This general classification includes any references to awareness of immediate stimulations from the body.

    S1. *Tension, agitation, trembling.*
        S1a. General (e.g., I feel tense all over).
        S1b. Specific (e.g., my stomach feels jumpy).

    S2. *Discomfort, pain, hurt.*
        S2a. General (e.g., I feel achy).
        S2b. Specific (e.g., I have a pain in my stomach).

    S3. *Tingling, throbbing.*
        S3a. Tingling (e.g., I can feel my skin tingling).
        S3b. Throbbing (e.g., my head throbs).

    S4. *Softness, weakness.*
        S4a. Softness (e.g., I just feel soft all over).
        S4b. Weakness (e.g., I feel very weak inside).

    S5. *Weight.*
        S5a. Heaviness (e.g., I feel heavy, sinking, pulled down).
        S5b. Lightness (e.g., I feel light, floating, buoyant).

    S6. *Fullness, emptiness.*
        S6a. Fullness (e.g., I feel very full, stuffed).
        S6b. Emptiness (e.g., I feel very empty, hollow).

    S7. *Temperature.*
        S7a. Hot (e.g., it feels hot, red, burning inside).
        S7b. Warm (e.g., I feel warm, there's a glow).
        S7c. Cold (e.g., it feels cold inside, a chill goes through me).

    S8. *Lack of or low tension.*
        S8a. General (e.g., my body feels completely relaxed).
        S8b. Specific (e.g., my legs, my neck just feels loose, relaxed).

    S9. *Pressure.*
        S9a. General (e.g., I feel I will burst or explode).
        S9b. Specific (e.g., my head feels as if it were in a vise).

    S10. *Energy level.*
        S10a. High (e.g., I'm full of energy, all charged up).
        S10b. Low (e.g., I feel sluggish, tired, drowsy, no drive, lazy).

PHYSICAL SYMPTOMS: This general classification includes directly experienced sensations that are part of an organized body system or the description of the working of such a system.

    PS1. *Cardiovascular.*
        PS1a. Heightened (e.g., my heart beats faster, pounds, blood rushes).
        PS1b. Depressed (e.g., my heart almost stops).
        PS1c. Disfunction (e.g., I felt the blood rushing to my stomach).

TABLE 6-1 (*continued*)

PS2. *Respiratory.*
    PS2a. Heightened (e.g., I start to breathe faster and faster).
    PS2b. Depressed (e.g., I just sigh, breathe very slowly).
    PS2c. Disfunction (e.g., I'm breathless, choking, grasping, suffocating).

PS3. *Digestive.*
    PS3a. Heightened (e.g., I'm ravenous, have a big appetite, want to eat).
    PS3b. Depressed (e.g., I don't feel like eating, no appetite).
    PS3c. Disfunction (e.g., I'm nauseous, feel like vomiting, stomach upset).

    PS4. *Increased sympathetic nervous system action* other than above (e.g., pale, sweaty, blushing, dry mouth, feel faint, dizzy, swallowing too much).

FUNCTIONING: This general classification includes all responses which essentially describe the individual's functioning or changes in functioning during the emotional experience in general, perceptual, motor, emotional, and cognitive areas. It differs from sensations and physical symptoms in that the responses are more the *S*'s interactional response to environmental stimulation, rather than aspects of physiological functioning.

F1. *General functioning and experiencing.*
    F1a. Heightened (e.g., I feel alert, ready to do things, looking forward to it).
    F1b.. Enhanced (e.g., I feel I've achieved something, enjoyed it, it was fun).
    F1c. Depressed (e.g., I don't feel like doing much, I'm slower).
    F1d. Disfunction (e.g., I feel blocked, paralyzed, frustrated, resigned, helpless).

F2. *Sensory functioning.*
    F2a. Heightened (e.g., I see, hear more acutely, clearly, quickly, sensitive).
    F2b. Enhanced (e.g., I perceive things better, more easily).
    F2c. Depressed (e.g., my sense of sight is duller, harder to see, focus).
    F2d. Disfunction (e.g., I just can't sense things right, normally, etc.).
    F2e. Other.

F3. *Motor functioning.*
    F3a. Heightened (e.g., I want to run, jump, dance, play, move around fast).
    F3b. Enhanced (e.g., I can move more easily, play sports better, balanced).
    F3c. Depressed (e.g., I don't feel like moving, move slowly, cautiously).
    F3d. Disfunction (e.g., I'm off balance, clumsy, can't move, I freeze, fall).
    F3e. Other.

F4. *Emotional functioning.*
    F4a. Heightened (e.g., I feel excited, strongly moved, boiling inside).
    F4b. Enhanced (e.g., I feel gay, glad, pleased, good inside, joyful, positive).
    F4c. Depressed (e.g., I feel dull, gloomy, moody, depressed, let down, blue).
    F4d. Disfunction (e.g., I feel numb, stunned, upset, disrupted emotionally, panicky).
    F4e. Other.

TABLE 6-1 (*continued*)

EXPRESSIVE BEHAVIOR: This general classification includes any extremely emotional motoric and nonverbal responses, as well as unique verbal or vocal responses that do not fall naturally into other functioning or interpersonal categories.

  EB1. Laughing.
  EB2. Crying, moaning, sobbing.
  EB3. Shouting, yelling, screaming (noninterpersonal).
  EB4. Singing.
  EB5. Facial expressions (e.g., smiling, grimacing, etc.).
  EB6. Gestures (e.g., wringing hands, waving, kicking, etc.).
  EB7. Other.

INTERPERSONAL: This general classification includes all responses which explicitly or implicitly describe an actual or desired relationship with another person which is a focal part of the emotional experience, or evoked by it. Responses are grouped according to whether they reflect a moving *toward*, moving *away from*, or moving *against* people.

  I1. Moving toward or close to people. Any positive form of relatedness.
     I1a. *Actual or desired general positive feeling toward others* (e.g., I feel very friendly, acceptant, liking, good toward them, positive).
     I1b. *Actual or desired strong identification with others* (e.g., includes desire to be with or close to another emotionally; fuse, merge, share feelings; admire, identify, become strongly attached to them).
     I1c. *Actual or desired communication of feeling with or to others* (e.g., want to talk with them, call up, tell what happened).
     I1d. *Actual or desired joint activity with others* (e.g., includes desire to be with or near others, do things *with* them rather than for them, play together, go with them).
     I1e. *Actual or desired helping, pleasing, or protection of others* (e.g., I want to do things for persons, be nice, kind, help them, please them).
     I1f. *Actual or desired physical contact with others* (e.g., I want to kiss, hug, touch, caress, cuddle the person).

  I2. Moving away from people. Avoidance, withdrawal, isolation responses.
     I2a. *Actual or desired lack of identification with others* (e.g., includes responses which establish distance without moving against; expressing doubt, skepticism, lack of agreement, separateness, mild criticism).
     I2b. *Actual or desired avoidance of interaction with others* (without physical withdrawal) (e.g., not wanting to join in activity with others or to interact with them, communicate, or acknowledge them).
     I2c. *Actual or desired physical withdrawal or escape* (e.g., I felt like running, leaving the room, walk out, hide from them, go away, etc.).
     I2d. *Actual or desired feelings of isolation, loneliness, or rejection* (e.g., feel alone, lonely, walled off, rejected, outside the group).

TABLE 6-1 (*continued*)

13. Moving against people.
    13a. *Actual or desired general negativism toward others* (e.g., I feel annoyed, irritated, displeased, want to get even, mean, angry at everyone, etc.).
    13b. *Actual or desired passive negativism or oppositionalism* (e.g., I want to pout, sulk, not cooperate, be stubborn, ignore, don't share, etc.).
    13c. *Actual or desired verbal aggression toward others* (e.g., I want to yell at them, complain, growl, scream at them, be sarcastic, say shut up).
    13d. *Actual or desired indirect or displaced aggression* (e.g., includes such indirect attacks as damaging possessions of the other person, or being angry at someone else or a pet).
    13e. *Actual or desired direct physical attack on others* (e.g., I felt like hitting, punching, slapping, kicking, hurting them physically, fighting and charging them).

ATTITUDES: This general classification includes all responses which reflect a system of beliefs, feelings, or dispositions to respond, usually bound to an object and involving evaluation of it. Attitudes may be expressed toward the self or the world in general.

At1. *Attitudes toward the self.*
    At1a. Positive (e.g., I feel important, strong, confident, worthwhile, secure).
    At1b. Negative (e.g., I feel worthless, self-conscious, inadequate, stupid).
    At1c. Heightening of specific feelings toward the self (e.g., hostility, love, pity, shame, guilt, etc.).
    At1d. Self-detachment (e.g., I feel removed, detached, outside myself, bored).
    At1e. Other.

At2. *General attitudes.*
    At2a. Positive (e.g., includes enhancement of the world or sense of positive feeling about the world, optism, etc.).
    At2b. Negative (e.g., includes responses reflecting pessimistic outlook, things look bad, nothing is going right, something bad will happen).
    At2c. Lack of involvement (e.g., not caring about anything, detached or removed from the world, uninvolved).
    At2d. Other.

CONTROL: This general classification includes responses which pertain to loss of or recognition of the need for emotional control, or lack of concern about it.

C1. *Loss of control* of behavior, feelings or thoughts (e.g., I feel unable to control my feelings, my thoughts ran wild, I felt out of control).

C2. *Lack of concern* over emotional control (e.g., I couldn't care less what happened, I feel carefree, no need to hold back, I say what I feel).

C3. *Recognition that control or the need for it exists* (e.g., I know I shouldn't do it though I want to, I stop myself, have to be careful).

TABLE 6-1 (continued)

SENSE OF TIME: This general classification includes responses which make reference to awareness or lack of awareness of the passage of time.

    T1. *Sense of expanding time* (e.g., time seems infinite, endless, could go on forever, the time passed in a flash).

    T2. *Sense of slowing time* (e.g., time seemed to stand still, I had no sense of the passage of time, I thought it would never be over, the minutes passed like hours).

AROUSAL OF OTHER EMOTIONS: This general classification includes responses which indicate that the feeling gives rise to another emotion, usually related to the initial state or reaction.

    Ar1. *Positive* (e.g., I feel happy, joyous).

    Ar2. *Negative* (e.g., I get angry, sad, disgusted).

---

[a] The content analysis systems used in several of the studies reported in this chapter differ slightly in certain subcategories, but follow the same overall outline. The particular version presented in this table is taken from Farmer, C. Words and Feelings: A developmental study of the language of emotion in children. Unpublished doctoral dissertation. New York, Teachers College, Columbia University, 1967. Pp. 25-33.

Development of the Language of Emotion*

Farmer (1967) studied four groups of 16 children each, 8 boys and 8 girls enrolled in the second, fourth, sixth, and eighth grades of a private school in New York City. Although there was some variability in age within each grade, by and large the second graders were 7 or 8 years old, with gradual progression to the 13- and 14-year-old eighth graders. The children came from middle and upper-middle class families in New York, and while no specific intelligence test data were analyzed, school records indicated that all of the children were at least normal in intelligence and many functioned at above average and superior levels. These qualifications, of course, limit the generalizations that can be made on the basis of these data, but as an initial developmental study in this line of investigation, it was desirable to begin with a verbally responsive sample.

Each child was interviewed individually, using open-ended questions

* This section is based on a study conducted by Capen Farmer for his doctoral dissertation at Teachers College, Columbia University. I am indebted to Dr. Farmer for his permission to use some of his data in this section. There are, however, major differences between Farmer's thesis and the analysis and presentation of data reported here, and I am of course responsible for this particular presentation. The reference to the thesis is: Farmer, C. Words and feelings: A developmental study of the language of emotion in children. Unpublished doctoral dissertation, Columbia University, 1967.

to obtain descriptions of the child's experience of Happiness, Sadness, Love, Anger, and Fear. After introducing the child to the situation and explaining the procedure, the child was asked, "How does it feel or what does it feel like inside when you feel happy?" If the child had any apparent difficulty in responding, the interviewer rephrased the initial question, asking, for example, "How else could you describe the feeling?" Descriptions of Happiness were then followed by questions about Sadness, Love, Anger, and Fear.

The interview technique has many advantages in this kind of research, and at this stage, perhaps it is the only technique that can be used meaningfully with younger children to obtain the data required. The interviewer had had considerable experience as a psychologist working with children and during the course of the interview, he neither asked questions other than those specified nor made evaluations or comments about any aspect of a child's response. As much as possible, he also avoided expressing nonverbal cues of approval or disapproval. Thus, within the limits required to establish rapport with each child, the interviewer's behavior was fairly well controlled and standardized. Nonetheless, this kind of research technique is susceptible to subtle but significant biases that operate without the experimenter's awareness, and while interviews are useful in collecting initial descriptive information, it would seem desirable in future research to use other techniques which can achieve more rigorous control in testing specific hypotheses.

The data were analyzed using the categories presented in Table 6-1. Two coders independently judged a sample of 435 responses and achieved 92% agreement in coding.

RESULTS

Quantity of Information. Each child's protocol was scored for the total number of subcategories mentioned in his descriptions of all five emotional states. This provided a basis for comparing the quantity of information given by boys and girls and by each age group.

Across all age groups, boys did not consistently differ from girls in quantity of information, though girls more often tended to mention subcategories dealing with speech and expressive behaviors. This would seem to be consistent with cultural norms which sanction somewhat greater expressiveness in certain kinds of emotional behavior (e.g., crying) among girls than among boys.

As indicated in Figure 6-1, there was a general tendency for quantity of information to increase with age, but the most marked shift occurred between fourth and sixth grades. In fact, using a Sign Test procedure comparing randomly paired *S*s from each of two groups (e.g., one from first

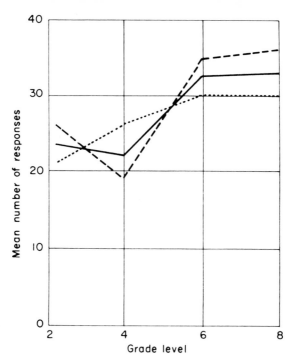

Fɪɢ. 6-1. Mean of total responses for all emotions for grades 2, 4, 6, and 8.

grade and one from fourth grade), Farmer found that second grade was not significantly different from fourth grade, and sixth grade was not significantly different from eighth grade. But fourth grade differed significantly from sixth grade ($p < .05$), and combined second and fourth grades differed significantly from combined sixth and eighth grades ($p < .05$). Thus, the data suggest that a major increase in capacity to describe emotional experiences (or perhaps in the "richness" of the experiences) occurs at about 10 or 11 years of age. Although changes in the experience of each emotional state probably do occur with increasing age, it is likely that the greatest part of the variance in productivity can be accounted for by increased verbal skills associated with age and grade. Thus, simply on the basis of greater facility with language, one would expect older children to produce a greater quantity of information.

Content of Descriptions. Farmer presents a detailed analysis of the description of each emotional state by each grade group in terms of the categories presented in Table 6-1 (Farmer, 1967, pp. 80–97). However, for purpose of the present discussion, the data were reanalyzed using the cluster categories identified in Chapter 4. Each child's description of an emotional state was coded in terms of the cluster categories mentioned in his description, and two independent coders analyzing the entire sample of protocols obtained over 90% agreement.

The results of this analysis are summarized in Table 6-2, which presents the number of children in each group who mentioned a given cluster in their descriptions of each emotion. Consistent with the procedure followed in establishing the definitions presented in the dictionary of emotional meaning (Chapter 2), a particular cluster was designated as part of each group's definition of an emotional state if at least one-third of the descriptions obtained from that group mentioned that cluster. Since there were 16 children in each group, frequencies of six or more reach this criterion and are reported in Table 6-2. In addition, the definition of each emotional state given by the 50 adults who comprised the sample upon which the dictionary was based is given in the first row under each emotion, listing the various clusters in order of relative emphasis in adults' descriptions of these emotions. Under each emotion in Table 6-2, the cluster listed in the first column (on the left) received greatest emphasis in adults' descriptions of that emotion; the cluster listed in the second column received the next greatest emphasis; continuing to the cluster in the last column (on the right), which received least emphasis in adults' descriptions.

Considered within this framework, the results indicate an orderly and consistent pattern in the development of children's verbal reports of emotion. The most striking characteristic of this pattern is the relationship between the relative emphasis of a particular cluster in adults' descriptions of an emotion and the age at which the cluster appears consistently in the verbal reports of children. In general, it seems reasonable to suggest that, for most emotional states, the more a cluster is emphasized in adults' descriptions, the earlier does it tend to appear among children's reports.

Consider, for example, the reports of Happiness as summarized in Table 6-2. *Activation* and *Comfort* received the greatest emphasis in adults' descriptions, and indeed both clusters appear with at least moderate frequency even among the youngest children in this sample. *Enhancement* was third in rank order of adult emphasis, and consistent with the general trend in these data, this cluster did not appear with any appreciable frequency until the sixth grade. Both *Hyperactivation* and *Moving Toward* were least emphasized in adults' descriptions, and among children's reports *Hyperactivation* does not appear at any age level in the present sample and *Moving Toward* is present only among the reports of the children in the oldest group.

A similar pattern appears for Sadness. *Discomfort* and *Hypoactivation* were emphasized most in adults' descriptions, and both appear in reports of children at all levels sampled. *Inadequacy* and *Incompetence:Dissatisfaction* received least emphasis in adults' descriptions, and among chil-

TABLE 6-2

Number of Children in Each Grade Who Mentioned Each Cluster in Adults' Definitions of Happiness, Sadness, Love, Anger, and Fear

HAPPINESS

Group	N	Clusters Contained in Adults' Descriptions[a]				
		Activation	Comfort	Enhancement	Hyperactivation	Moving Toward
2nd grade	16	12	6	—[a]	—	—
4th grade	16	13	6	—	—	—
6th grade	16	12	10	6	—	—
8th grade	16	6	9	9	—	9

SADNESS

Group	N	Clusters Contained in Adults' Descriptions			
		Discomfort	Hypoactivation	Inadequacy	Incompetence:Dissatisfaction
2nd grade	16	7	6	—	—
4th grade	16	6	8	—	—
6th grade	16	6	9	—	6
8th grade	16	6	11	—	8

LOVE

Clusters Contained in Adults' Descriptions

Group	N	Moving Toward	Comfort	Activation	Enhancement	Hyperactivation	Inadequacy
2nd grade	16	9	—	—	—	—	—
4th grade	16	12	6	—	—	—	—
6th grade	16	12	8	—	—	—	—
8th grade	16	12	7	—	—	—	—

ANGER

Clusters Contained in Adults' Descriptions

Group	N	Hyperactivation	Moving Against	Tension	Inadequacy
2nd grade	16	—	11	—	—
4th grade	16	—	14	—	—
6th grade	16	—	16	6	—
8th grade	16	6	11	6	—

TABLE 6-2 (continued)

FEAR

Group	N	Clusters Contained in Adults' Descriptions				
		Inadequacy	Hyperactivation	Tension	Moving Away	Incompetence: Dissatisfaction
2nd grade	16	—	—	6	7	—
4th grade	16	—	—	6	8	—
6th grade	16	8	—	11	8	—
8th grade	16	9	6	11	6	—

[a] These clusters are presented, from left to right, in order of relative emphasis of the several clusters in the definitions based on adults' descriptions. Thus, for example, in adults' descriptions of Happiness, *Activation* received greatest emphasis and *Moving Toward* least emphasis. Reference may be made to Table 4-2 for a summary of the relevant data on emphasis of each cluster.

[b] Frequencies less than 6 are not included.

dren's reports *Inadequacy* does not appear consistently at any age sampled and *Incompetence:Dissatisfaction* appears only in the sixth and eighth grades.

Essentially the same pattern appears for Love. *Moving Toward* was emphasized most in adults' descriptions, and indeed this cluster is present consistently in the reports of children at all levels. *Comfort* was emphasized next by adults, and following the general trend in other emotions, this cluster appears by the fourth grade and continues through sixth and eighth grades. The other clusters, which received progressively less emphasis in adults' descriptions simply do not occur with appreciable frequency at any level of the children sampled.

Thus, the results for Happiness, Sadness, and Love clearly support the proposed relationship between degree of emphasis in adults' descriptions and age at which the cluster appears in children's reports. The greater the emphasis among adults, the earlier the cluster appears in children's reports.

But this single proposition obviously does not account for all of the data. In Anger, for example, the cluster most emphasized by adults, *Hyperactivation,* occurs with any consistency only in the eighth grade. *Moving Against,* however, which ranked second in emphasis among adults, occurs at all levels among children. Thus, there is something of a reversal of the general trend noted for Happiness, Sadness, and Love.

In Fear, this difference is even more striking. *Tension* and *Moving Away* ranked third and fourth in adults' descriptions, but appear at all levels among children. *Inadequacy* and *Hyperactivation,* however, were most emphasized by adults, but do not appear consistently among childrens reports until the sixth or eighth grade.

Thus, the initial statement of the proposition relating emphasis by adults and age at which the cluster appears in children's reports must be modified to account for these deviations. Specifically, it would seem that these deviations can be accounted for by the conditions under which adults and children are likely to experience a particular emotional state. In Anger, for example, *Moving Against* is a central feature for both adults and children. Among adults, however, it seems likely that there is at least some degree of impulse control, in a sense allowing an opportunity for activation level to increase to a state of *Hyperactivation.* Among children, particularly younger children, one might expect less impulse control or inhibition and thus less opportunity for heightened activation level to become a central feature of the child's state of awareness. For a child, then, the central feature of Anger is acting, *Moving Against* something or someone in the environment. For an adult, impulses to *Move Against* something or someone are also a prominent feature of Anger, but socially acquired controls of these impulses may lead to increased awareness of one's state of *Hyperactivation.* The differences between adults' and children's reports of Anger might thus reflect the child's tendency to act out his angry impulses more readily, without the impulse control and blocking of expression that might lead to an adult's sense of "exploding inside."

Differences among adults and children in descriptions of Fear also seem to be accounted for in terms of different conditions or expectations associated with this emotional state. Among children, threat elicits *Tension,* and the child tries to escape or *Move Away* from the threat. Adults, however, who are more likely to be expected to deal somehow with the threat, experience a sense of *Inadequacy* and an increased level of activation. Escape, *Moving Away* from the threat, is probably not as easily or widely an accepted adult response to threat as it is among children. Thus, adults are expected to "stand and face the music," feeling inadequate and hyperactivated, while fearful children feel tense and escape.

In general, then, it would seem that as children mature, their reports of emotional experiences increasingly resemble the descriptions given by adults. In the present sample, as one might reasonably expect, reports of the eighth graders more closely resembled adults' descriptions than did those of second or fourth grade children. This, of course, can hardly be considered a surprising or particularly noteworthy finding.

However, the pattern of increasing resemblance is of some interest, in that it appears to follow a relatively orderly process of growth. That is, other things being equal, those clusters most emphasized by adults appear earlier in children's reports, and clusters least emphasized by adults tend to appear at later ages among children. The consistency of this relationship, however, is somewhat mitigated for particular emotional states as a consequence of the varying conditions and social expectations for adults and children associated with these emotional states.

Individual Differences in Reported Emotional Experiences and Perceptual–Cognitive Style*

The definitions of emotional terms in Chapter 2 are based on the consensus found among 50 subjects who contributed data to the dictionary.

* This section is based on a study conducted by Janet A. Weinberg for her doctoral dissertation at Teachers College, Columbia University. I wish to express my appreciation to Dr. Weinberg for her permission to report the material in this section. The reference to this study is: Weinberg, J. A. Relationships between the organization of reported emotional experience and the organization of perceptual–cognitive processes. Unpublished doctoral dissertation. Columbia University, 1968.

While there was a fair amount of consensus among these reports, there were also obvious individual differences among subjects in the number of items checked for each term and in the specific items chosen. Since the principal aim of that phase of the research was to identify areas of agreement for each emotion, the individual differences observed were not pursued *post hoc* with the data obtained from that sample. However, the study reported in this section represents a followup of some observations made in the earlier work.

Weinberg (1967) began with the general hypothesis that reports of emotional experiences involve perceptual–cognitive processes; therefore, certain characteristics of these reports should be related to the style of perceptual–cognitive responses to nonemotional stimuli. On the basis of observations made in collecting data for the dictionary and suggestions derived from the work of Perls, Hefferline, and Goodman (1965), two aspects of reported emotional experiences were selected for study. These were: (*a*) *Complexity,* defined by the number of different descriptive ideas contained in the report of an emotional experience; and (*b*) *Differentiation,* defined by the degree to which an individual's description of one emotional state differs from his descriptions of other emotional states. Thus, a person manifested high *Complexity* if his reported emotional experiences contained a relatively large number of different descriptive ideas, and he manifested high *Differentiation* if his report of each emotional state contained a relatively large proportion of ideas that uniquely defined a given emotion.

The perceptual–cognitive variables were based on research reported by Gardener, Holzman, Klein, Linton, and Spence (1959) and by Witkin, Lewis, Hertzman, Machover, Meissner, and Wapner (1954). Three such variables were selected: (*a*) *Equivalence Range,* which pertains to the subjective criteria used to categorize experience—so that a so-called broad range is based on relaxed, inclusive criteria of similarity and a narrow range reflects more exacting, precise critera (Gardener *et al.,* 1959, p. 39); (*b*) *Field Independence–Dependence,* which is concerned with a person's ability to respond selectively to a figure apart from its ground (Witkin *et al.,* 1954); and (*c*) *Leveling–Sharpening,* which refers to "differentiation in memory organization as a function of the extent to which successive stimuli assimilate to each other" (Gardner *et al.,* 1959, p. 100).

Since people who use a narrow *Equivalence Range* presumably use more exacting and precise criteria in judging similarity of experiences, high *Differentiation* of emotional reports was expected to be associated with narrow *Equivalence Range.* In addition, assuming that selective direction of attention is an important aspect of *Field Independence,* high *Differ-*

entiation of emotional reports was also expected to be associated with *Field Independence*. And finally, since the reports of emotional experiences depend upon memory and the degree to which each experience has been maintained as a distinct experience, high *Complexity* of emotional reports was expected to be associated with a relatively *Sharpening* rather than *Leveling* style. These predictions may be summarized as follows: (*a*) High *Differentiation* associated with narrow *Equivalence Range;* (*b*) High *Differentiation* associated with *Field Independence;* (*c*) High *Complexity* associated with *Sharpening.*

METHOD

The subjects of this research were 27 male and 43 female graduate students in education, most of whom were teachers and only part-time students. The mean age was 26.9 years and English was the native language of all subjects.

Using a critical incident technique, subjects wrote descriptions of their experiences of the following emotional states: Anxiety, Love, Sadness, Fear, Contentment, Anger, Contempt, Joy, Boredom, and Shame. These descriptions were content analyzed, using essentially the category system presented in Table 6-1, and two relevant scores were based on this analysis:

1. *Complexity* was operationally defined by the number of specific categories in a subject's descriptions of all emotional states.

2. *Differentiation* was operationally defined as the proportion of categories mentioned uniquely for each of the ten emotions, i.e., the proportion was obtained by dividing the number of unique categories by the total number of categories mentioned.

Each subject was seen individually and in small groups to obtain measures of *Equivalence Range, Field Independence–Dependence,* and *Leveling–Sharpening*. These measures were as follows:

1. *Equivalence Range* was operationally defined by performance on the Object Sorting Test requiring a subject to sort 73 objects. The score consisted of the number of groups used, a large number of groups indicating narrow *Equivalence Range* (Gardener *et al.,* 1959).

2. *Field Independence–Dependence* was measured by Jackson's shortened form of the Embedded Figures Test, in which a subject is required to locate a simple figure within a more complex ground. The time required for each task operationally defined this variable, with relatively shorter times indicative of *Field Independence* and longer times indicative of *Field Dependence* (Jackson, 1956).

3. *Leveling–Sharpening* was measured by the schematizing test, which

requires subjects to judge the relative size of squares. The degree to which a person's judgments were based on *Sharpening,* rather than *Leveling,* was operationally defined by the number of stimuli that he ranked correctly (Gardener *et al.,* 1959).

Because of the verbal nature of the emotional description task, two additional measures were obtained to investigate their relation to *Differentiation* and *Complexity* of reported experiences. These were: (*a*) *Verbal intelligence,* as estimated by the Gallup-Thorndike Vocabulary Test (Thorndike, 1942); and (*b*) *Fluency,* estimated by the number of words written by each subject in response to the question, "What psychological questions do you have about education?"

RESULTS

To estimate reliability of the measures of the two emotional report variables, *Differentiation* and *Complexity* scores were computed for five of the ten emotions and compared to the parallel scores computed on the other five emotions. For *Differentiation,* the correlation between these two sets of scores is .77; for *Complexity,* the correlation is .94. Thus, there would seem to be adequate evidence in support of the internal consistency of both these measures—if a person's descriptions of one set of emotional experiences tend to be highly differentiated (or highly complex), his descriptions of a second set of emotional experiences also tend to be highly differentiated (or highly complex). To evaluate reliability of the content analysis, ten randomly selected protocols—each containing descriptions of ten emotional states—were analyzed independently by two judges and scores computed for each of the two emotional report variables. For *Complexity,* a correlation of .99 was obtained between these two sets of scores; for *Differentiation,* a correlation of .92 was obtained.

As indicated in Table 6-3, all three predictions are supported by data from the female sample; for males and the total group, only the correlation between *Field Independence–Dependence* and *Differentiation* is statistically significant.*

Of all the correlations between either verbal intelligence or fluency and each of the perceptual–cognitive and emotional report variables, only the correlation between verbal intelligence and *Complexity* in the female sample is significantly different from zero ($r = .33$, $p < .05$). Par-

---

* Field Independence–Dependence was measured by the time required to distinguish a relatively simple figure from a more complex ground. The less time required, the more field independent is the subject. Thus, a negative correlation indicates that greater Field Independence is associated with more Differentiation of reported emotional experiences.

TABLE 6-3

Correlations between Perceptual-Cognitive Variables and Characteristics of
of Reported Emotional Experiences

| | Correlation coefficient[a] | | |
| | Total group (N = 70) | Males (N = 27) | Females (N = 43) |
Variables			
Equivalence range and differentiation	.20	−.08	.31[b]
Field independence-dependence and differentiation	−.39[c]	−.48[d]	−.33[b]
Leveling-sharpening and complexity	.24	.00	.35[b]

[a] Product moment correlation.

[b] $p = .05$.

[c] $p = .005$.

[d] $p = .025$.

tialing out verbal intelligence in the correlation between *Leveling–Sharpening* and *Complexity* for the female sample does not reduce it substantially ($r = .30$, $p < .05$).

The data also provided an opportunity to compare males and females in terms of the emotional report variables. Among the 25 male and 25 female subjects who comprised the sample on which the dictionary was based, the female subjects tended to check a somewhat larger number of items in their descriptions. However, in the present sample of 27 males and 43 females, there was very little difference between males and females either for *Complexity* (males: $\bar{X} = 68.5$, S.D. $= 32.8$; females: $\bar{X} = 70.3$, S.D. $= 33.2$) or Differentiation (males: $\bar{X} = .55$, S.D. $= .15$; females: $\bar{X} = .52$, S.D. $= .16$).

DISCUSSION

The results generally support the central hypothesis regarding the relationship between perceptual–cognitive and emotional report variables—particularly for the female sample and at least partially for the male sample. This clearly reinforces the view that perceptual–cognitive processes are involved in emotional experiences, thus contradicting the use of theoretical dichotomies such as thinking versus feeling, cognition versus affect, or rational versus emotional. It seems more reasonable to view *perceptual–cognitive processes as part of emotional phenomena,* recognizing that certain aspects of perceptual–cognitive functioning are probably independent of emotion and certain aspects of emotion are likely to be independent of perceptual–cognitive functioning. Moreover, the socially learned rules of cognition—which presumably define "rational" thought—are different from the "rules" of emotion, though undoubtedly the structure of emotional experience is also determined, in part, by social learning.

It is possible, of course, that the relationships obtained in this study are a function of the fact that the measures were derived from *reports* of emotional experience, and that the use of verbal language mediated the relationships between the perceptual–cognitive and emotional report variables. On the basis of the present research, this possibility cannot be refuted, though it should be noted that the two measures most directly concerned with the use of language—verbal intelligence and fluency—did not appreciably influence the relationships between the perceptual–cognitive and emotional report variables. Nevertheless, to clarify this issue, further research must investigate this problem, perhaps using various non-verbal modes of describing emotional experiences. In a cross-cultural study presented in a subsequent section of this chapter, the influence of specific language differences on emotional reports will be discussed.

The results also support Witkin's interpretation of *Field Independence–Dependence* as a major dimension of perceptual–cognitive functioning related to a variety of diverse phenomena (Witkin *et al.*, 1962). In previous research, Field Independence–Dependence has been related, for example, to variables such as resistance to reversal of perspective (Haronian and Sugerman, 1966); response to group pressure (Rosner, 1957); and passive–dependent needs (Marlowe, 1958). In the present study, for both males and females, *Field Independence* was consistently related to *Differentiation,* such that persons who were able to distinguish graphically presented figure from a more complex ground with relatively greater speed also tended to report more differentiated emotional experiences.

The results, however, are not nearly so consistent for either *Equivalence Range* or *Leveling–Sharpening.* The predicted relationships were obtained for the female sample but not for the males, and this difference cannot be accounted for by sample size or any substantial difference between males and females in the varibility of any of the measures concerned. These results, therefore, suggest some interaction between sex of the subject and the relationship between perceptual–cognitive and emotional report variables. There are at least two obvious possibilities which must be explored in the light of these results. On the one hand, among men it is possible that perceptual–cognitive functioning, other than in terms of the *Field Independent–Dependent* dimension, is unrelated to emotional functioning. Perhaps men in the culture sampled are indeed more "compartmentalized," so that their styles of perception and cognition are independent of their styles of emotional experience—while women, in contrast, are more consistent in style across all areas of functioning. On the other hand, it is also possible that the appropriate variables, either for perceptual–cognitive or emotional functioning, were simply not identified in this research. Consider, for example, some of the perceptual–cognitive factors that might possibly be involved in reporting an emotional experience. First, of course, one has to observe one's own reactions, which not only involves the ability to observe a complex and rapidly changing pattern of stimuli, but requires the capacity to maintain a certain perspective in perceiving one's self during the course of an emotional experience. Then, upon being asked to report and describe the experience, one must be able to recall, perhaps after a considerable length of time, the details of events that have occurred in the past and verbally describe these events. Thus, while gross measures of verbal ability—such as the vocabulary and fluency tests used in this study—are apparently not productive in this line of inquiry, more specific measures designed to evaluate the individual's ability to describe events verbally might well be worth investigating. In short, then, one might expect *Complexity* of emotional reports to be related to: (*a*) the ability to observe a complex and rapidly changing pattern of stimuli; (*b*) the capacity to achieve and maintain perspective about one's self during an emotional experience; (*c*) the ability to recall the details of events after periods of considerable delay; and (*d*) the ability to describe events verbally. These variables, of course, do not stem directly from the present study, but they offer potentially useful leads for further investigation.

Similarity of Reported Emotional Experiences and Genetic Background*

Allerand (1967) began with the assumption that emotional reactions involve physiological events, such as changes in heart rate, blood pressure, etc. Therefore, it seemed reasonable to expect that people who are physiologically similar to each other tend to have emotional reactions that are also similar. An individual's physiology at any given time is influenced by a variety of factors, but among these, certainly genetic background is a major determinant. Thus, extending the argument one step further,

---

* This section is based on a study conducted by Anne-Marie Allerand for her doctoral dissertation at Teachers College, Columbia University, and I am indebted to her for permission to report the material presented in this chapter. The reference to this study is: Allerand, A. M. Rememberance of feelings past: A study of phenomenological genetics. Unpublished doctoral dissertation, Columbia University, 1967.

other things being equal, people who are genetically identical would be expected to have emotional reactions that are more similar to each other than those of people who have different genetic backgrounds.

Moreover, it would seem likely that the areas of similarity in emotional reactions would extend beyond those directly related to physiology. If a person, for example, tends to function physiologically at a relatively high level of activation and becomes hyperactivated as a consequence of only slight stimulation, one might expect his relationships with others and perhaps even his sense of competence to be affected in some ways. Surely in contrast to another person who is physiologically sluggish and tends to remain at a fairly hypoactive level, it would be reasonable to expect differences in emotional reactions that extended beyond those aspects of emotion most immediately related to physiology.

Therefore, assuming that reports of emotional experiences indeed reflect emotional reactions, Allerand tested the notion that monozygotic twins report emotional experiences that are more similar to each other than do either dizygotic twins or nontwin siblings.

METHOD

The study involved a comparison of three groups: (a) monozygotic twins; (b) dizygotic twins, and (c) nontwin siblings. There were 24 pairs in each group, 12 pairs of males and 12 pairs of females. Their ages ranged from 13 to 18, with a mean age of 16 for each of the three groups.

The following data were obtained from each subject:

1. Written descriptions of the experience of Affection, Anger, Delight, Disgust, Excitement, Fear, Sadness, and Worry.

2. An estimate of verbal intelligence, using the Gallup-Thorndike Vocabulary Test (Thorndike, 1942).

3. A report of the degree to which each pair shared friends, clothes, activities, etc. using a check list inventory.*

The reports of emotional experiences were content analyzed using essentially the category system presented in Table 6-1. Similarity of reported emotional experiences was evaluated for each pair by the proportion of total categories mentioned by both members that were identical in their descriptions of each of the eight emotional states.

---

* In addition to these data, a self-description of each subject and a description of his cotwin or sibling was obtained using a 50-item adjective check list. However, these data were not treated in relation to similarity of emotional reports—though it is interesting to note that monozygotic twins assume greater similarity between themselves and their twin than do either dizygotic twins or siblings. In fact the differences among groups in actual similarity is not statistically significant.

RESULTS

The emotional reports of monozygotic twins contained, on the average, about 20% identical categories, while the reports of dizygotic twins contained an average of about 15%, and siblings about 13%. An analysis of variance revealed a significant difference among groups ($F = 5.86$, $p < .01$), and t tests indicated a significant difference between monozygotic twins and dizygotic twins ($p < .02$), and between monozygotic twins and siblings ($p < .02$); but the difference between dizygotic twins and siblings was not statistically significant.

The differences among groups in verbal intelligence was not statistically significant. On the check list of shared activities, monozygotic twins reported that they shared significantly more activities, friends, etc. than did dizygotic twins ($t = 9.62$, $p < .001$); however, this estimate of shared activities was independent of the emotional similarity index ($r = -.11$, $p < .05$).

DISCUSSION

The results clearly support the expectation that genetic identity is related to similarity of emotional reports, and presumably this relationship is mediated by the relatively similar physiological reactions of persons with the same genetic background. This assumption, however, might well be tested in further research by actually measuring similarity of physiological reactions between people and studying these similarities in relation to similarities of emotional reports.

Once again, it must be recognized that genetic identity does not account for a great deal of the variance in similarity of emotional reports. Thus, while it seems evident from this research that physiological factors influence reported emotional experiences, other variables relevant to language, the individual's history of learning, and the particular conditions under which he experiences emotional reactions perhaps play an even greater part in determining reports of emotional experiences. In the next study we shall consider cultural differences in relation to the language of emotion.

A Comparison of Emotional Experiences Reported by Adolescents in Uganda and the United States

During the summer of 1967, I participated in a research program at the Institute of Education, Makerere University College in Kampala,

Uganda.* This provided an opportunity to collect data on emotional experiences from students in Ugandan schools and to compare these reports with those obtained from an approximately equivalent sample of American adolescents. In addition, since English is the official language of instruction in Uganda, and Luganda is the vernacular of the students sampled, differences in emotional reports could be studied as a function of the language used for report—that is, Luganda versus English.

At the outset of this research it was assumed that emotional experiences reflect relevant characteristics of a particular culture. Thus, differences in the emotional reports obtained would presumably parallel other differences in the two cultures sampled. However, in the absence of previous research on this specific topic, predictions about the exact nature of differences expected did not seem warranted. Rather, the study was viewed as an exploratory investigation guided by the general thesis that emotional experiences are at least in part culture bound.

Similarly, in regards to differences in language, no specific predictions were made. Nevertheless, a bilingual sample such as that available in Uganda affords an especially valuable opportunity to investigate one aspect of an important methodological question—*viz.* since emotional experiences in this line of inquiry are studied by means of verbal reports, what characteristics of these reports are determined by the language of report *per se?* If we can identify the effects of language, a potentially major source of variance in verbal descriptions of emotional experiences can be controlled. Thus, assuming that the language of report influences verbal descriptions of emotion, the purpose of this phase of the research was to identify possible differences between the reports given in Luganda versus those given in English by the Ugandan sample.

Method and Procedures

The subjects of this research were 60 adolescents sampled in Uganda and 60 sampled in the United States. There were 30 males and 30 females in each group. The Ugandan sample was obtained from the highest grade in primary school (P-7) and the first year of a secondary boarding school (S-1), approximately half of the sample coming from each of these levels. All Ss were Buganda, the major tribe living in the south-central part

* I would like to express my appreciation to Mr. W. Senteza Kajubi, Director of the Institute of Education, Makerere University College, and to Mr. Jackson Kaswa-Lyazi, Mr. J. E. Kasujja, and Mr. Pafula Kiwanuka, who assisted me in this research.

of Uganda. The schools from which Ss were obtained are located in and around Kampala, the capital and major city of Uganda, and the students came to these schools from the area in and around Kampala. Their ages ranged from 12 to 20, with a mean of 14.8 years. While there is as yet no empirically established way of identifying social class of the students, the occupations of their fathers (or mother, if father was deceased) ranged from professionals, such as physician or member of the local government, to unemployed. Without systematic evidence, it seems reasonable to suggest that the primary school sample was fairly representative of the African urban population, while the secondary school students tended to come from backgrounds somewhat wealthier than the average.

The American sample was obtained from grades 9, 10, and 11 (mean age, 15.6 years) in two schools in the New York City area. One of these is a public school with a predominantly lower and lower-middle class student population; the other is a private school with a middle and upper-middle class student group. Approximately half the sample came from each school. It would be practically impossible, at this point, to establish the equivalence of samples from Uganda and the United States on the basis of the usual criteria; in any event, both groups represent primarily an urban population with a socioeconomic distribution somewhat skewed in the upper-middle class direction.

During the initial phase of research in Uganda, an attempt was made to collect data by means of individual interviews. These were conducted both by me and by my African colleagues, but none of us was able to obtain much information from the majority of students interviewed. They seemed pleasant and apparently cooperative in conversation, but when it came to describing their emotional experiences in a face-to-face interview with an adult, they became obviously tense and unable to communicate.

As a next preliminary step, therefore, another group of students were asked for written descriptions of their emotional experiences. These were written anonymously in a group setting. In marked contrast to the interviews, the students showed no difficulty in describing their experiences, and in fact wrote fairly lengthy reports that contained a good deal of information. Therefore, the data for the present study were obtained by written reports collected in classroom groups.

Descriptions were obtained of three emotional states: Happiness, Sadness, and Anger. For each state, the subject was asked to think of a particular time he experienced the emotion, to describe briefly the situation, and to describe his experiences as fully as possible.

Among the Ugandan subjects, half the males and half the females wrote in Luganda, and the other half wrote in English. All of the United States subjects, of course, wrote in English.

TABLE 6-4a

Number of Subjects in the Uganda Sample Who Mentioned Each Category
in Their Descriptions of Happiness: A Comparison of Reports
Written in English and Luganda

Category	Group		
	English	Luganda	Total
Activation	13	12	25
Hyperactivation	3	4	7
Move toward others			
General	8	6	14
Absence of negative	5	0	5
Inadequacy			
General dysfunction	2	2	4
Speech dysfunction	2	1	3
Sensory dysfunction	0	2	2
Cognitive dysfunction	4	1	5
Motor dysfunction	1	1	2
Self-enhancement			
General	10	8	18
Strength	0	2	2
Discomfort			
General	0	1	1
Heat, fever	1	3	4
Comfort			
General	5	7	12
Freedom, pain, etc.	12	9	21
Attitude			
Positive	5	4	9
Expressive behavior			
Laughing, smiling	17	10	27
Crying	6	4	10
Self-awareness			
Self-absorbed	4	3	7
Loss self-awareness	0	3	3
Hunger			
Absence of hunger	0	3	3
Not eat	3	1	4
Sense of unreality	3	4	7
Other feelings			
Anxiety, fear	0	1	1
Situation			
Academic achievement	10	10	20
Family	5	4	9
Social	2	2	4
Gifts, presents	5	4	9
Other	2	5	7
Not specified	6	5	11

TABLE 6-4b

Number of Subjects in the Uganda Sample Who Mentioned Each Category
in Their Descriptions of Sadness: A Comparison of Reports
Written in English and Luganda

Category	Group		
	English	Luganda	Total
Hypoactivation	10	8	18
Move away from others			
Escape	15	6	21
Wish to die	8	4	12
Move against others			
Extreme aggression	0	1	1
Moderate aggression	1	0	1
Agression toward self	3	2	5
Inadequacy			
General inadequacy	1	1	2
General dysfunction	3	4	7
Speech dysfunction	1	2	3
Sensory dysfunction	1	1	2
Cognitive dysfunction	5	6	11
Obsessive thoughts	9	10	19
Motor dysfunction	3	1	4
Random activity	1	1	2
Discomfort			
General	7	6	13
Heat, fever	3	2	5
Cold	1	0	1
Tension	1	1	2
Attitude			
Negative	8	7	15
Expressive behavior			
Crying	18	15	33
Sense of unreality	1	1	2
Other feelings			
Anxiety, fear	0	1	1
Guilt	1	2	3
Self–awareness			
Loss	1	2	3
Hunger			
Not eat	9	9	18
Situations			
Death—relative, friend	16	18	34
Academic failure	3	2	5
Social problem	0	2	2
Other	4	6	10
Not specified	7	2	9

TABLE 6-4c

Number of Subjects in the Uganda Sample Who Mentioned Each Category
in Their Descriptions of Anger: A Comparison of Reports
Written in English and Luganda

Category	Group		
	English	Luganda	Total
Hypoactivation	1	1	2
Activation	2	1	3
Hyperactivation	6	2	8
Move away from others			
Escape	12	10	22
Wish to die	1	4	5
Move against others			
Impulse extreme aggression (killing, mutilation)	12	6	18
Impulse moderate aggression (striking out, hurting)	10	7	17
Aggressive behavior (persons)	7	4	11
Aggressive behavior (objects)	2	4	6
Nonphysical aggression	6	4	10
Aggression toward self	0	2	2
Control of aggression	4	0	4
Inadequacy			
General inadequacy	1	1	2
General dysfunction	0	2	2
Speech dysfunction	1	2	3
Sensory dysfunction	2	1	3
Cognitive dysfunction (general)	4	5	9
Cognitive dysfunction (obsessive thoughts)	1	1	2
Motor dysfunction (random activity)	2	0	2
Self-enhancement			
Strength	6	3	9
Discomfort			
General	7	5	12
Heat, fever	2	1	3
Cold	1	0	1
Tension	1	0	1
Attitude			
Negative	3	4	7
Expressive behavior			
Laughing, smiling	1	0	1
Crying	9	12	21

TABLE 6-4c *(continued)*

Category	Group		
	English	Luganda	Total
Self-awareness			
Loss self-awareness	1	1	2
Hunger			
Not eat	3	3	6
Other feelings			
Sadness, depression	0	2	2
Situations			
Frustration, aggression			
(by adult)	8	12	20
Frustration, aggression			
(by child or adolescent)	15	7	22
Other	1	3	4
Not specified	6	8	14

The descriptions of each emotional state were content analyzed using a simpler modification of the category system presented in Table 6-1. Agreement between two independent judges who analyzed the reports was 92%. In each of the tables summarizing the results, frequencies are reported in terms of the number of Ss in each group who mentioned a given category.

RESULTS

Since no predictions regarding specific differences were made prior to collecting the data, statistical significance tests were not computed. With the usual accompanying probability levels, reporting such tests lends results an aura of conclusiveness that they sometimes do not warrant. In the present instance, therefore, inspection of the frequencies presented in each table must suffice as a basis for formulating hypotheses to be tested in further research.

Luganda versus English. Tables 6-4a, 6-4b, and 6-4c summarize the frequencies obtained for each category in the Ugandan sample's descriptions of Happiness, Sadness, and Anger. For the most part, the frequencies for reports written in English differ from those written in Luganda by only one or two, and the few larger differences are most likely due to chance. In descriptions of Happiness, for example, the reports in English somewhat more often mentioned smiling and laughing. In descriptions of Sadness, the English reports more frequently mentioned an impulse to move away from others. And in describing Anger, the reports in English contained a higher frequency of extremely aggressive statements. But in analyzing the descriptions of the three emotional states, over 90 categories were used, and the relatively few apparent differences found must be considered chance findings. Therefore, at least in terms of the fairly gross level of analysis used in this study, the data *do not* support a hypothesis that the content of emotional reports is influenced by the language of report *per se*. Instead, the data suggest that other determinants of emotional reports, including the referent experiences, are so compelling that they either obscure or cancel out gross content differences that might result from linguistic variables.

Sex Differences. Since no consistent differences were obtained between reports written in English and those written in Luganda, the results for all 60 *S*s in the Ugandan sample were combined. Tables 6-4d, 6-4e, and 6-4f summarize the frequencies obtained for males, females, and total group for the Ugandan and United State samples.

Inspection of the frequencies for males versus females in each national group reveals no consistent differences. As in the preceding analysis of possible language differences, most of the relatively few apparently substantial differences between males and females are probably chance findings. Others reflect obvious cultural stereotypes. For example, in descriptions of Sadness written by the United States sample, females more often than males mentioned crying (females, 14; males, 7). In descriptions of Anger written by the Ugandan sample, males more often than females mentioned impulses to extreme aggression (males, 13; females, 5) and enhanced strength (males, 9; females, 0). But other than these few differences, the frequencies for males and females within each national group were substantially the same.

Differences between the Ugandan and United States Samples. In view of the similar frequency patterns obtained for males and females in each group, attention may be focused on the results for each total group in comparing the descriptions of the Ugandan versus United States samples. At the outset, it should be noted that the reports by the Ugandan *S*s consistently contained a higher number of content analysis categories. These data are summarized in Table 6-4g. It is difficult to interpret this finding with much confidence at the present time. Perhaps these results reflect a difference in the richness or complexity of the experiences described; perhaps they reflect a difference in sensitivity or recall of the experiences; or perhaps they reflect a difference in the motivation and industry with which the *S*s in the two national groups attended to the descriptive task. In any event, the overall quantitative differences suggest that, rather than compare absolute frequencies for each category, the relative frequencies of various categories within each group should be con-

TABLE 6-4d

Number of Subjects Who Mentioned Each Category
in Their Descriptions of Happiness

Category	Uganda Male	Uganda Female	Uganda Total	United States Male	United States Female	United States Total
Activation	13	12	25	15	11	26
Hyperactivation	5	2	7	0	1	1
Move toward others						
General	6	8	14	7	11	18
Absence of negative	3	2	5	0	0	0
Inadequacy						
General dysfunction	0	4	4	0	0	0
Speech dysfunction	1	2	3	0	0	0
Sensory dysfunction	2	0	2	0	0	0
Cognitive dysfunction	2	3	5	0	0	0
Motor dysfunction	1	1	2	0	0	0
Self-enhancement						
General	9	9	18	9	9	18
Strength	2	0	2	0	0	0
Discomfort						
General	1	0	1	0	0	0
Heat, fever	4	0	4	0	0	0
Comfort						
General	7	5	12	7	5	12
Freedom from pain, etc.	13	8	21	3	5	8
Attitude						
Positive	6	3	9	5	3	8
Expressive behavior						
Laughing, smiling	15	12	27	2	3	5
Crying	7	3	10	0	0	0
Self-awareness						
Self-absorbed	3	4	7	0	0	0
Loss of self-awareness	2	1	3	0	0	0
Hunger						
Absence of hunger	2	1	3	0	0	0
Not eat	1	3	4	0	0	0
Sense of unreality	4	3	7	0	0	0
Other feelings						
Anxiety, fear	1	0	1	0	0	0

sidered. Thus, using an arbitrary cutoff point of 12 (one-fifth of each sample), the most frequently mentioned categories for each emotional state for the two national groups were identified. These data are summarized in Tables 6-4h, 6-4i, and 6-4j, which present the categories for each group in rank order of frequency. Thus, using frequency as the

TABLE 6-4d (continued)

Category	Uganda Male	Uganda Female	Uganda Total	United States Male	United States Female	United States Total
Situation						
Academic achievement	12	8	20	2	2	4
Achievement (other than academic)	0	0	0	9	8	17
Social	2	2	4	8	14	22
Family	4	5	9	5	2	7
Gifts, presents	2	7	9	2	0	2
Other	5	2	7	4	4	8
Not specified	5	6	11	0	0	0

key, some sense of the degree to which various categories were emphasized by Ss in each national group can be obtained from Tables 6-4h, 6-4i, and 6-4j.

In the descriptions of Happiness (Table 6-4h), there is considerable similarity between the Ugandan and United States samples. Both emphasize Activation, Moving Toward Others, General Enhancement, and Comfort. But among the Ugandan Ss, there is clearly greater emphasis on expressive behaviors (smiling, laughing) and freedom from pain and worry. Most striking, though, are the differences in situations associated with Happiness. Among the Ugandan Ss, academic achievement was mentioned most often. For the United States Ss, however, social situations (e.g., dating, parties, etc.) were mentioned most frequently, with nonacademic achievement (e.g., learning to drive) a close second.

A somewhat similar pattern (Table 6-4i) is apparent in descriptions of Sadness—there is a core of similarity in the experiences reported by the two groups, and there are certain obvious differences. For both groups, crying, a sense of inadequacy, moving away from others, a negative attitude towards the world, and feelings of hypoactivation are mentioned. These aspects of the experience, of course, are quite consistent with the definition of Sadness contained in the dictionary of emotional meaning (Chapter 2). However, among the Ugandan Ss the sense of inadequacy was expressed much more often in terms of having obsessive thoughts. Also, the Ugandan Ss specifically emphasized an inability or lack of desire to eat and a wish to die. Neither of these appeared in the descriptions of the United States sample.

Among the situations associated with Sadness, death of a relative or friend was clearly the most frequent situation mentioned by the Ugandan Ss. In contrast, social problems, disappointments, and failures were men-

TABLE 6-4e

Number of Subjects Who Mentioned Each Category
in Their Descriptions of Sadness

Category	Uganda			United States		
	Male	Female	Total	Male	Female	Total
Hypoactivation	10	8	18	5	7	12
Activation	0	0	0	0	1	1
Move toward others						
General	0	0	0	0	1	1
Move away from others						
Escape	10	11	21	7	11	18
Wish to die	5	7	12	0	0	0
Move against others						
Extreme aggression	1	0	1	1	0	1
Impulse moderate aggression	0	1	1	2	1	3
Aggression toward self	3	2	5	2	3	5
Inadequacy						
General inadequacy	1	1	2	8	12	21
General dysfunction	3	4	7	1	0	1
Speech dysfunction	2	1	3	0	0	0
Sensory dysfunction	2	0	2	0	0	0
Cognitive dysfunction	7	4	11	0	0	0
Obsessive thoughts	6	13	19	0	0	0
Motor dysfunction	2	2	4	0	0	0
Random activity	1	1	2	0	0	0
Discomfort						
General	7	6	13	10	7	17
Heat, fever	4	1	5	0	0	0
Cold	1	0	1	0	0	0
Tension	2	0	2	1	0	1
Attitude						
Negative	6	9	15	8	7	15
Expressive behavior						
Crying	15	18	33	7	14	21
Self-awareness						
Loss	2	1	3	0	0	0
Hunger						
Not eat	6	12	18	0	0	0
Sense of unreality	1	1	2	0	1	1
Other feelings						
Anxiety, fear	1	0	0	0	1	1
Guilt	3	0	3	0	0	0

TABLE 6-4e *(continued)*

Category	Group					
	Uganda			United States		
	Male	Female	Total	Male	Female	Total
Situations						
Death—relative, friend	18	16	34	4	4	8
Death—other (public figure, pet)	0	0	0	3	5	8
Academic failure	2	3	5	2	0	2
Social problem	0	2	2	5	12	17
Family problem	0	0	0	3	4	7
Other	6	4	10	11	4	15
Not specified	4	5	9	2	1	3

tioned most often by the United States sample. This, of course, parallels the results in the United States sample obtained for Happiness, which was often associated with social success.

The results for Anger (Table 6-4j) also reveal a clear-cut similarity between the two groups, in that some form of aggression was mentioned by a larger majority of Ss in both the Ugandan and the United States samples. But in the Ugandan sample, both moving away from others and crying were reported more often than aggression. Moreover, impulses to extreme aggression (e.g., killing, severe mutilation), general discomfort, and various subcategories of inadequacy were far more frequent in the Ugandan sample. Among the United States Ss, impulses to moderate agression (striking out, hurting), a sense of hyperactivation, and aggressive behavior were emphasized. The gross breakdown of situations associated with Anger revealed no substantial differences between the two groups.

DISCUSSION

Recognizing that the specific differences found in this study cannot be generalized, but rather, serve as a basis for formulating hypotheses to be tested in subsequent studies, the overall findings support two general propositions. First, the similarities between the emotional reports of the two national groups suggest a core of experiences associated with various emotional states that cuts across different cultures. Thus, paraphrasing Gertrude Stein's dictum that a rose is a rose is a rose—to a certain extent, Happiness is Happiness is Happiness. On the other hand, the differences between the two national groups also suggest that Happiness in Uganda is *not quite* the same as Happiness in the United States—which in turn

TABLE 6-4f

Number of Subjects Who Mentioned Each Category
in Their Descriptions of Anger

	Group					
	Uganda			United States		
Category	Male	Female	Total	Male	Female	Total
Hypoactivation	1	1	2	0	0	0
Activation	1	2	3	0	0	0
Hyperactivation	5	3	8	11	7	18
Move away from others						
Escape	10	12	22	4	9	13
Wish to die	1	4	5	0	0	0
Move against others						
Impulse extreme aggression (killing, mutilation)	13	5	18	1	2	3
Impulse moderate aggression (striking out, hurting)	8	9	17	18	16	34
Aggressive behavior (persons)	4	7	11	6	6	12
Aggressive behavior (objects)	2	4	6	1	1	2
Nonphysical aggression	2	8	10	2	3	5
Aggression-self	1	1	2	0	0	0
Control of aggression	3	1	4	3	2	5
Inadequacy						
General inadequacy	1	1	2	1	4	5
General dysfunction	0	2	2	0	0	0
Speech dysfunction	2	1	3	0	0	0
Sensory dysfunction	2	1	3	0	0	0
Cognitive dysfunction (general)	6	3	9	0	0	0
Cognitive dysfunction (obsessive thoughts)	0	2	2	0	0	0
Motor dysfunction (random activity)	0	2	2	0	0	0
Self-enhancement						
General	0	0	0	2	0	2
Strength	9	0	9	3	0	3
Discomfort						
General	8	4	12	1	1	2
Heat, fever	2	1	3	0	0	0
Cold	1	0	1	0	0	0
Tension	1	0	1	1	4	5

TABLE 6-4f (*continued*)

	Group					
	Uganda			United States		
Category	Male	Female	Total	Male	Female	Total
Attitude						
Negative	3	4	7	2	1	3
Expressive behavior						
Laughing, smiling	0	1	1	0	0	0
Crying	10	11	21	0	5	5
Self-awareness						
Loss self-awareness	2	0	2	0	0	0
Hunger						
Not eat	1	5	6	0	0	0
Other feelings						
Sadness	1	1	2	0	0	0
Situations						
Frustration, aggression (by adult)	11	9	20	7	11	18
Frustration, aggression (by child or adolescent)	9	13	22	9	7	16
Other	3	1	4	8	7	15
Not specified	7	7	14	6	5	11

is probably not quite the same as Happiness in Afghanistan or in any other culture. And these differences in emotional experiences reflect other relevant differences in the various cultures.

Consider, for example, the descriptions of Happiness. There is considerable overlap in the reports given by the two national groups, and it would be extremely unlikely that an American would mistake a Ugandan report of a happy experience for another emotional state such as Anger or Sadness. Yet, the Ugandan adolescent's stress on freedom from pain and worry as a significant part of Happiness reflects an important contrast with the culture of the American adolescent. Childhood and adolescence in Uganda are certainly not constantly fraught with pain and worry—there is obviously a good deal of play, fun, and satisfaction. But in comparison to life in the United States, the typical Ugandan child undoubtedly encounters basic difficulties in living far more frequently, and perhaps with greater intensity, than the typical American child. Freedom from hunger, from illness, from all the realistic worries associated with poverty in a relatively underdeveloped country simply are more common facts of daily life for the Ugandan child than they are for most American children. Thus, it is not at all surprising that freedom from pain and worry should

TABLE 6-4g

Number of Categorized Ideas in Descriptions of Each Emotional State

Emotional state	Uganda sample	United States sample
Happiness	$\overline{X}$ = 3.3 (S.D. = 1.3)	$\overline{X}$ = 1.6 (S.D. = 0.8)
Sadness	$\overline{X}$ = 3.4 (S.D. = 0.9)	$\overline{X}$ = 1.9 (S.D. = 1.0)
Anger	$\overline{X}$ = 3.3 (S.D. = 1.6)	$\overline{X}$ = 1.9 (S.D. = 0.8)

TABLE 6-4h

Categories Emphasized by Each National Group in Their Descriptions of Happiness

Uganda		United States	
Category	Frequency	Category	Frequency
Smiling, laughing	27	Activation	26
Activation	25	Move toward others	18
Freedom from pain, worry	21	General enhancement	18
General enhancement	18	General comfort	12
Move toward others	14		
General comfort	12		
Situations		Situations	
Academic achievement	20	Social	22
		Nonacademic achievement	17

TABLE 6-4i

Categories Emphasized by each National Group in Their Descriptions of Sadness

Uganda		United States	
Category	Frequency	Category	Frequency
Crying	33	Crying	21
Move away from others—		General inadequacy	20
escape	21	Move away from others—	
Obsessive thoughts	19	escape	18
Hypoactivation	18	General discomfort	17
Not eat	18	Negative attitude toward	
Negative attitude toward		world	15
world	15	Hypoactivation	12
General discomfort	13		
Wish to die	12		
Situations		Situations	
Death of relative, friend	34	Social problems	17

TABLE 6-4j

Categories Emphasized by Each National Group in Their Descriptions of Anger

Uganda		United States	
Category	Frequency	Category	Frequency

Move away from others—
    escape
	22	Impulse to moderate aggression
		    (striking out, hurting)
			34

Crying	21	Hyperactivation	18
Impulse to extreme aggression (killing, mutilating)	18	Aggressive behavior	12
Impulse to moderate aggres- sion (striking out, hurting)	17		
General discomfort	12		
Various subcategories of inadequacy	23		
Situations		Situations	

Frustration, aggression by
    child or adolescent
	22	Frustration, aggression by
		    adult
			18

Frustration, aggression by
    adult
	20	Frustration, aggression by
		    child or adolescent
			16

play a significant role in the Happiness experienced by Ugandan adolescents.

Even more striking is the difference in situations that are the occasion of Happiness in the two cultures. No one familiar with education in Uganda can be at all surprised by the importance of academic success in accounting for happy occasions in the Ugandan child's life. Of course the data were collected in school settings, which may have biased the results somewhat—though apparently the bias did not operate in the United States sample. Regardless of any possible bias, however, the frequency with which academic success was mentioned as the occasion for Happiness is even more noteworthy when one recognizes that Ss were asked to think of *any* happy experience at *any* time in their lives. Clearly, academic success is of prime importance in the lives of Ugandan adolescents. In fact, it would not be difficult to substantiate the proposition that school achievement is the single most important activity for most urban children in Uganda. For the vast majority of children, success in school is the only way out of a lifetime of poverty, unemployment, or menial labor. And success, which primarily means passing examinations, is a thoroughly public affair—as is failure—with lists of results posted, family celebrations, gifts, admiration, and often love are rewards for academic achievement.

It would certainly be incorrect to minimize the significance of academic achievement for many American children, but rather than Happiness, perhaps school success in the United States is more typically associated with other emotional states—pride, confidence, or satisfaction. Be that as it may, the United States adolescents associated Happiness with nonacademic achievement and social success, with learning to drive a car, for example, or dating a particularly attractive boy or girl. Perhaps nothing so obviously distinguishes the two cultures of Ugandan and American adolescents as these differences in the occasions of Happiness.

That a majority of Ugandan adolescents associated Sadness with the death of a friend or relative reflects one of the facts of day-to-day existence experienced by many Ugandan children. In the first place, the death rate is considerably higher than that in the United States. Moreover, in contrast to the American culture, in which death of a distant relative in many instances is not interpreted as an immediately personal event for a child, within the extended family among the Buganda, death of any member of a large family is more likely to be associated with a gathering of most members of the extended family and relatively lengthy period of mourning characterized by dramatic expressions of grief. In addition, death of a parent, particularly the father, may well have traumatic consequences in the child's life—not only psychological, but also economic and social. Thus, death of a relative or friend is not uncommon for many Ugandan children, and represents a major and possibly traumatic experience in the child's life.

Lost in the quantitative data of the content analysis is the intensely dramatic flavor of the descriptions of Sadness written by the Ugandan sample—the pain and the sense of utter helplessness are perhaps captured a bit in the categories that deal with obsessive thoughts and the wish to die as a means of escaping from the pain and suffering of the experience. It would be interesting to study comparable experiences of American children who have experienced the death of a relative or friend, to determine whether or not their reactions parallel those of the Ugandan sample. In the present United States sample, Sadness was most often associated with social problems (e.g., being rejected by others), and while many of the categories emphasized by the Ugandan group were also mentioned by the United States sample, the apparent intensity of the descriptions seemed to be nowhere near as great. This observation, of course, is merely impressionistic and does *not* derive directly from the quantitative results. At most, it merely suggests a line of inquiry in terms of intensity of experiences for further investigation.

Perhaps of greatest psychodynamic interest are the descriptions of Anger. Among Ugandan children, overt respect for adults (including older siblings) is one of the principal characteristics of all adult–child relationships. Adults may very well punish a child, sometimes severely, with little justification, and the punishment is generally viewed by most adults as simply the "natural" and certainly accustomed way of dealing with children. But in the Ugandan culture, there are strong inhibitions against the child expressing overt hostility towards adults. Thus, if the child is punished or frustrated by his parent or headmaster, he is likely to try to escape from the situation, perhaps cry, feel uncomfortable, inadequate—and suppress impulses to aggression, which rather frequently in fantasy take extreme forms of violent killing and mutilation.

These data suggest a number of hypotheses, assuming, of course, that the present findings are corroborated in further research. One would expect, for example, occasional outbreaks of apparently "irrational" hostility among children and adolescents, a relatively high incidence of psychosomatic illnesses, and perhaps greater concern with problems of guilt and depression associated with aggressive impulses. Obviously the present data offer no way of testing these hypotheses, but merely suggest potentially fruitful avenues for further research.

In a sense, the failure to find differences in emotional descriptions as a function of the language of report (English versus Luganda) was something of a disappointment. But from another point of view, the absence of differences related to language *per se* is somewhat encouraging because it suggests that the definitions of emotional states obtained in other phases of this line of inquiry are not as susceptible to linguistic influences as one might have expected.

Certainly further research must be done on this particular topic with other language groups, and perhaps a more refined analysis of the data will reveal more subtle influences of the language of report. It should be noted that the Ugandan Ss were bilingual, and perhaps the knowledge of both Luganda and English mitigated differences that might have appeared among those who knew only one language. One might compare the present Luganda descriptions with those obtained in Luganda from Ss who did not know English, but of course, one would also have to account for major subcultural differences between those who knew both English and Luganda and those who knew only Luganda. At any rate, at least insofar as gross content categories are concerned, the present data do *not* support a hypothesis of significant linguistic effects on emotional reports.

In summary, the present study, though clearly exploratory and descriptive, suggests both similarities and differences among reported emotional experiences in two cultures. More important than the specific results obtained, however, is the impetus this study may provide for further research along similar lines, with the aim of clarifying our understanding of emotional experiences as well as deepening our insights into cross-cultural similarities and differences.

Questions for Further Investigation

The studies reported in preceding sections of this chapter are only beginnings in research along several interrelated lines of inquiry, and each of these studies suggests a number of questions for further investigation. For example, now that the general lines of development in the language of emotion have been established, more specific, theoretically focused investigations would seem to be called for. In general, it would be profitable to design these investigations against the broader background of more general developmental points of view, such as those presented by Erikson or Piaget.

Assuming that emotional experiences reflect significant events that a person has encountered, one would expect from Erikson's theory of life stages (1963) a systematic shift with age in the nature of reported emotional experiences. At the locomotor–genital stage of later childhood, ACTIVATION might be expected to play a predominant role in emotional experiences; later in development, with latency, and perhaps even more during the identity crisis associated with adolescence, the dimension of COMPETENCE should become increasingly important. And in young adulthood, when the individual presumably is concerned with problems of intimacy versus isolation, RELATEDNESS should come into the foreground of more and more of a person's emotional life. These predictions, of course, assume normal development in Erikson's sense of a sequence of developmental crises or conflicts, and one would expect disruptions in this line of personality development—such as unresolved conflict at some early stage—to be reflected in the nature of an individual's emotional experiences. Thus, if conflicts involving autonomy versus shame and doubt have not been adequately resolved, one would expect certain subsequent emotional experiences to be characterized by an emphasis on *Inadequacy* and also perhaps *Incompetence:Dissatisfaction*.

This line of investigation would relate a more general theory of personality with the view of emotion thus far developed in this research, and as such, might serve as one basis for integrating previously diverse aspects of psychology.

Weinberg's study of cognitive style and style of emotional reports strongly supports Schachter's emphasis on the importance of perceptual–cognitive factors in emotional experience. In Piaget's terms, the experience of emotion depends upon the cognitive *schemata* involved in the perception and interpretation of internal and external events, and thus emotional phenomena cannot usefully be conceptualized without considering the influence of perceptual–cognitive variables.

If this view is valid, research can be meaningfully focused, for example, on identifying those cognitive variables which contribute to an individual's ability to report emotional experiences. These might involve the capacity to perceive and recall details of complex events; the capacity to describe verbally a series of nonverbal phenomena for which there are no readily available, conventional labels; the capacity to shift perspectives, so that one can experience emotions fully and directly, without mediating labels (that is, without a constant process of self-conscious labeling, "Now I'm happy; now I'm sad"), and yet later view these events with enough perspective to permit a full verbal report of the experience.

Allerand's results with monozygotic twins supports the assumption that physiological similarity between people is positively related to similarity of their emotional experiences. But a more direct test of this proposition would involve measures of physiological reactions to standard stimuli, which could then serve as a basis for evaluating the degree to which specific physiological factors contribute to similarity of emotional reaction. With further work, perhaps this line of research could lead to a more precise specification of the physiological variables that influence various aspects of emotional experience. The results of previous research aimed at identifying physiological correlates of particular emotional states have not been especially promising, but a reformulation of this kind of research in terms of dimensions of emotional experience, ACTIVATION, COMFORT, etc., may lead to more rewarding findings. That is, rather than attempt to identify the physiological correlates of Fear or Anger, it may be more meaningful to search for physiological reactions associated with reports of *Tension, Discomfort,* or *Hyperactivation.*

Throughout this research we have been concerned with verbal reports of emotional experiences, first in terms of the consensus among such reports and later in terms of certain individual differences. But all of the work reported thus far has been correlational or cross sectional, neglecting important questions concerned with changes in an individual's ability to report his emotional experiences. Assuming, for the moment, that increased awareness of emotional experiences and increased capacity to report these experiences is a desirable goal for some purposes (as in various forms of psychotherapy), one might focus research on evaluating the effectiveness of a variety of techniques presumably designed to enhance the ability to describe emotional experiences. Using the content analysis measures of complexity and differentiation developed in this research, one might investigate changes in emotional reports as a function of practice, simple verbal reinforcement of descriptive statements, modeling procedures, empathic reflection of feelings, and a wide variety of techniques derived from learning or psychotherapeutic models. In a sense, reporting emotional experiences represents one aspect of a patient's performance in psychotherapy, and by limiting one's concern to changes in this behavior, an experimental paradigm for studying the effects of various techniques of psychotherapy becomes available.

Another important line of experimental investigation involves the study of changes in emotional states under controlled laboratory conditions. To a large extent, experimental manipulation of emotional states has been fairly gross and frequently concerned with inducing states such as fear or anxiety. But the structure of emotional meaning discussed in Chapters 4 and 5 (e.g., see Propositions 5 and 6 in Chapter 5) suggests a conceptual scheme that could conceivably provide a useful basis for designing experimental procedures to elicit with greater precision a wider range of emotional states. Thus, instead of being concerned with inducing a relatively broad and amorphous emotional state associated with some common emotional label, the experimenter might design and focus his procedures in terms of influencing particular dimensions or cluster aspects of emotional meaning. The experimenter's task, then, is not to induce Anxiety or Happiness *per se,* but rather, to design experimental conditions that are likely to induce a sense of *Activation, Tension, Discomfort,* or *Self-Enhancement,* or any other specific aspect of emotional states. It would seem much more likely that effective experimental procedures can be designed to achieve these more specific and delimited goals than to elicit global and more diffuse emotional reactions with any reasonable degree of reliability.

While the single cross-cultural study of American and Ugandan adolescents clearly represents only a preliminary beginning in this line of research, a number of exciting possibilities in this direction are apparent. The results thus far obtained clearly support the general notion that emotional experiences reflect significant characteristics of an individual's culture; the differences between the emotional reports of the American and Ugandan samples mirror obvious differences in the two cultures. But one need not travel to Africa, of course, to study significant cultural differences. In fact, perhaps some investigation of American subcultures in terms of similarities and differences in emotional experiences might enhance our understanding of current conflicts in American society.

In conclusion, this report represents a minor beginning in a direction of research that could conceivably have some implications for a broad range of psychological and social problems. If this work has any value, it will be determined by the degree to which the promises of these early steps in investigation are fulfilled in future research.

Bibliography

Allerand, A. M. Remembrance of feelings past: A study of phenomenological genetics. Unpublished doctoral dissertation, Columbia University, 1967.

Arnold, M. *Emotion and personality.* Vols. I, II. New York: Columbia Univ. Press, 1960.

Bakan, D. Clinical psychology and logic. In J. R. Braun (Ed.), *Clinical psychology in transition.* (Rev. ed.) Cleveland: World Publ., 1966. Pp. 10–17.

Beebe-Center, J. G. Feeling and emotion. In H. Helsen (Ed.), *Theoretical foundations of psychology.* New York: Van Nostrand, 1951.

Block. J. Studies in the phenomenology of emotions. *Journal of Abnormal and Social Psychology,* 1957, **54,** 358–363.

Burt, C. The factorial study of emotions. In M. L. Reymert (Ed.), *Feelings and emotions.* New York: McGraw-Hill, 1950. Chapter 46.

Cannon, W. B. *Bodily changes in pain, hunger, fear and rage.* (2nd ed.) New York: Ronald Press, 1929.

Davitz, J. R. (ed.) *The communication of emotional meaning.* New York: McGraw-Hill, 1964.

Duffy, E. The conceptual categories of psychology; a suggestion for revision. *Psychological Review,* 1941, **48,** 177–203.

Duffy, E. *Activation and behavior.* New York, Wiley, 1962.

Erikson, E. H. *Childhood and society.* (2nd ed.) New York: Norton, 1963.

Farmer, C. Words and feelings: A developmental study of the language of emotion in children. Unpublished doctoral dissertation, Columbia University, 1967.

Freud, S. Papers on metapsychology. In *Collected Papers.* Vol. IV. London: Hogarth Press, 1949. Pp. 109–111.

Gardener, R. W., Holzman, P. S., Klein, G. S., Linton, H., & Spence, D. P., Cognitive control; a study of individual consistencies in cognitive behavior. *Psychological Issues,* 1959, **1,** No. 4.

Hall, R. A. *Leave your language alone.* Ithaca: Linguistica, 1950.

Harlow, H. F., & Stagner, R. Psychology of feelings and emotions, II. Theory of emotions. *Psychological Review,* 1933, p. 191.

Haronian, F., & Sugerman, A. Field independence and resistance to reversal of perspective. *Perceptual and Motor Skills,* 1966, **22,** 543–546.

Horney, K. *Our inner conflicts.* New York: Norton, 1945.

Jackson, D. N. A short form of Witkin's embedded figures test. *Journal of Abnormal and Social Psychology,* 1956, **53,** 254–255.

Mandler, G. Emotion. In Brown, R., Galanter, E., Hess, E., & Mandler, G. *New directions in psychology.* New York: Holt, Rinehart, and Winston, 1962.

Marlowe, D. Some psychological correlates of field independence. *Journal of Consulting Psychology,* 1958, **22,** 334.

193

Nowlis, V., & Nowlis, H. H. The description and analysis of moods. *Annals of the New York Academy of Science* 1956, **65,** 345–355.

Perls, F., Hefferline, R. F., & Goodman, P. *Gestalt therapy.* New York: Dell, 1965.

Pervin, L. A. Existentialism, psychology, and psychotherapy. In J. R. Baun (Ed.), *Clinical psychology in transition.* (Rev. ed.) Cleveland: World Publ. Co., 1966. Pp. 210–214.

Plutchik, R. *The emotions: facts, theories, and a new model.* New York: Random House, 1962.

Rosner, S. Consistency in response to group pressures. *Journal of Abnormal and Social Psychology,* 1957, **55,** 145–146.

Sartre, J. P. *The emotions: Outline of a theory.* (translated by Bernard Frechtman) New York: Philosophical Library, 1948.

Schachter, S. The interaction of cognitive and physiological determinants of emotional states. In Ph. H. Leiderman & D. Shapiro (Eds.), *Psychobiological approaches to social behavior.* Stanford: Stanford Univ. Press, 1964.

Schachter, S., & Singer, J. E. Cognitive, social and physiological determinants of emotional state. *Psychological Review,* 1962, **69,** 379–399.

Schachter, S., & Wheeler, L. Epinephrine, chlorpromazine and amusement. *Journal of Abnormal and Social Psychology,* 1962, **65,** 121–128.

Schlosberg, H. Three dimensions of emotion. *Psychological Review,* 1954, **61,** 81–88.

Stagner, R. *Psychology of personality.* New York: McGraw-Hill, 1948.

Thorndike, R. L. Two screening tests of verbal intelligence. *Journal of Applied Psychology,* 1942, **26,** 128–135.

Tryon, R. C. *Cluster analysis.* Ann Arbor: Edwards Brothers, 1939.

Weinberg, J. A. Relationships between the organization of reported emotional experience and the organization of perceptual-cognitive processes. Unpublished doctoral dissertation, Columbia University, 1968.

White, R. W. Motivation reconsidered: The concept of competence. *Psychological Review,* 1959, **66,** 297–333.

Witkin, H. A., Dyk, R. B., Faterson, H. F., Goodenough, D. R., & Karp, S. A. *Psychological differentiation.* New York: Wiley, 1962.

Witkin, H. A., Lewis, H. B., Hertzman, M., Machover, K., Meissner, P. B., & Wapner, S. *Personality through perception.* New York: Harper, 1954.

Wundt, W. *Grundriss der psychologie.* (7th rev. ed.) Leipzig: Engelmann, 1905.

Young, P. T. Affective arousal: Some implications. *American Psychologist,* 1967, **22,** 32–40.

Author Index

Numbers in italics refer to the pages on which the complete references are listed.

Allerand, A. M., 151, 170, *193*
Arnold, M., 128, 129, *193*

Bakan, D., 139, *193*
Beebe-Center, J. G., 149, *193*
Block, J., 128, 133, *193*
Burt, C., 128, 133, *193*

Cannon, W. B., 134, *193*

Davitz, J. R., 1, *193*
Duffy, E., 128, 130, 148, *193*
Dyk, R. B., 169, *194*

Erikson, E. H., 190, *193*

Farmer, C., 151, 156, 158, *193*
Faterson, H. F., 169, *194*
Freud, S., 137, *193*

Gardener, R. W., 165, 166, 167, *193*
Goodenough, D. R., 169, *194*
Goodman, P., 146, 165, *194*

Hall, R. A., 141, *193*
Harlow, H. F., 128, 133 149, *193*
Haronian, F., 169, *193*
Hefferline, R. F., 146, 165, *194*
Hertzman, M., 165, *194*
Holzman, P. S., 165, 166, 167, *193*
Horney, K., 132, *193*

Jackson, D. N. 166, *193*

Karp, S. A., 169, *194*
Klein, G. S., 165, 166, 167, *193*

Lewis, H. B., 165, *194*
Linton, H., 165, 166, 167, *193*

Machover, K., 165, *194*
Mandler, G., 90, 137, 139, *193*
Melssner, P. B., 165, *194*
Marlowe, D., 169, *193*

Nowlis, H. H., 128, 130, 133, *194*
Nowlis, V., 128, 130, 133, *194*

Perls, F., 146, 165, *194*
Pervin, L. A., 141, *194*
Plutchik, R., 134, *194*

Rosner, S., 169, *194*

Sartre, J. P., 134, *194*
Schachter, S., 129, 146, 148, *194*
Schlosber, H., 129, 133, *194*
Singer, J. E., 129, 148, *194*
Spence, D. P., 165, 166, 167, *193*
Stagner, R., 128, 133, 149, *193, 194*
Sugerman, A., 169, *193*

Thorndike, R. L., 167, 171, *194*
Tryon, R. C., 107, *194*

Wapner, S., 165, *194*
Weinberg, J. A., 151, 164, 165, *194*
Wheeler, L., 129, 148, *194*
White, R. W., 134, 135, *194*
Witkin, H. A., 165, 169, *194*
Wundt, W., 129, 133, *194*

Young, P. T., 129, 132, *194*

Subject Index

Words in italics refer to clusters identified in structural analysis; words in capital letters refer to dimensions of emotional meaning.

Activation, 108
ACTIVATION, 128, 148
Adaptive behavior, 134
Adequacy of definitions, 13, 85
Adjustment, 133
Admiration, 32
Affection, 33
Affective intensity, 128
Amusement, 34
Anger, 35
Anxiety, 36
Apathy, 36
Atomistic model, 6, 88
Attention-rejection, 130
Awe, 37

Behaviorism, 4
Boredom, 38

Check list, 7, 15–31, 90
  revised version, 92
Checking tendencies, 91
Cheerfulness, 39
Cluster analysis, 106
Clusters, 108
  emphasis of, 115
  interrelationships, 114
  score, 115
Cognitive events, 7, 131, 146
Comfort, 109
Commonalities of experiences, 85
Commonalities of meaning, 3
Commonality of verbal reports, 13, 85
Communication of emotion, 1
COMPETENCE, 148
Complexity, 165
Confidence, 41
Conscious states, 136
Contempt, 42
Content analysis, 151

Contentment, 43
Control of behavior, 7, 151
Critical incident technique, 11
Cross-cultural comparisons, 172

Delight, 44
Depression, 45
Determination, 47
Differentiation, 165
Dimensions of emotional meaning, 121
  ACTIVATION, 121
  COMPETENCE, 121
  HEDONIC TONE, 121
  RELATEDNESS, 121
Discomfort, 109
Disgust, 48
Dislike, 49
Distortion, 91

Educational level, 9
Efficacy, feeling of, 135
Elation, 49
Embarrassment, 51
Emergency theory, 134
Emotional energy, 128
Emotional similarity index, 172
Energy mobilization, 129
English, 8
Enhancement, 109
Enjoyment, 52
Equivalence Range, 165
Etymology, 13
Excitement, 54
Existential view, 140
Experience of emotion, 2, 89
Expressive behaviors, 151
External situation, relation to, 7

Factor analysis, 115
Fear, 54

Field independence–dependence, 165
Formal aspects of emotion, 7
Friendliness, 56
Frustration, 57

Gaiety, 58
Genetic background, 170
Gratitude, 60
Grief, 60
Guilt, 62

Happiness, 63
Hate, 64
HEDONIC TONE, 148
Hope, 65
Hyperactivation, 108
Hypoactivation, 108

Inadequacy, 114
Incompetence:Dissatisfaction, 113
Impatience, 66
Impulses to behave, 7
Individual differences, 138
Inspiration, 67
Interpersonal relations, 151
Interviews, 5
Irritation, 68

Jealousy, 68

Labels of emotions, 1, 6, 10, 141
Language 2, 138, 141
   development of, 156
   learning, 146
   limitations of, 89
Learning, 149
Leveling, 91, 165
Love, 70
Luganda, 173

Manifest emotions, scales of, 93–105
Modal meanings, 141
Moving against, 109
Moving away, 109
Moving toward, 108

Negative emotional states, 118
   Type 1, 118
   Type 2, 118
Nervousness, 72

Overlap of definitions, 87

Panic, 73
Passion, 74
Pattern of definitions, 143
Perceptual-cognitive style, 164
Phenomenology, 4
Phi coefficient, 107
Physical sensations, 7, 151
Physical symptoms, 151
Pity, 75
Pleasure, 128
Positive emotional states, 115
Pride, 76
Psychoanalytic theory, 136

RELATEDNESS, 129, 148
Relief, 77
Remorse, 78
Resentment, 79
Response bias, 91
Response sets, 5, 142
Reverence, 79

Sadness, 80
Serenity, 81
Shame, 83
Sharpening, 91, 165
Social orientation, 130
Solemnity, 84
Specificity of definitions, 87
Structural analysis, 127
Structure of emotional meaning, 142
Surprise, 84

Tension, 109
Tension reduction, 133
Time, sense of, 151

Uganda, 173
Unconscious, 136
Unpleasantness, 128

Valence, 115
Verbal ability, 5, 8, 167
Verbal fluency, 167
Verbal report, 3
   errors in, 142

Word count, 87